CSSCI 集刊
CNKI 来源集刊

学术支持单位 | 南京大学外国语学院

外国语文研究:
语言与传播

南京大学出版社

《外国语文研究》编辑委员会

主　任：高　方　何　宁

委　员（按姓氏笔画排列）：

　　　　孔德明　王加兴　王守仁　文秋芳　石　坚　申　丹
　　　　叶　琳　冉永平　朱　刚　许　钧　庄智象　刘云虹
　　　　束定芳　杨金才　何　宁　何成洲　陈新仁　金　莉
　　　　殷企平　徐　昉　高　方　黄国文　蒋洪新　魏向清

主　编：陈新仁

副主编：曹丹红　张　翼

编辑部主任：张　翼

秘　书：俞　希

通信地址：南京市栖霞区仙林大道163号（邮编210023）
　　　　　　南京大学仙林校区外国语学院
电　话：025-89683243
电　邮：wgywyj@126.com

目 录

公共健康与语言传播

Health Promotion Discourse: The Voice for New Good / Michael Rinn …… 1

An Argument for Public Health: The Centrality of Communication Theory in Making Comprehensive and Effective Public Health Messages / Jessica Mudry …………………………………………………………………… 14

Developing Rational Empathy in Health Care Policy: The Usefulness of Online Comments / Fabienne Baider ……………………………………… 29

语言学与应用语言学研究

现代汉语副词"相互/互相"联系义用法的涌现 / 郝 琦 郭 锐 …… 52

基于词语法的汉语论元结构阐释 / 张智义 ………………………… 67

哈尔滨市中心与郊区楼盘名称的语音、语用研究 / 郭思文 柳君丽 …… 82

中英文社交媒体不礼貌话语的同异性探究：以微博、Twitter 为例 / 刘胜男 侯 涛 ………………………………………………………… 91

美国 ACTFL 外语能力指导方针研究及启示 / 张蔚磊 ……………… 109

外国文学研究

"灰姑娘反串版"的四种现代叙事变体 / 张俊萍 …………………… 121

无法逃离的精神藩篱——艾丽丝·门罗《逃离》的文体学分析 / 张淑玲 …… 129

神话中的觉醒——《野猫精》中的反乌托邦思想解读 / 赵 杨 …… 144

翻译研究

"被××"反讽句的跨文化阐释及英译 / 姚 俊 ……………………………… 152

前沿动态

基于 CiteSpace 的国外语言学领域立场研究 / 夏 秸 陈新仁 …………… 162

《劳特利奇语用学手册》与语用学研究前沿 / 黄立鹤 祝 琳 …………… 178

《语用翻译学：寓意言谈翻译研究》简评 / 王才英 ……………………… 186

《面向"一带一路"建设的外语规划研究》介评 / 杨金龙 ………………… 192

公共健康与语言传播

Health Promotion Discourse:
The Voice for New Good

Université de Bretagne Occidentale   Michael Rinn*

Abstract: This article will analyze how the creative power deployed by the health promotion discourse against HIV/AIDS can be explained by its hybrid nature. It is both functional in its maximization of efficiency and its anticipation of reception, and normalizing in its unification of behavior. In this regard, we understand the health promotion discourse as a major component of what Marc Angenot broadly calls "social discourse" (2009: 8). This discourse governs citizens' way of living, by organizing, unifying and fixing limits on what is said, debated and discussed in a given society (Rinn & Sherlaw, 2018). Our analysis will show how health promotion goes beyond the cognitive dimension of social discourse. Public authorities, by showing the image (we will call ethos) of responsibility, knowledge and performance, aim not only to impose a discursive dominance, in order to develop and legitimize the way of framing social life, as the dominant Zeitgeist, but also to provide ways of acting of each citizen. It is this combination of cognition and action that gives the health promotion its persuasive power.

Key words: HIV/AIDS; social reality; ethos; persuasion; power

---

* Michael Rinn, Professor of Département des Lettres modernes, Université de Bretagne Occidentale. Email: michael.rinn@univ-brest.fr.

1 Introduction

HIV/AIDS has marked history at the end of the 20th century and the beginning of the 21st century, for the havoc it has wreaked and the anxiety it has provoked since its discovery in the early 1980s (Grmek, 2005; Kingman & Connor, 1989; Pépin 2011), as well as for the clash of cultures (Cooper, 2017), ideologies (Kello, 2017) and habits (Shilts, 1987) it has given rise to. For almost forty years now public authorities have designed new health promotion discourses (Bunton & Macdonald, 2002; Scirven, 2010) aiming to change citizens' social hygiene beliefs to avoid the exclusion of vulnerable communities (e.g. drug addicts or prostitutes) and behaviors (safer sex practices) (Rinn, 2002) and incite them to purchase items (medicine, condoms, etc.) and services (doctor's appointments, hospice care, psychotherapy treatment). In this article, we define this discourse as a way of creating social reality, with which the political authorities address the issue of governability of contemporary societies (Ollivier-Yanniv & Rinn, 2009). We will discuss the concept of creation through the rhetorical strategies used by state agencies to build a social reality adapted to public health requirements in the age of HIV/AIDS.

Thus, when launching prevention campaigns in the 1980s, faced with the fact that they had little or no established knowledge about the disease, public authorities had to create a new social environment, in order to reduce the spread of HIV/AIDS by establishing new rules of living. The visual and conceptual design of these campaigns broadly borrows from the social marketing: "Social marketing (...) refers primarily to efforts focused on influencing behaviors that will improve health, prevent injuries, protect environment and contribute to communities" (Kotler & Lee, 2008: 7). But it is especially the use of **transparency** underlying the information and communication technologies that emerged in the end of the 20th century (Breton, 1997: 63–90) that helps us to understand why the public authorities focused on the discursive construction of the image of the self, called **ethos** in ancient Greek. Since Aristotle's Rhetoric (2006: 1378), the image of the self (ethos), by which the speaker presents himself as a model of virtue, expertise and knowledge, by showing the audience example how to behave for **common good** (Garver, 1995), is considered as one of the three modes of persuasion, the other principles being the discourse by itself (**logos**) and the use of emotions (**pathos**) (Meyer, 2004). In this article, we will analyze how the public authorities in Switzerland have made use of the ethos as a discursive strategy in the STOP AIDS campaign launched in the early 1980s.

The article consists of 6 sections. Section 2 gives the research background on ethos as well as the specificities of the data related to the STOP AIDS campaign in Switzerland. Section 3 analyses the persuasive process of the implicit ethos. Section 4 addresses the presentation of self in discourse. Section 5 will illustrate what is called the verbalized ethos. Finally, Section 6 discusses and concludes the outcome of our study on the discursive construction of ethos in public health promotion campaigns.

2　On the ethos in the *Stop Aids* campaign in Switzerland

The problem of this study spans many countries today and can be generalized. Indeed, as the study of the data provided by the Swiss *Stop AIDS* campaign (1987—2004) (https://www.lovelife.ch/en/campaign/archive/) (Rinn, 2000: 19 - 48)—renamed *Check Your Lovelife*, and then since 2005, *Love Life* (http://www.lovelife.ch/en/) will show, the persuasive power of health promotion discourse becomes effective when the public authorities interfere in the private life of each citizen. We will discuss the following hypothesis: The public authorities undertake action in the interest of all, while, in reality, it can only be in the interest of certain people, as much of a majority as they may be. In other words, health promotion discourse, founded on the ideal of **common good**, aims paradoxically at **individual good**. Our case study will show, health promotion discourse produces increasing inequality between those who are doing well—because they have adopted the safety instructions they have been instilled with … and the others. This discourse creates a social reality from which "the others" will be excluded, not only socially, but also economically.

Our first theory is that, in order to be truly efficient, the institutional advertiser has to provide proof of its civic nature, an oratory procedure which refers to the rhetorical concept of ethos, meaning the way the speaker presents himself or herself to the public (Amossy, 1999, 2010). It is significant that the discourse on AIDS often refers to an ethic based on the concept of *responsibility to oneself* and others, a premise that underlies any action undertaken in a social marketing context. Our second theory consists in showing that the argumentation strategy adopted by public authorities aims to validate the idea of *freedom of choice*, based on the standards of social rationality. One must distinguish between ethics, conceived as a set of social values shared by a community of speakers at a given moment, and ethos, an oratory posture adopted by the public authorities (Hyde & Schrag, 2004).

In the following section, analysis of the data will show how the public health discourse has adopted a socio-economic ideology of distinction based on personal merit; an ideology whose outcome leads to discrimination against those who will have failed in their civic duties①. Our approach is based on the idea that health promotion discourses build self-image by successive steps, starting with a non-verbalized advertising concept, in order to impose a fully verbalized ethos, after having gone through several levels of intermediate discursive situations.

3 The persuasive process of the implicit ethos

The signature of the Swiss campaign STOP AIDS (1984—2004) illustrates one of the processes of what we call implicit, preexisting ethos, that is a self-image of the public authorities that anticipates speech. Situated below the logo, which enjoys a worldwide reputation (a condom in the shape of a pink icon) (https://www.youtube.com/watch? v=d_dRnkzpRHo), the syntax "*Aide Suisse contre le sida*" ("The Swiss AIDS Federation") (https://www.aids.ch/en/), in collaboration with the Swiss Federal Office of Public Health" does the strategic work of pinning down the ad. This core phrase allows highlighting the double affiliation of the advertiser. The Federal Office of Public Health (OFSP), one of the sections of the Swiss Federal Department of Interior, is responsible for national AIDS prevention campaign. The Swiss AIDS Federation (AHS) is an NGO of more than 40 organizations committed to HIV/AIDS. AHS was founded in 1985 by members of the gay community of Zurich. Co-signatories of the campaign STOP SIDA, with l'OFSP from its launch in 1987 until 2004, the AHS plays a leading role in the integration of people living with HIV/AIDS

---

① To broaden the discussion, see John Kemm (2014) *Heath Promotion: Ideology, Discipline, and Specialism*, which brings up the contradiction between the displayed purpose of prevention and well-being of an individual, and the hidden goal of controlling the population.

into all aspects of society. The choice of this partnership between the ministry of public health and the Swiss AIDS Federation (AHS) speaking in the name of marginalized communities, offers one element that, based on the rhetorical concept we call the **VOICE**, builds public trust in the ability to take action together, for the good of all.

The Federal Office of Public Health, like Swiss AIDS Federation, has a level of expertise widely acknowledged by the general public. Its roots in collective programs bringing prevention and protection from infectious diseases to the whole of the population are underpinned by a theme of **solidarity**. Providing a second reason for credibility, according to the rhetoric, the advertiser, shown to be in solidarity, displays **kindness, thoughtfulness** and **sympathy** towards its audience. Finally, in conferring legal status to this mixed advertiser, representing all the major players affected by AIDS, the legislator demonstrates **honesty** and **sincerity**. The adoption of the **right balance of voices** in the campaign offers a third reason to trust the advertiser, putting together all elements defined by Aristotle as ethos.

We thus note that the preexisting ethos of solidarity campaigns are based on a fundamental argumentation approach. All the rhetorical traditions since the Rhetoric of Aristotle are sustained by **common sense, virtue and kindness**. The process behind the self-image of the advertiser is made up of several corresponding elements: the moral and deontological reputation of the advertiser, its institutional status, its political and legal mandate, the success of the majority of past public health campaigns, and even the choice of the theme of solidarity (which theoretically refers to loving one's neighbor, a fundamental principal of Christianity, dominant religion in Switzerland).

4 Presentation of self in the discourse

We will now analyze ads that put the representation of self of the speaker progressively into a language situation. We can distinguish the image of a speaker representing an institution from that built through the discursive strategy of ethos. In regards to the former, it involves a process of presentation of self that integrates certain elements of preexisting ethos: the social prestige that it represents, one's good reputation and one's ethical motivation. As for building a self-image through a speech act, it is constructed through verbal interaction with the receiver, meaning through the argumentative scope of the discourse. The former tries to convince the public through demonstration of the high morality and the irreproachable character of the speaker discussing the institution he or she is representing. The latter aims to persuade through the merits of its arguments. The authoritative moral argument is certainly the most promising approach in terms of an orator speaking on behalf of an institution. Thus, relative to the overall aim of a prevention discourse that consists in winning the trust of the public at large, convincing it of the value of the solidarity message, the advertiser emphasizes its moral and institutional authority. As in the enclosed example, the expectation provoked by preexisting ethos is reinforced when the advertiser calls upon a figure well known for his or her intellectual and moral integrity. We will look at the following example:

"Discrimination of AIDS patients is irreconcilable with the gospel."
(*The Swiss AIDS Federation* and The Federal Office of Public Health, Switzerland) https://wellcomecollection.org/works/k6jukzqc (consulted on October 10, 2019)

Displayed in large format (270 × 128 cm), the poster shows the portrait of Cardinal HenriSchwery, bishop of Sion. Henry Schwery is known as a moral authority, not only for the high office he holds in the Catholic Church, but also for the courageous stance he has taken, largely surpassing his episcopal mandate. Thus the prelate's statement has more of an impact than would a simple evocation of the gospel. This semantic extension shows that the advertiser does not wish to moralize on debates about AIDS. The cardinal's widely known reputation strengthens the ethos of the advertiser, that the public has every reason to consider as honest, and to be acting selflessly from the bottom of its heart and who must, after all, be right. For the good of society, discrimination against people with AIDS must be rejected. Ethos based on fairness strives to remind us more of good than of harm suffered, in order to emphasize the relativity of value judgments against others. This oratorical process aims to convince that the advice offered is adapted to a given communicative situation. We can suppose that the implied advice in this ad consists in saying that it is better to join together in a spirit of solidarity than to stand facing a wall. In regards to the second way of building self-image, it is no longer the institution, which the orator is speaking on behalf of, that guarantees the ethical value linked to the advertising message, but the discourse act. It is a matter of convincing the public, by developing communicative ethos through discussion. As the next example shows, the advertiser can use the inherent argumentative nature of language. This can be seen in the following passage.

Can we kiss someone who is HIV positive? (Ⅰ) Yes. (Ⅱ) It takes more than kisses to get AIDS. (Ⅲ) Let's finish with prejudices. (Ⅳ) STOP AIDS. (Ⅴ)
(*The Swiss AIDS Federation* and the Swiss Federal Office of Public Health, 1992)
https://www.rts.ch/galeries/3881758-les-campagnes-de-lutte-contre-le-sida-de-1987-a-2014.html? image=3881726 (page 22, consulted on October 2, 2014)

This ad is from a series of posters distributed in December 1992. All the ads in this series involve a discursive pattern in five successive movements: The first phrase (Ⅰ) asks a precise question about how to relate to a person who has HIV and the dangers involved (working or living together, kissing, etc.). This question leads to a positive, exclamatory answer (Ⅱ). The third phrase (Ⅲ) consists in supporting the answer, while the fourth movement (Ⅳ) of the debate sequence delivers a general maxim. Finally (Ⅴ), the prevention campaign logo plays the role of theme changer. It indicates the final goal of the message: Stop propagation of the epidemic. A first look at these phrases shows the polyphonic nature of the message, successively articulating the voices of one or more speakers, anxious about the idea of meeting someone who is HIV positive: the advertiser, who takes the role of speaking partner from the scientific community, authorized to address the issue; all of the speakers present who call for an ethical approach; and lastly, society itself, threatened by AIDS. The speaking network woven into the rhythm of the debate movement contributes to integrating the verbal interaction between the speaker—public and the speaker—advertiser, into a general opinion authorized to judge fairly and competently. This staging of a verbal exchange allows the advertiser to block counter-arguments coming from a receiver-speaker, who might have doubts about bio-medical research, which can certainly boast progress in the treatment of the disease, but still lacks knowledge as to the cause and inner workings of the virus. Thus, the dubious position of the advertiser is neutralized by the ethical merit of calling upon a sense of community spirit whose preventive interest concerns everyone.

Another strategy of persuasive discourse consists in using arguments *outside* of language. Such is the case, in the following example signed by The Swiss AIDS Federation and the Swiss Federal Office of Public Health. This ad bears witness to a fate that most receivers could share. The layout of this double page magazine ad is presented as an autobiographical photo narrative, commented by a mother of three. Entitled, "I'm Fighting for my Life," the narrative respects rules of the genre, maintaining certain characteristics of oral language and story telling, progressing by successive ellipses. The points of the argumentative process are connected by progressively putting the reader into the place of the "I" identified by the narrator.

This example allows us to conclude that this sort of argumentation process aims to develop strong public conviction, through mirroring effects between the different images in play. The ethos of the advertiser is built up in the message, through the roles of advisor or mediator that it takes on. The non-manipulative persuasive power that the advertiser thus acquires depends on the appeal of this portrayal. However, this sort of reasoning by generalization, which exploits existing stereotypes and counters others, should not allow us to forget that the argument is not truly persuasive unless it deductively confirms a rationalist axiom, namely that humankind has a natural inclination towards the true, the good and the fair. The assumption of this anthropological ideal seems particularly problematical in the field of prevention against AIDS, an epidemic that reveals the conflicting ideological, political and historical forces found throughout Western countries.

5 Verbalized ethos

Evaluation of verbalized ethos can only be addressed hypothetically. It is up to each receiver to get a clear picture of the sender aiming to demonstrate the validity of a message. However, nothing keeps the advertiser from staging the outcome of this work of reciprocal, simultaneous portrayal between speaker and receiver. It is a matter of making it seem as if the creation of the social reality had already happened. The following ad is an indicative example:

A Storybook Image①.

The image is beautiful. It is that of a country in which, side by side, the healthy and the handicapped sing and spin the flag together, in a land where those who are seropositive or have AIDS are not excluded, where there is no isolation, nor solitude, nor discrimination, neither in terms of work, nor in terms of housing. Yet, the image is misleading. One could almost forget that reality falls short.

UNITED IN SOLIDARITY

(*Nouveau Quotidien*, December 12, 1997) https://www.youtube.com/watch? v=lon7E3RIe3A (video consulted on October 10, 2019)

This double page ad in a French Swiss daily newspaper was part of a solidarity campaign jointly launched by the Swiss Federal Office of Public Health, *Aide Switzerland contre le sida* and by *Pro Infirmis*, a NGO that works for better integration of handicapped people into society. On the bottom left hand corner of the page, the text is divided into two parts, one that is denotative and postmodern and the other that is connotative and utopian. This opposition is indicated by the title, "A Storybook Image", and the closing phrase, "united in solidarity". The term "Storybook Image" refers to the iconic image, representing a mixed choir in traditional folk dress. In the foreground we see two Swiss alpine horns, while the background is dominated by mountains. At first glance, it looks like a tourist snapshot. This impression is strengthened by the opening sentences in the text area. ("The image is beautiful ... "). However, as of the word "handicapped" in the second sentence, the receiver's attention is drawn to the person in a wheelchair in the first row of the choir.

The sense of idyllic representation connected to this "storybook image" therefore shifts in nature, to better denounce the utopian nature of a society that claims to be in solidarity with all people who are marginalized or becoming so. The referential relationship between text and image starts the simultaneous deconstruction of the project of a united community, such as it is extolled in the text, and depicted by the iconic image of the choir. (No one is excluded and no one will experience isolation,

---

① In the original ad, the expression *Image d'Epinal* is used, evoking 19th century regional French Epinal prints; the expression meaning, "idealize image".

solitude, discrimination, etc.) Indeed, among the singers, we seem to make out some with Down syndrome, others who are visually impaired and yet others with reduced mobility. The choir would equally include members living with HIV/AIDS, as the text states. It is precisely this gaze that starts to scrutinize, define and, in some cases, judge and stigmatize whatever does not correspond to established norms of society, which is made impossible, through the diverse social reality represented by the image-symbol. Anticipating the interpretive process begun by the receiver, the advertiser aims to channel criticism about its message of solidarity. In denouncing the utopian aspect of a united society, this ad enhances the ethos of both the sender and the receiver, by praising the lucidity of each of them, to finally affirm the ethical project: be responsible for oneself, for one's own *Weltbild*, one's way of being and living in a society made up of a sum total of unique individual players. This analysis shows that since the early 2000s, public awareness campaigns have presented HIV/AIDS as a largely banalized social reality, which could potentially affect each one of us, just like a handicap or an accident, but which would now be considered a private matter. This can be noted in the 2004 poster that says:

No action without protection. LOVE LIFE—STOP AIDS.
(Federal Office of Public Health, Switzerland, 2010)
https://www.youtube.com/watch?v=dbQJdf1OEto (consulted on October 10, 2019)

The voice of the state, through the advertiser, solicits the passerby directly, with an appeal to a sense of civic duty, without clarifying whether referring to responsibility for oneself or others. The campaign titles, successively "Love life/Stop AIDS", followed by "Love Life" in 2005, confirms the trend to exclude those living with HIV/AIDS. In leaving its historical partner, the association Swiss Aids Federation, the political authority is now concerned only with each citizen's self-preoccupation, warning them about the danger of STD transmission. It thus reinforces its role as creator of lifestyles in society, presenting itself as a guardian of the well-being of each individual. This allows it to incarnate the new model citizen, worried about maintaining perfect health, in *"Le Manifeste Love Life"* Manifesto Love Life"("The), distributed during the launch of the 2014 campaign. Now, as the cover of the Manifesto illustrates, everyone aside from me, living with HIV/AIDS or not, will henceforth be excluded from social reality:

> I LOVE MY LIFE. I TAKE CARE OF IT. I LOVE MY BODY. I PROTECT IT. I REGRET NOTHING. I AM CAREFUL.
> (Federal Office of Pubic Health, Switzerland, 2014)
> https://www.lovelife.ch/fr/le-manifeste (consulted on October 10, 2019)

6 Discussion and conclusion

This article aims to consider how the health promotion discourse, conceived as producer of a new social reality, operates. Our study has focused on the construction of discursive ethos by which public authorities, together with an NGO, have presented themselves as the VOICE, in the context of prevention campaigns against HIV/AIDS since the early 1980s. Through its nonverbal positioning of self-image, its discursive scenario and its verbalized evaluation of ethos, the VOICE presents to the receiver the example of recognized moral and civic authority, counselor, mediator or partner in verbal interaction. In reality, these different images, which are, by definition, suspended between preexisting ethos and discursive ethos, aim to get citizens taking over new social standards, in order to radically change their behaviors and practices, their ideological concepts and their religious beliefs. The creation of social reality occurs through the persuasive power of discourse and the social prestige of the public authorities and it is partners on behalf of whom the VOICE is speaking, borrowing from the ancient ideal of the "person of virtue", the upstanding speaker and the model citizen.

In addition, the advertiser's ethos aims to convince receivers of the validity of its argumentations. The credibility of the approach resides in the fact that it purports to give the public the choice of agreeing or disagreeing. Here, the discursive strategy consists in accentuating the concept of communication transparency, which reigns in contemporary societies. The staging of a discursive presentation of self, which appears as a negotiation of meaning, shared with the general public, modifies the anthropologic preconceptions that consider that people are naturally inclined towards truth, goodness and justice. However, our analysis indicates that the power of the rhetorical process, used in solidarity campaigns in the context of health promotion discourses against HIV/AIDS, keeps the receivers from being in disharmony with the public health ideology of the VOICE. The examples of solidarity campaigns show how political authorities seek to impose their understanding of social reality, by exercising both moral and civic pressure on public opinion. Thus, as our analyses have shown, the power of inclusion, deployed through argumentation strategies based on ethos, holds, in itself, the contradictory movement between social inclusion and exclusion. The question is how the VOICE manages this conflict on the rhetorical level. In our study, analysis of verbalized ethos has shown how it tries to anticipate a negative reaction from the receiver, by apparently proceeding with self-criticism. But the power displayed in this ad indicates the real goal of this discursive strategy. The reinforcement of the moral burden exercised by this sort of ethos produces the opposite of what the message advocates: an increasing lack of solidarity and an agonic decline of social ethics. Thus, the result of our study shows that the health promotion discourse against HIV/AIDS builds a social reality governed by an ethic of happiness of those who deserve to be happy, because they have adopted civically proper, self-interested behavior. It is then a selective, exclusive happiness, showing that the VOICE, speaking in the name of common good, has proceeded at a major shift in terms of ethos: the promotion of the individual good.

References

[1] Amossy, R. (éd.), 1999. *Images de soi dans le discours. La construction de l'ethos*[M]. Lausanne-Paris, Delachaux et Niestlé.

[2] Amossy, R., 2000. *La présentation de soi. Ethos et identité verbale*[M]. Paris, PUF.

[3] Angenot, M., 2009. «Rhétorique, théorie du discours social, histoire des idées, dix-neuvième siècle»[J]. *Discours social*, vol. XXXII.

[4] Aristotle., 2006. *On Rhetoric* (Transl. G. A. Kennedy)[C]. Oxford, Oxford University Press.

[5] Breton, P., 1997. *Utopie de la communication*[M]. Paris, La Découverte.

[6] Bunton, R. & G. Macdonald. (eds.), 2002. *Health Promotion*[C]. New York, Routledge.

[7] Garver, E., 1995. *Aristotle's Rhetoric: An Art of Character*[C]. Chicago, University of Chicago Press.

[8] Grmek, M., 2005. *Histoire du sida*, Paris, Payot.

[9] Hyde, M. J. & C. O. Schrag. (eds.), 2004. *The Ethos of Rhetoric*[C]. Columbia (SC): University of South Carolina.

[10] Kello, L., 2017. *The Virtual Weapon and International Order*[M]. New Haven, Yale

University Press.

[11] Kemm, J., 2015. *Health Promotion: Ideology, Discipline, and Specialism* [M]. Oxford, Oxford University Press.

[12] Kingman, S. & S. Connor., 1989. *The Search for the Virus* [M]. Harmondsworth [Eng.], Penguin.

[13] Kotler, P. & N. R. Lee., 2008. *Social Marketing. Influencing Behaviors for Good* [M]. London, Sage.

[14] Melinda, C., 2017. *Family Values: Between Neoliberalism and the New Social Conservatism* [M]. Cambridge (MA), Zone Books.

[15] Meyer, M., 2004. *La rhétorique* [M]. Paris: Presses Universitaires de France, coll. «Que sais-je?».

[16] Ollivier-Yanniv, C., & Rinn, M. 2009. (eds). *Communication de l'état et gouvernement du social* [C]. Grenoble, P. U. G.

[17] Pépin, J., 2011. *The Origins of AIDS* [M]. Cambridge, Cambridge University Press.

[18] Rinn, M., 2002. *Les discourse sociaux contre le sida. Rhétorique de la communication publique* [M]. Bruxelles, De Boeck Université.

[19] Rinn, M. & Sherlaw, W., 2018. Santé publique et communication [J]. *MEI*, n° 44 - 45 (Specialissue).

[20] Scriven, A., 2010. *Promoting Health: A Practical Guide*, (6th edition) [M]. Edinburgh, Balliere Tindall/Elsivier.

[21] Shilts, R., 1987. *And the Band Played on: Politics, People, and the AIDS Epidemic* [M]. New York, St. Martin's Press.

An Argument for Public Health: The Centrality of Communication Theory in Making Comprehensive and Effective Public Health Messages

Ryerson University　Jessica Mudry[①]

Abstract: This paper calls for the centrality of the rhetorical processes of communication as fundamental to public health, and it argues that the study of rhetorical theory, techniques of argumentation and the histories and limits of language is fundamental and, indeed, ethical to successful public health. This paper will propose a practical, epistemological framework for the co-creation of public health messages within populations. Bolstered by a deliberative process, this paper proposes the reclaiming of the public nature of public health, by examining context, tropes, and cultural/rhetorical tools to make for a more robust and constitutive model for effective public health messages.

Key words: public health; Communication Theory; argumentation; rhetorical tools

1　Introduction

Communication is both a theoretical field of study and an applied set of techniques

---

① Dr. Jessica Mudry is an associate professor at School of Professional Communication, Ryerson University, Toronto, Ontario, Canada. email: jessica.mudry@ryerson.ca.

that become instrumental in operationalizing human action. Put simply, good communication helps us move people to action. As for the effectivity of communication, we ask ourselves what has resulted from our communication; is the outcome of human action in line with the intention of the words we used? This fundamental question has no greater bearing on the wellbeing of humankind as in the case of public health communication.

Conceptually, public health forgoes treating the individual (such is the domain of medicine), and instead aims to examine populations and approach health as a collective goal. Public health succeeds when it prevents diseases, increases lifespans, and improves the collective quality of the lives of a population. As such, the goals of the research and practices of public health are to improve, to save, and to protect the well-being of a population. But to consider the discursive structure within which public health operates, the delicate ether of language, means that where we do public health is not in the clinic, mobile health bus, or urban vaccination hub, rather through the construction and communication of arguments to various audiences. Thus, understanding how communication through language and argumentation works can allow for a more comprehensive approach to understanding and constructing effective and innovative public health messages. Thus, understanding basic communication and argumentation theories within the context of public health can teach us much about what public health is, the narrative framework within which it exists, and the ways in which campaigns and professionals can make better arguments in the name of public health.

Language is a constructive force in the world. It makes things true or false, knowable or mysterious, data points or anomalies. We identify a virus in a lab, note an epidemiological trend within a population, or map the movement of food poisoning but we use language to articulate these ideas and to propose action. Language circumscribes and constitutes both the concept of "public" and the concept of "health," making the study of communication theory and argumentation and the functions of language and discourse, fundamental and necessary for public health practitioners. The goal here is not to outline a blueprint for public health messaging. Rather, the goal here is to point out some primary aspects of communication theory that are fundamental for public health practitioners to integrate into their field. At the core, public health is a practical art that aims to move people to action; so is communication.

2 Models of communication

Understanding how to make public health messages aimed at particular populations means first understanding workable models of communication and, second, taking into consideration how language and arguments resonate with the public of the populations. A scan of published materials written to public health professionals about how to "do" public health communication yields step-by-step plans that often involve identifying the target audiences, strategically designing a plan, testing messages among a population or measuring a message's impact. Health communication textbooks ask public health professionals to identify behaviors that they hope to change with a campaign, the conditions under which this change will occur and the "amount of behavior change" that needs to be measured in order to deem a campaign successful. (O'Sullivan et al., 2003: 82) These texts encourage public health professionals to measure "impacts," "outcomes" and "objectives" in order to judge the success of the campaign or communication program. (U. S. Department of Health and Human Services-National Cancer Institute, n. p., n. d.) Applied health communication encourages the use of both qualitative and quantitative methods: "in-depth interviews" and focus groups, surveys and randomized trials that observe and catalogue behaviors that become markers for a successful or unsuccessful public health campaign. (Schiavo, 2013) When the statistical data of a methodological evaluation of an audience's understanding becomes the marker of a successful public health campaign, governmental programs, NGOs and university programs run the risk of seeing populations as a de-animated mass. This reductive view of a "successful" public health campaign is dangerous and short-sighted. In this model, and at a policy level, behavioral change among a population becomes a quantity upon which professionals make economic, social or political decisions. Both the public and health become targets for epidemiologists or data analysts, who may point to a successful campaign through markers of reduced incidence of a disease, or an increase in healthy behavior. What gets lost here, however, is the impact that those increases and decreases have on the lived experience of the public, the "public"-ness of the population.

We could look at these models that call for the observation and notation of changed behaviors, or the evaluation of the audiences' understanding as being holistic, comprehensive or inclusive models of communication. The audience is, of course, made up of people who receive a message, populations whose behaviors the campaigns are hoping to change. A closer look reveals that "how-to" guides for public health communicators' use provide a model of communication that treats the communication process as uni-directional. The United States Center For Disease Control, for example, relies on a power structure of experts and the "non-expert public." (Centers for Disease Control, "Everyday Words", p. 1) This is a telling moniker. Underpinning the distinction between "expert" and "non-expert" is a patriarchal view of health. The calling of populations of people "non-experts" about something that can be considered deeply individual creates impotence among the public in feeling healthy unless they enact the policies in place. These kinds of language divisions create public health campaigns that quantify success based on a population "getting" the message as though it were a discrete packet of information. Discursively, communicators must pay attention to "short sentences," the "active voice" and "everyday words and pronouns." (Centers for Disease Control, "Everyday Words" p. 1) Asking public health communicators to pay heed to the grammatical structure of a message, or the length of the sentence is useful and important, but it demonstrates a two-dimensional understanding of language, with little attention paid to long-term discursive effects or processes shaped by language or argument. Rhetoricians and communication scholars understand the communication processes of many campaigns as falling into the category of communication outlined by James Carey in his seminal work from 1989 Communication as Culture as a transmission model of communication. Some of the least successful public health campaigns rely solely on the transmission model of communication. A prominent example is in "abstinence-only" public health campaigns that aim to curb teenage pregnancy. The United States has the highest teenage pregnancy and birth rates in the developed world a result of which, one could argue, comes from a top-down, transmission model of communication. In the early 2000s the United States teenage pregnancy rate was 72.2 pregnancies per 1000, 2.5 times the rate of Canada (at 29.2) and almost 7 times as high as the Netherlands at 11.8. Both the Netherlands and Canada have socialized medicine and a national strategy around sexuality that is integrated into health education as early as kindergarten. The United States relied on a strategy of avoidance, and a unidirectional message of "no" around sexuality, effectively shutting down any communication processes. This strategy failed. As Stanger-Hall and Hall

(2011) point out in their paper: "[T]hese data show clearly that abstinence-only education as a state policy is ineffective in preventing teenage pregnancy and may actually be contributing to the high teenage pregnancy rates in the U. S." As an example of a poor model for public health communication, simply telling teenagers to abstain from having sex, instead of having frank conversations with them, or providing an integrated education plan that encourages a contextual conversation, fails terribly. At its core, the transmission model fails to contextualize and situate health among populations and delivers information as though it was a rigid object, and not a malleable concept that is subject to interpretation. In the case of abstinence-only campaigns, political will and religious strong-arming create a reticence to engage in a two-way discussion about sexuality among teenagers. This results in a public health campaign that deems itself successful because the information has been "delivered" to the audience, but ultimately fails when the information is not integrated into the population it aims to serve because it is inconsiderate to cultural, social, economic, educational, historical or political contexts.

One could understand why the tidy but flawed transmission model of communication is appealing to the public health profession. The transmission model makes quantitative public health audiences research easy, and makes the "results" of communication measurable or seeable. The model fits into an ideological framework of bureaucratic efficiency, in which communication is conceived of as a thing that happens in and through the space between people. In industrial societies the idea of sending something and having it marked as "received" either by email confirmation, text message, or by focus group consensus is a marker of successful communication. The quantification of public reaction to epidemics, patient compliance or concordance, or even public awareness of issues as measures of the "success" of a public health program, perpetuates the transmission model of communication as a viable construct of how communication happens. The problem with such quantification is that it treats communication as an "achievement"—a terminal process with a measurable end. But the measurement of public awareness or public action around health makes knowledge static, more like a data point than nuanced human behavior. For example, a chapter in the *Routledge Handbook of Global Public Health* by Bertrand et al., writes that "the level of effectiveness of health campaigns ... have an average effect size of 5 percentage points ($r=0.05$). That is, if 60 percent of the target population performed the desired behavior before the campaign, the percentage post-campaign would be

65." (p. 320) Indeed, it is true that public health communicators can go back and see their successes or failures and attempt to correct their campaigns by examining data such as "propensity score matching," or "triprobit regression" (Babalola & Kinkaid, 2009). But a communication scholar could see these kinds of data sets as dangerous as to what constitutes public health communication. Such a model of communication bolsters a biopolitics of public health in which a healthy population becomes a constructed representation for a healthy state. Once "health" becomes an objective construct through datasets, intangible and immeasurable markers of health like happiness, community engagement, and friendships may fail to make the checklist what constitutes health for a public health professional.

A communication strategy born of, and shaped upon, the transmission model is abetted by the rise in the professional status of public health, wherein the formalization of the discipline through university training programs, governmental standards and bodies of professional oversight make public health an authoritative voice in its own right. Specialization makes the "things" of public health the knowledge of how to be healthy, and makes public health professionals the gatekeepers of this information; information that is inaccessible to those lacking training or experience: the "non-expert." Thus, the transmission model, where how to behealthy is somehow a knowable, finite packet of data becomes the capital of public health with the goal of a successful public health campaign to generate this capital. Where this model falls down is the idea that knowledge of how to be healthy can be somehow delivered and received, and that communication moves from sender to receiver with no interference from human factors such as language, context, culture, history or geography.

Is there a better way to conceive of communication in a public health context? In short, yes, and this conception relies on the questions we ask around the process of communication. Instead of asking if the public "gets" a message, the question to ask is "what **effect** did the message have?" Public health involves the actions and words of people, and neither language nor people are static. If we consider public health communication as a dynamic system wherein individuals and professionals communicate with each other instead of the top-down model of professionals communicating to groups of people, then we can approach communication not as a thing that is finished when words are spoken, but rather as an on-going process that a) has no end and b) has no authoritative "source" of the message. Thus, public health professionals, and the public mutually constitute public health messages. This constitutive model does not privilege the source of the message and, necessarily, places both the public health professional and the community in the role of generating knowledge, and making meaning, together. What results are public health messages that are multi-dimensional and contextual, wherein the public feels interpolated, empowered and contributory. In this model, the content of the message itself is less important than the integration and extension of societal values from the public. This is not to say that this model cannot move the public to act on particular public health issues. Instead, the power of this model of communication comes through the mobilization of people, and their participation and commitment to a narrative within which they see themselves. Depending on the community, these kinds of messages can use linguistic tropes, music, regional history and geography, humor or discursive gravity to communicate ideas about public health to people. The success of Australia's SunSmart Campaign for sunscreen "Slip, Slop, Slap" relied on alliteration, and a cartoon seagull to appeal to adults and children. Anti-smoking campaigns that use images of cancerous lungs, or rotting teeth, rely on both a societal aversion to the decay of the human body, and a societal norm of beauty, as well as a political ideology of self-care and wellness. (Kremer, 2014)

3 Argumentation in public health

The discretionary tools of public health are manuals, guides and textbooks, at their core, asking public health professionals to make an argument. A loose academic definition of making an argument involves understanding how to organize and present information with the hopes of changing the ideas or behaviors of the audience, the aforementioned, rhetorically defined, "effect." Understanding the structure and organization of argumentation is crucial for public health professionals because these structures appreciate language as an imperfect conduit for communication. In public health, as in most disciplines, problems of communication become most obvious in moments of turmoil or discord. In these moments communication fosters collective deliberation, decisions, and judgments. The ancient Greeks categorized communication, as a practical art of discourse—and scholars of rhetoric understand deliberation and argument as modes of persuasion that are necessary to address any given situation and to resolve problems. Arguments offer a way **through** a moment. While there are multiple models of argumentation, here I highlight two in particular with which we can explore argumentation in public health.

3.1 A classical approach to argumentation

The classical or Aristotelian framework of argumentation works to identify and employ patterns of communication to demonstrateto an audience why they should adopt the speaker's point of view. The classical approach, based on Aristotle's *Rhetoric*, relies heavily on the use of different appeals in order to have an effect on others and, ultimately, move them to action. Aristotle wrote *Rhetoric* as an account of the mind, and his interest lay in why the mind believes one thing and not another. This question is ubiquitous in public health. *Why* are some communities receptive to particular public health campaigns, and not others? Why do some government public health initiatives fail, and others succeed? We find answers to these questions when one understands that the quality of argument does not solely come from data, but also from timing, emotion, language and place.

Aristotle was interested in the relationship and tension between emotion and reason, and for Aristotle it was emotion, not reason, that formed the foundation for morals and ethics in any given set of circumstances. Knowing how to respond to certain appeals implicates emotion in discourse, decision-making and action. Rational arguments exist, but are both tempered, and often superseded, by emotional ones. As such, Aristotle arrived at three different kinds of argumentative appeals: ethos, pathos and logos, all of which are implicated in any argument. It is fair to say that any effective argument is a combination of each of the following three appeals, and the weight of each appeal is context-dependent.

3.1.1 Ethos

The concept of ethos can be translated in myriad ways, but it is commonly translated into the authority of the person or organization making a claim. It is the answer to the question: why should I trust what you are saying? Ethos, thus, is constituted by the audience's sense of the speaker's good sense, good will and good character. Moving an audience to action with an appeal to the speaker's ethos requires first that the speaker or organization demonstrate a level of intelligence that resonates with the worldview of the audience. Put another way, the speaker or organization needs to be in possession of good sense. Second, ethos is most effective when the audience understands that the speaker has their best intentions in mind: good will. Finally, ethos' appeal works on the good character of the speaker. Does the speaker share the same sense of right and wrong, of *how* to live, and a shared sense of ethics? To sum up, ethos is the "*who says*" factor of an argument's effect. When a city like Berkeley, California, issues an excise tax on sugar-sweetened beverages in efforts to combat obesity, they do so with the blessing and support of legions of professors, doctors, and public health professionals. Statements from the political movement establish ethos by promoting support from the American Academy of Pediatrics, the American Heart Association, and the Alameda County Public Health Commission. Alternatively, public health movements like Mothers Against Drunk Driving rely on a social recognition of the mother as a trustworthy authority, who has the best interest of her children in mind. Public health professionals ignore the ethos of non-experts at their peril. The challenge that the concept of ethos faces in public health communication is when the scientific and medical voices compete with other trusted voices within communities who may understand health outside of a medical-scientific paradigm. In 2019, the World Health Organization reported a 300% global increase in measles with significant increases in countries with mass vaccination plans. Western Europe and North America have seen outbreaks in communities who have perceived vaccinations as a risk for a variety of reasons: a fear of mercury in the vaccines eluent, a fear that the vaccines cause autism, or fears that the vaccines themselves cause the disease they are aimed at preventing. As well, certain communities eschew vaccinations for their children for religious or cultural reasons. Celebrities, politicians and community religious leaders' ethos resonates among certain populations. A parent who chooses not to vaccinate their child does so on the advice of what the medical establishment may call a "non-expert" but their voice and opinion has had an effect, and it has moved a public to action. To a particular public, a celebrity may be an expert because their likability, ability to relate, and their sensibility (whether or not it goes against the grain of medical truth) precludes any public health messages about the topic.

3.1.2 Pathos

Aristotle's second proof considers the emotional state of the audience. Aristotle used the word pathos, meaning emotion or feeling, to describe this proof. In order for pathos to work, the speaker must have sensitivity to the audience's emotional state. In the case of an acute public health concern the audience may be afraid, excited, or worried. Authors of public health campaigns that employ pathos, then, must know how to use language to excite or suppress the audience's emotions using texts and images that fit into an emotional narrative with which the audience is familiar. Understanding narratives and stories with cultural and social resonance, and having sensitivity to connotation in language and the power of words to move people to action makes pathos effective. Appeals for the safety of children employ pathos, aimed squarely at parents to modify their or their children's practices to keep children safe. A television advertisement from the Department of the Environment of Northern Ireland about road safety and speeding is one example of this. Deemed "triggering," and "troubling," the minute-long advertisement cuts together footage of young children on a field trip in the forest. Scenes of children playing and laughing are cut with a young male losing control of his speeding car. The car rolls through a wall and into the class of children, sitting in the grass. The advertisement is horrifying, and an acoustic version of the popular rock'n'roll song "Sweet Child 'O Mine" makes it even more so. The Department justified the ad because, according to them, "the fear of killing a child was one of the few factors that influences drivers to cut their speed." (Gayle, 2014). Pathos can be a powerful appeal for behavioral change, if the audience's ideological position towards the narrative is culturally favorable. The narrative of children as innocent, protectable and vulnerable works in this campaign's advertisement. This narrative can also backfire in a case where the public health intervention might be deemed a potential risk to the "innocent" child. Again, anti-vaccination parents choose to do so because they deem the invisible "risk" of the vaccine greater than the risk of contracting the mumps or the measles. In these cases public health administrators and practitioners must learn to work within certain cultural narratives, understand the social and discursive traction of particular messaging, and manage health outcomes through understanding and appreciating the element of emotions that are fundamental to effective communication.

3.1.3 Logos

While the ethos and pathos proofs are useful, Aristotle placed emphasis on the process of deliberation, a rational process of reasoning, and the justification of an argument with the presentation of evidence. Logos, the third proof, then, is about methodical and practical reasoning. When a speaker uses logos, they present evidence to show that their argument is somehow external to them. In the case of proof by logos, rationality and practicality create a framework for discourse. Evidence-based medicine, statistics and data, and quantitative rationality as justification for behavioral change are all logos arguments wherein facts "speak for themselves." In much scientific, medical and technical writing the presentation of facts, delivered in a passive voice, foster an aura of objectivity and make ethos and pathos less effective in these kinds of milieu. India's recent deworming campaign poster, published by the national Ministry of Health and Family Welfare, shows a series of rational arguments for deworming: "reduced economic productivity," "reduced physical and cognitive development" and "reduced school attendance." The cartoon depiction of a child does little to incite emotion in the audience. The practical reason of national "economic productivity" depicted by a cartoon rupee is the rational reason for deworming. This example demonstrates that scientific framework within which much public health communication happens, abstracts actual people from the political construct of a "population." (WHO, 2016) Strictly rational arguments encouraging healthy behavior rarely stand alone, and generally need political, cultural, social or personal messaging alongside. Even statistics designed to "scare" populations into acting—like risk or probability statements around contracting a particular disease—require the population to adopt a medico-scientific framework for understand power relationships with a society. Those quantitative statements, whether they are issued from a governmental body, a medical professional or a community member, require ethos working in tandem with logos to move people to action.

3.2 A modern approach to argumentation

Aristotelian proofs are a time-honoured way of understanding argumentation, and a useful tripartite structure for public health professionals to consider when crafting messages. But the structure of much public health discourse rests upon a foundation of repeatable science, rationality and reason, and a more granular picture of how the Aristotelian proof of logos works can offer a different model for public health communication. Fundamentally, scholars concerned with justification recognize that absolute "truth" is not the goal of argumentation. Put another way, when addressing an audience, communicators need to have access to an audience's perception, belief or understanding of what is true. Underpinning a population's beliefs are reasons, some rational, some irrational. The important question answered by a modern approach to reason, then, is "how do I convince you to believe something is true?" Public health professionals can benefit from understanding the architecture of a model of reasoning that begins with beliefs that reflect a social and cultural context.

3.3 A theory of justification: the model of warranted assent

If we consider how reasoning works, we can start with belief, akin to starting with a conclusion, or a claim. A claim is a something that not everyone believes to be true; this matter or uncertainty or controversy almost always invites a response. In models of justification, argumentation is a way of justifying a particular claim, of supporting it, and of making sure it responds to challenges from dissent.

Oxford philosopher Stephen Toulmin was interested in the process of reasoning and argued that formal logic could not explain how people made decisions. People often acted irrationally, but within architecture of rationality. That is, they could explain, in a structured way, why they believed what they did. For example, anti-vaccination adherents can explain, in a reasoned way, why they believe that vaccines "cause" autism. Public health, evidence-based medicine and policy-makers may dismiss such a group's argument for not vaccinating as "irrational" scientifically, but the structure of the anti-vaxxers argument fits into a model of reasoned discourse. Toulmin's architecture of argumentation, often called the Model of Warranted Assent, gives us a picture of how reasoning, justification and ultimately argumentation, works.

The Toulmin model's most important tenet is that arguments are "field dependent," meaning that there is no universal audience for a claim. For some people a claim can be reasonable, and for others, not. While an audience's beliefs may be fluid and field-dependent, Toulmin saw the structure of a reasoned argument as fixed. A speaker makes a *claim*, a statement that you want the audience to believe. *Data or grounds* are the facts or information upon which the claim rests—data answers the question "what do we have to go on?" Finally, the warrant is the general rule that creates the relationship between the facts and the claim. The warrant is implied, field-dependent, historical, geographical, social and cultural. Toulmin's model is easily illustrated if we make a claim like "the force is 10 Newtons" with the data/grounds of "the mass is 5 grams, and the acceleration is 2 meters per second squared." The warrant, for anyone familiar with basic physics, is that the principle of force is equal to mass multiplied by acceleration. Toulmin's model is useful when an argument fails because the audience does not recognize the warrant the speaker uses to link the data and the claim. In the case of the anti-vaccination controversy, the claim was from Dr. Andrew Wakefield, who published a fraudulent [now retracted] paper in the British journal *The Lancet* linking the measles, mumps, rubella vaccine to "hyperplasia, non-specific colitis, and pervasive developmental disorder." (Wakefield et al., 1998). Understanding the Model of Warranted Assent means that Wakefield's data presented in the form of a scientific paper and in a medical journal, becomes the symptoms manifested in the children. Wakefield wrote "[W]e have identified chronic enterocolitis in children that may be related to neuropsychiatric dysfunction. In most cases, onset of symptoms was after measles, mumps, and rubella immunization. Further investigations are needed to examine this syndrome and its possible relation to this vaccine." The warrant here, which links the grounds with the claim, is that certain sets of medical symptoms are recognized by the medical "field," as being a disease or malady. We take much of these warrants in medicine for granted: small itchy spots, a fever, and a positive test for the varicella-zoster virus means chicken pox, and not a manifestation of weak morals as may have been the warrant several hundred years ago. Textbooks of clinical diagnoses are, from a Toulmin standpoint, texts of claims, data and warrants. This model of medicine with a professional and epistemological system that explains symptoms and diagnoses through warrants of Western medicine explains why, when Wakefield's study identified nine out of twelve children as having "gastrointestinal disease and developmental regression" as a possible result of having the MMR vaccine, it had argumentative traction. The warrants in medicine are studies (preferably repeatable) that attempt to link symptoms and diagnoses within certain measurable frames of time or geography. Wakefield's claim fit neatly into an argumentative structure of medicine with which most of Western society was familiar, leading the research group to make a "claim" in *The Lancet*, with the evidence being a series of symptoms.

4 Conclusion

The MMR-autism case is a cautionary tale, but it is also a moment that points to the importance of teaching public health professionals communication theory, structures of argumentation, various rhetorical appeals, and communication context. If public health professionals can understand basic categories of rhetorical appeals, the structure of warrants, and the constitutive model of communication, they can better understand how and why some public health initiatives succeed, and others fail.

Underpinning all of this is a call for public health to recognize the importance of training in communication theory for professionals. Effective and successful public health campaigns require sensitivity to and a respect for the media of language, symbols and argument. Such a sensitivity to the tools and structures of communication can help public health practitioners better understand their discipline, their campaigns, and, hopefully, their "publics."

References

[1] Babalola, S., & L. Kincaid., 2009. New methods for estimating the impact of health communication programs[J]. *Communication Methods And Measures*, 3: 61–83.

[2] Carey, J., 1989. *Communication as Culture: Essays on Media and Society* (Vol. 1, Media and Popular Culture)[M]. London, UK: Psychology Press.

[3] Gayle, D. (2014, June 22). The road safety advert so shocking it's been banned from screens until after 9 p.m. Retrieved April 24, 2017, from http://www.dailymail.co.uk/news/article-2664537/Watch-The-road-safety-advert-shocking-banned-screens-9pm.html.

[4] Kremer, W. (2014, November 24). The battle for control of the cigarette packet. Retrieved April 24, 2017, from http://www.bbc.com/news/magazine-30061952.

[5] O'Sullivan, G. A., J. A. Yonkler., W. Morgan., & A. P. Merritt. (2003, March). *A Field Guide to Designing a Health Communication Strategy*, Baltimore, MD: Johns Hopkins Bloomberg School of Public Health/Center for Communication Programs.

[6] Parker, R. &M. Sommer (eds.)., 2011. *Routledge Handbook of Global Public Health*[M]. New York, NY: Routledge.

[7] Schiavo, R., 2013. *Health Communication: From Theory to Practice* (2nd ed., Jossey-Bass Public Health)[M]. New York, NY: John Wiley and Sons.

[8] Stanger-Hall, K. F. & D. W. Hall., 2011. Abstinence-Only Education and Teen Pregnancy Rates: Why We Need Comprehensive Sex Education in the U.S. PLoS ONE 6(10): e24658. https://doi.org/10.1371/journal.pone.0024658.

[9] *United States, Centers for Disease Control and Prevention, Office of the Associate Director for Communication.* (2015, October 1). *Everyday Words for Public Health Communication*. Retrieved April 24, 2017, from https://www.cdc.gov/other/pdf/everydaywordsforpublichealthcommunication_final_11-5-15.pdf.

[10] *United States, U.S. Department of Health and Human Services, National Cancer Institute.* (n.d.). *Making Health Communication Programs Work* (Pink Book). Retrieved from https://www.cancer.gov/publications/health-communication/pink-book.pdf.

[11] Wakefield, A., 1998. RETRACTED: Ileal-lymphoid-nodular hyperplasia, non-specific colitis,

and pervasive developmental disorder in children[J]. *The Lancet*, 351(9103), 637–641.

[12] *World Health Organization. New Measles Surveillance Data.* Retrieved October 18, 2019. Retrieved from https://www.who.int/immunization/newsroom/measles-data–2019/en/.

[13] *World's largest deworming campaign targets 270 million children in one day.* (2016, February 10). Retrieved April 24, 2017, from http://www.who.int/neglected_diseases/news/270_million_children_treated_in_one_day/en/.

Developing Rational Empathy in Health Care Policy: The Usefulness of Online Comments

University of Cyprus　Fabienne Baider[①]

Abstract: Studies of interactions have gained an increasing importance in research related to healthcare. Most empirical studies have explored the dynamics of exchanges between patients and practitioners (Barry et al., 2001, Beach et al., 2001). This study is devoted to the analysis of discussions in two forums to investigate how to develop what we call 'a rational empathy' so as to understand the attitudes and beliefs which constitute the basis of these opinions.

Key words: rational empathy; health care policy; online comments

1　Introduction

On the 4th of July 2017, the French Health Minister Agnès Buzyn announced that eleven vaccines (eight more than the three usual ones) will be compulsory for all babies in France during their first two years of life from the first of January 2018 onwards. Such measure was declared as being 'incidental', because, as it was officially argued, '80% of babies in France receive already 8 of these injections'. Not quite so incidental was this measure felt and thought by some doctors and the parents.

[①] Dr. Fabienne H. Baider is an associate professor at Department of French Studies and European Studies, University of Cyprus, Cyprus. Email: helenafab @ yahoo.fr.

Indeed studies of interactions have gained an increasing importance in research related to healthcare, most empirical studies have explored the dynamics of exchanges between patients and practitioners (Barry et al., 2001; Beach et al., 2001). Developing an emotionally sensitive rapport with patients has also grown in importance in health care studies and practice (Charles et al., 1999; Mead & Bower, 2000; Stivers et al., 2009). However, we believe that studying debates among the public is as useful to develop an emotionally sensitive rapport with the public when health policies are put into place.

In this paper we investigate how to develop what we call 'a rational empathy', against what could appear as being 'overt coercion' exerted by politicians against the public they are supposed to serve. To do so we collected online data so as to understand the attitudes and beliefs which constitute the basis of these opinions. More precisely the objectives of this article are twofold: (1) What emotions and rational are used by the side of the pro-government measure? (2) What emotions and rational are used by the anti-vaccine group to explain and convince of the 'folly' of vaccines?

2 Context of the vaccine issue

The socio-cultural context iskey to the analysis of our online data. In this section we give a brief description of what Fairclough (1995) calls the macro context, i.e. the discourse, which circulates at the time of the study regarding the topic investigated. Taking into account Fairclough's proposals regarding the importance of contextualizing a communication event we give here the main facts in relation to the general social climate regarding the vaccine issue in Europe and then more specifically in France.

2.1 Socio-cultural context of the vaccine issue in the EU

Vaccine confidence is defined as 'the trust in the effectiveness and safety of vaccines and trust in the healthcare system that delivers them' (The Vaccine Confidence Project or VCR, 2018)①. Many surveys and reports are carried out to test vaccine confidence; most found that some European regions have low levels of

---

① These study and report were commissioned and paid by the European commission.

confidence in the safety and effectiveness of vaccines (Larson et al., 2016). More precisely in a number of settings, confidence has significantly decreased and concerns regarding vaccines have significantly increased in Poland, the Czech Republic, Finland, and Sweden. Therefore vaccine refusal has been increasing in many EU member states: for example in the last 15 years what has been called routine immunization coverage (the measles-containing vaccine) has been on the decrease in 12 European states, and this trend goes on intensifying①. As Mc Donald (2015: 4162) explains 'Acceptance of vaccination is an outcome behavior resulting from a complex *decision-making process* that can be potentially influenced by *a wide range of factors*' (my italics). This complexity and this need for contextualization should therefore be addressed when deciding health policies and communication strategies to convey such policy. Indeed results from the different survey (reports from VCR 2016, 2018, for instance) and research on the topic of vaccination (Dubé et al., 2015; Oku et al., 2016) have highlighted the importance of addressing public concerns around vaccination to maintain optimal coverage rates. These reports and articles show that the medical professions are quite aware that '*public confidence* in vaccination is fundamental for ensuring high vaccination uptake' (cf. Larson et al., 2018, 8, my italics).

2.2 Reasons for resistance to vaccine

The reasons for such mistrust are numerous and we can cite the growing role of alternative medicine such as homeopathy, such alternative medicine not being all pro vaccine, and previous vaccination disasters (Chen & Fu, 2019). Public confidence or lack of confidence depends a lot on how much the public trusts the vaccination and how much they have political confidence in the government enforcing it to accept such medical intervention. To observe and evaluate confidence in vaccination scientists have developed a 3 Cs model—Confidence, Complacency and Convenience—to capture the different factors which have to be watched when discussing trust in vaccine. We will only mention the *confidence* parameters which are the ones that will be motivating the comments which we analyze in this paper.

Confidence is based on trust. Trust has been suggested to be working on a triple basis (Mc Donald, 2015: 4162) as far as vaccination is concerned:

---

① These estimates are taken from the 2018 EU report which quotes WHO-UNICEF 2017 figures.

(i) Trust in the effectiveness and safety of vaccines;

(ii) Trust in the *system* that delivers them (health services and health professionals);

(iii) Trust in *the sincerity and well-founded motivations of policy-makers* who decide on the needed vaccines.

In the next section weanalyze these three factors in the French context. The factors are not as independent from each other's as this list may imply: once the policy makers are distrusted we may have a snowball effect on the two other parameters, i. e. the health system being considered as complicit in the deceit and then fear regarding the safety and effectiveness of the vaccines can be the consequence.

2.3 Objectives of this study

France had known already in 2016 (VCP, 2016) a decrease in confidence as far as the safety of vaccines is concerned; as matter of fact France is one of the ten countries with the lowest levels of safety-based confidence issues within the European region (Larson, 2016). As such France is a country known to be one of the most anti-vaccinecountry in the EU and even in the world according to a 2019 recent study[①]. When the decision for 11 vaccines was taken, according to polls, 56% of the parents were against the measure; 2,500 complaints were sent to the government regarding the measure and a petition was signed by 1,500,000 people. This discontent was also felt among the medical staff since 25% of doctors were against the announced. Such mistrust and resistance could be explained by the triple parameter system described in the previous section, i. e. trust in the vaccine's efficiency, in the *system* that delivers them and in the *policy-makers* who decide on the needed vaccines.

The additions and intersections of all these parameters revived disbelief and mistrust over any decision made tomultiply vaccination and to render them compulsory. Reports highlight the costs of such disbelief and lack of confidence: loosing trust of the public is quick (Peretti-Watel, 2013), but rebuilding it is a lengthy task, hence the communication prudence that such decision deserves. Moreover any such decision is extremely context dependent, i. e. the necessity when thinking of communication strategies to be taking into account the public, the historical moment as well as the

---

① https://www.lemonde.fr/societe/article/2019/06/19/les-francais-sont-les-plus-sceptiques-face-aux-vaccins-selon-une-enquete-mondiale_5478259_3224.html.

type of vaccination (Raude & Muller, 2017; Chen & Fu 2019). Therefore identifying the beliefs, attitudes and knowledge of the public following the Minister's decision and the ways these concerns have been addressed on online forums could be the first move to assess the success (or lack of) of the government communication strategy in this matter. This is the aim of this paper.

3 Theoretical framework and methodology

Our analysis is anchored in frame semantics which will guide our discourse analysis of data collected online. We will adopt a socio-cognitive approach and as such centering our analysisaround the 'frame' concept. This concept has been put forward by sociologists such as Goffman (1974) and cognitive psychologists such as Minsky (1975) to explain how we process information and make sense of events, people and ideas which surround us.

3.1 Concept of frame and salience

The concept of frame was discussed as early as the 70's if one recalls Goffman's concept of 'schemata' (1974) which according to the sociologist 'organize, and interpret our life experiences to make sense of them'; such conceptual devices enable individuals to locate, perceive, identify, and label the events, people, concepts and information around them (Goffman, 1974: 21). This guiding of the information process making it quicker and more efficient *simplifies* as well evaluations (Tadlock et al., 2007: 196, our italics; Cravens, 2015); it has been called in psychology 'template', 'data structure', script (Fiske & Taylor, 1991; Minsky, 1975). The *framing effect* has been proven to be one of the strongest biases in making a judgment (Wallin et al., 2016; Fagley & Miller, 1997). Tadlock et al. (2007:196) have worked on the dialectics between individual frames and society frames: each of us relies on our *own* personal frames which is based on our own personal *values* to interpret events, things and individuals; on the other hand, we acknowledge that a society tends to favor specific knowledge, beliefs and attitudes, which are then promoted in the mainstream media and perpetuated in the institutions governing the life of individuals in that same society. Any online exchanges will be a negotiation between one's own frames (pro, anti or neutral regarding vaccine) and the society's frame in which the exchanges occur (in our case the French vaccine social resistance to vaccine). Therefore analyzing framing of the vaccine issue is also analyzing the development of online social relations and circulation of ideologies (van Dijk, 1993).

As we see in our data such ideologies lead to and feed intense emotions and allow violent or contemptuous exchanges creating or reinforcing in group andoutgroup formation (Allport, 1956; Stephan et al., 1999, 2009). Working on frames is also discovering an underlying system of evaluation which is the objective of our paper.

3.2 Concept of salience in frame semantics

The notion of 'frame' is in fact grounded in our cognitive and epistemological knowledge, which itself has been formed by our previous (linguistic and non-linguistic) experiences (Barsalou, 1992; Fillmore, 1982: 112). Because frames are so contextualized they play a major role in our appraisal of events and ideas. We could refer to a specific *sociocultural arena of frames*.

How can we track such a schemata in text? We will be using the two concepts put forward by earlier research on frames: the centrality of a frame and its power of selecting or excluding other information. Centrality of one idea is what qualifies a frame for Gamson & Modigliani, since they consider a frame a "*central organizing idea (...) that provides meaning*" to events (Gamson & Modigliani, 1987, 143, my italics). For Gitlin the "*persistent selection*, emphasis, and exclusion" of ideas, events (Gitlin, 1980: 7) would qualify for being a frame. For example framing the vaccination decision as putting in danger babies would encourage discussions of previous health scandals, previous causalities because of vaccination, and encourage as well research on other motives than the well-being of children.

For that matter we argue for frame semantics in the same way that Charteris-Black (2004) argued à propos metaphors: they simplify complex issues using well-known cultural references and familiar values specific to the socio-cultural content; because of the proximity of these references and values, it becomes easier to stir emotions among the audience and therefore to persuade. Indeed among the five typical rhetorical tropes which are used to build frames we find metaphors (cf. Gamson & Modigliani, 1989). How practically examining frames?

Frame Semantics (Fillmore, 1982; Huckin, 2002; Langacker, 1991) examines lexical choice as a way to uncover framing strategies which have been described as being unique ways for each community to perceive and construct events and ideas

(Fairclough, 1989; Wodak & Meyer, 2016), as mentioned as well by sociologists and psychologists above as defined by Fillmore, a frame refers to: any system of concepts related in such a way that to understand any of them you have to understand the whole structure in which it fits; when one of the things in such a structure is introduced into a text or into a conversation all of the others are automatically made available. ①(1982:11, our italics)

We believe that to discover the 'one of the things' which will trigger a whole system of evaluation or in other words the 'centralorganizing idea' can be uncovered with firstly identifying frequencies and specificities among the lexicon. The *persistent selection* and exclusion of events and information defines how a frame functions within the texts; this functioning can then be assessed when going back to the context where the most frequent or specific lexical items are used. To do so our methodology comprises corpus linguistics which enable us to identify the most salient words in our data. Salience is here understood as the most frequent and the most specific (i. e. not expected) (cf. Giora, 2003; Kecskes, 2004), the concept of salience being core to such linguistic choices.

Words or phrases are salient either because of their frequency and familiarity in the public discourse (strong presence in the mainstream media), because of their prototypicality and representative of the society under study or their specificity (i. c. they should not appear in the data). Both high frequency and prototypically can be representative of the community belief and attitudes for the issue under study (Giora, 2003). This methodology is consistent with frame semantics theory which involves working on co-occurrence of words (called semantic preference by Sinclair, 2004).

3.3 Concept of empathy

Once we have identified the frames on each side of the debate, we will argue for a solution to solve such hardened positions on both sides. Most studies acknowledge that empathy is useful for understanding the perspectives, needs and intentions of others. Different from sympathy which does not require a simulation of the other or insight into his state of mind, but does require a positive attitude of being "for" the

---

① This concept can be also defined, as mentioned by Fillmore himself (1982:11), with the words *schema, script, scenario* or *cognitive model*. However we prefer to use the word *frame* itself because of the rigidity and squareness it evokes, which captures the constraints imposed on the bodies and behaviors.

other (Chismar, 1988).

Empathy is described as the way in which one responds to another's physical or emotional experience. More precisely, Hodge and Myers (2007) define empathy as 'understanding the other person's experience as if it were being experienced by the self, but without the self actually experiencing it. A distinction is maintained between self and other.' Most of the literature concurs regarding the two types of empathy, cognitive and emotionali. e as having both cognitive and affective components (Decety and Jackson, 2004; Eisenberg and Fabes, 1990). The cognitive dimension involves awareness of the internal state of another person; empathy is about "imagining how it feels to experience something" (distanced-analytical cf. Halpern, 2001:85). Cognitive empathy is also called empathic accuracy in that it refers to the potential of an individual to perceive and understand the emotions of another, including the understanding of how the person feels (Strayer, 1987). The affective dimension involves the emotional response toward the other person, and is about caring for the other (simulative-emotional). For Hoffman (1987, 2000), empathy is the act of "feeling into" another's affective and cognitive experience.

4 Data and results

4.1 Data collection and Identification of frame

A three step methodology, which we explained in detail below, was followed:

a. First we identified the frames with corpus linguistics tools i. e. the specificities and the frequencies;
b. Secondly we analyzed the functioning of those frames on the emotional level and more precisely what emotional ethos is constructed within these frames by both groups pro and anti-vaccines;
c. Thirdly we suggest a different communication strategy so as to develop a rational empathy.

We aimed at triangulating the sources of our data so as to get different point of views or standpoints on the issue (Cohen, Manion & Morrison, 2000: 254; Wodak &

Meyer, 2009). Cohen and Manion (2000) define triangulation as an "attempt to map out, or explain more fully, the richness and complexity of human behavior by studying it from more than one standpoint". In our case we have collected in our previous section the point of views of reports and scientific articles. In this section we focalize on online data.

We collected our data from two discussion forums focused on the measure (Doctissimo, YouTube). The two of them genuinely debate the pro and the cons of such measure. The first data were collected in YouTube comments regarding a program titled *France 24*, well known in France to debate current issues (3,566 words). The second body of data comprises discussions on a mainstream medical forum (8,950 words), a forum where parents were overwhelmingly present. We anchor the analysis of our data in the Computer Assisted Discourse Analysis (CADS) approach, combining Critical discourse analysis (CDA, Fairclough, 1995, *inter alia*) and argumentation theory (Amossy, 2008, *inter alia*) applied to data collected with Corpus linguistic tools (Partington et al. , 2013). Retrieval of the most frequent words was done in order to define the salient *paradigm or frame* used to evaluate such decision. This was achieved with the concordancer *Antconc*.

Once we gathered the keywords we went back to extract where the keywords were sued so as to proceed to our argumentative analysis. We focus specifically on the emotional ethos built on each side of the debate.

4.2 Results

In the table below we give the frequencies we found in two lists of discussion, one is made of all the comment posted under a well-known station France 24 discussing current social and political issues and in this case the vaccine decision. Two people are discussing, a female lawyer defending an association who wants the right to refuse vaccinations (such as the hepatitis B[①]) but also stipulates she is not against vaccination. She is especially against any vaccination coating the booster made of aluminum and asks for more studies about consequences. Her association collected

---

[①] Which is generally only for sexually transmissible disease (STD) and some studies have established the causality between the vaccination and the multiple sclerosis within the vaccination (Dipheteria, tetanos and polio).

2,500 signatures against the Minister decision which were forwarded to the State council①. She is a professor of medicine and head of the Academy of Science who defends the need for all vaccinations. Both are fierce adversaries; the professor denies any of the dangers mentioned by the lawyer.

Table 1 Corpus presentation

Name of list	date	Number of words	Link
Vaccins obligatoires en France: une nécessité de santé publique? You Tube	13 July 2017	62 comments 3,566 words	https://www.youtube.com/watch?v= UEP9f59xBKg
Vaccins obligatoires Doctissimo	July 2017	8,950 words	http://forum.doctissimo.fr/grossesse-bebe/ futures-mamans/Les-novembrettes-2017/vaccins-obligatoires-2018-sujet_370273_1.htm http://forum.doctissimo.fr/grossesse-bebe/ futures-mamans/Les-novembrettes-2017/vaccins-obligatoires-2018-sujet_370273_1.htm

Interestingly the journalist mentions the categorization of people questioning vaccinations as being in *obscurantism* [to which the professor answers that 'reason will be stronger' (*c'est la raison qui l'emporte*) and whether the fact that vaccination has become an obligation is not a problem]. Both will be the focus in the second discussion found on the Doctissimo which we present in Table 2. This discussion is not focused on an article but on the Minister decision.

Table 2 Frequencies of lexical items in discussions in semantic fields

Comments, general public You Tube		Parents discussions, *Doctissimo* (8,950 mots)	
Aluminium	24	Risks (Risques, 27), Unwanted consequences (effets indésirables) **Autism (autisme, 18)**,	70
Health Well being Diseases	29	hepatitis (hépatite, 14) measles (rougeole, 11)	
France	9	Doctors (médecins), laboratories (laboratoire, injection, etc.),	65

---

① She mentions a DOXA opinion pool revealed which shows that 56% of French people are against the Minister decision although 75% already give such vaccinations to the children. They seem to resent the obligation to do it.

Comments, general public You Tube		Parents discussions, Doctissimo (8,950 mots)	
Dosage	8	Obligation (10) Study (Étude) (8)	57
Children 15 People 9	24	Parents People (Gens, Monde, personnes), Children (Enfants), bodies (corps), babies (bébés)	
Brain	7	Health (santé), diseases (maladies)	32
USA	6	Life (Vie), time (temps)	26
Industry	6	**Money (Argent)**	22

In bold letters we have the lexical items which are specific to the discussion, i. e. not expected when discussing vaccination.

4.3 Quantitative analysis: Identification of frames and salience

The France 24, YouTube video

For the discussion commenting the France 24 debate, the expected frames are quite distinct from the unexpected frames put in bold such as Brain, Industry and Aluminum. Actually the three items describe a chain of events apparent in the context in which they are used: the brain is said to be attacked by the aluminum, which is an adjuvant used in some vaccines by the pharmaceutical industry and such aluminum presence would have for consequence autism.

We can observe with this list of keywords that the Argumentative frame on the You Tube that the anti-vaccines have managed to put at the center of the debate their positioning, since we find much about the negative effects and not about the positive ones. Regarding the Emotive Frame, the frame of fear dominates regarding the safety of the vaccine (aluminum) and the pharmaceutical industry (rumors of corruption).

The discussion on the Doctissimo forum

For *Doctissimo* parents are worried and discuss the pros and cons of this measure. We observe again the usual frames for a debate on vaccination (health, doctors, diseases, children), the high frequency of negative frames related to health such as specific diseases as well as an unusual frequency of words related to risks, obligation, etc.). Another unusual frame for health is the frame of money. All in all we find the same pattern as we have found for the previous debate. When looking at clusters around the word vaccine the emotional frame of fear is very present with the most frequent coordinated noun being *décès* (death). The most frequent adjective is obligatory, therefore the *obligatory* nature of the vaccine is the most controversial dimension of the procedure, because of the possibilities of disease and death according to the frequencies we have observed. Moreover the most frequent verb *pouvoir* (can, may) is associated with the possibilities of risks and the phrase *faire le vaccin* (to do the vaccine) is embedded in 90% of the cases in a negative context. These quantitative results point at indeed the main reasons for refusing the vaccine or questioning the Minister decision.

If these frames give us a general picture of the main point of discussion regarding vaccination, we have not with those frames any of the arguments given by the pro-vaccine group. The qualitative analysis, which is done by going to the context of the most frequent words and analyzing the threads which areenfolding will give us this missing information.

5 Qualitative analysis of the emotional ethos

Both discussions involve very different participants. On the Doctisimo the emotion of fear for their children health is quite present and most parents agree that protecting their children is their first responsibility. Their argument is that the pro-vaccine group to impose a medical gesture which is unsafe on unwilling children. This fear is met by the anger of the pro-vaccine camp who argues that prevention of spreading diseases is also the first duty of a citizen so as to protect all other children, accusing therefore anti-vaccine parents of lethal irresponsibility.

5.1 Discursive construction of the emotion of fear (anti vaccine)

To understand the strategies deployed by both camps to display their fear/anger, we have gone back to the context of the most troubling key word, *aluminum*. If we look at the Keyword in context (*KWIC*) (Annex1) it shows balanced interactions about the danger and reassuring messages on the part of the other participants. However are these reassurances convincing the parents?

The emotion of fear is generally expressed through two most common reactions which we could describe as being visceral: 1. babies seem to be used as Guinea pigs (Qu'est ce qu'ils veulent faire sur nos bébés? [What do they want to do to our babies?]) and in 2. such a number of vaccines in less than two months of life is too much for a new-born:

> 1) What do they want to do on our babies? This doctor must be sincere with his Hippocrates oath. (Qu'est ce qu'ils veulent faire sur nos bébés? Ce médecin doit être sincère avec son serment Hippocrate)
> 2) Children are too fragile for so many vaccines. (Lesenfants sont trop fragiles pour tant de vaccins)

In the next two quotations below 3) and 4) arguments are put into place by the anti-vaccine group to explain where their fear is founded and logical. The first one is the scientific argument, explaining that aluminum is used in some vaccine as adjuvant (which is true) and that such substrate can be toxic (which is also true but under certain conditions). It is even mentioned that it is prohibited in vaccination for pets (with providing no proof for such a statement). The comment plays on the reasoning that children are treated less well than animals, which would obviously trigger some reactions from parents.

> 3) Do you know that aluminum is found in certain vaccines for children and infants while it is a toxic substance that the body cannot evacuate? Do you know that legislation prohibits aluminum in pet vaccines but not in human vaccines?

Even though the argument is not sustained by any proof, the emotional dimension may be enough to trigger strong opposition on the parents' side. Although appealing to rationality (Why would pet vaccine be safer than infant vaccine?), it actually plays on emotion of indignation, unfairness, regarding this illogical decision etc. and at the same attacking the ethos and credibility of the laboratories who seem to be willing to put in danger the babies' life.

The second argument is an argument from authority (*argumentum* ab *auctoritate*) which is much more sustained than the previous one. It appeals to a well-known figure (the European Commissioner for Health) who is used as evidence for an argument's conclusion. This claimed authority's support is also sustained by the use of a hyperlink which leads to damming article against the vaccine, citing almost 2000 people adults and children having been strongly affected by the swine influenza A vaccine:

> 4) Vytenis Andriukaitis, European Commissioner for Health: "Children suffer from terrifying experiences related to the side effects of swine influenza A (H1N1) vaccine. Nearly 1,700 adults and children across Europe are now registered in the EU Adverse Drug Reaction Database. They suffer from neurological disease for life, narcolepsy caused by this vaccination." https://inews.co.uk/essentials/news/health/eu-health-commissioner-narcolepsy-swine-flu-vaccine/[①]

The emotion of fear for the children life is obviously present here. The social media specificities such as possibilities of sharing hyperlinks provide the opportunity to share as well an argument of authority more or less related, i.e. the consequences of another vaccine which was administered against the swine influenza.

To this basic instinct (to protect my child) and to the expression of a primary emotion (fear) the following typical arguments are given as follows:

> 5) Vaccination protects (Levaccin est très protecteur)
> 6) To get vaccinated is also protecting others: A case of measles makes 17 contaminations (Sevacciner c'est aussi protéger les autres: Un cas de rougeole fait 17 contaminations)

The quotation 5) tries to reassure the parents in a very succinct way, asserting only that vaccination protects. The following quotation 6) though emphasizes the responsibility of the parents towards other children who would be put at risk if they come into contact with children who are not vaccinated[②]. This argument puts into an

---

① Vytenis Andriukaitis, commissaire européen pour la santé: «Des enfants souffrent d'expériences terrifiantes, liées aux effets secondaires du vaccin contre la grippe porcine A (H1N1). » Près de 1.700 adultes et enfants à travers l'Europe sont à présent enregistrés dans la base de données des effets indésirables des médicaments de l'Union européenne. Ils souffrent de maladie neurologique à vie, de narcolepsie causée par cette vaccination. https://inews.co.uk/essentials/news/health/eu-health-commissioner-narcolepsy-swine-flu-vaccine/.

② Although it is not clear how a vaccinated child would then contaminate other children if those children are vaccinated?

emotional double bind the parents. On the one hand they want to avoid possible danger for their children and do not want either to put in danger other children. This double bind though does not answer the fear they have expressed. It does not take into account either the infant-mother relationship which is decisive for all mammals. We would then conclude that such argumentation cannot convince.

Finally on the anti-vaccine side the mistrust towards companies, laboratories and the government is tangible: the frequency of the word *money* in the Doctissimo data and of industry in the YouTube data shows how important in the anti-vaccine discourse is the idea that vaccination is firstly business for the government and not children wellbeing. Moreover the fact that the Minister imposed the decision so abruptly and her links with the laboratories do not help in convincing sincerity as it is obvious in the quotation 7:

> 7) The unofficial reason for 11 compulsory vaccines Emmanuel Macron has publicly benefited from an intensive help for his campaign from Serge Weinberg, president of Sanofi, the leading French producer of vaccines! His Health Minister Agnès Buzyn has been paid many years by the giants of the pharmaceutical world (Sanofi, Novartis, Bristol Myers-Squibbs). Agnès Buzyn was caught by Médiapart for justifying the researchers' "conflicts of interest": according to one of her statements, there is no problem for scientists who evaluate drugs for the public to be paid at the same time by the industry fabricating them.

It motivates in some cases the conspirational theory such as the 'new order' theory, with the quotation 8:

> 8) This is to make people stupid and weak.

5.2 Discursive construction of the emotion of contempt (pro-vaccine group)

The amalgam of anti-vaccine arguments and conspiracy theory is one of the most frequent arguments of the pro-vaccine. Anti-vaccine people are accused of repeating fallacies about laboratories and vaccination, in other words they are accused of spreading fake news. In 9, the presence of aluminum and its noxiousness is here described as false:

9) This rumor about theallu is FALSE and has no scientific support whatsoever. It's only about conspiracy. (Cette rumeur sur l'allu est FAUSSE et n'a aucun appui scientifique quel qu'il soit. C'est juste de la théorie du complot.)

The emotion of contempt is palpable in the pro-vaccine camp: describing anti-vaccineas living in the dark ages, of being illiterate and not knowing what are the functions of vaccines. To these 'obscurantists' is opposed the pro-vaccine described as the camp of the sciences, of progress and of 'the enlightened' as explicitly mentioned in 10 and 11:

10) I see obscurantism, the result of smear campaigns. This attitude of French opinion must be attacked and scientists will help the minister to make scientific truth triumph.
11) What do you want theantivax, return back to the 17th century when rabbies was everywhere? The vaccine if you do not mind serves to protect you from diseases. It is his role and its unique role. (Vous voulez quoi les anti, retourner au 17eme siècle ou sévissait partout le rage et autre? Le vaccin ne vous en déplaise Sert à vous protéger des maladies C'est son rôle et son unique rôle)

When expressing genuine fear and meeting contempt, one does not feel heard but hurt. Empathy and fear for a baby's life safety cannot be defeated by contempt: the higher order of emotion wins. However the most important is that this attitude is not convincing. Only rarely do we find arguments or real attempts to answer fear one the logos level as in 12), where the presence of aluminum is acknowledged but the level of its presence cannot be hurtful:

12) In fact there is aluminum but that micrograms not hurt our health. (En faitil y a de l'alu mais que des micro-grammes, pas de quoi nuire à notre santé)

If for Michel Meyer rhetoric is about negotiating difference by individuals on a specific issue, we could conclude from our brief analysis above that in such forums there is only differences and no negotiation, nor compromise.

6 Discussion

6.1 Usefulness of analyzing comments

Our data illustrates how mistrust is built in dialogues. As far as trust in *medical efficiency* is concerned a controversial historical health context feeds the messages. If previous health scandals have not been forgotten by the general population, the one which has been referred to in our data is what is called the 'tainted blood scandal' (1998) in which the Health Minister at the time and has been proved guilty of mismanagement. As for vaccines especially, an important controversy that surrounded the AH1N1 pandemic influenza vaccination campaign[①] in 2009 was also mentioned. This unfortunate development compromised the level of trust in safety of the seasonal influenza vaccine and vaccine in general.

To these real scandals we add *mistrust in the policy-makers*. We can see the preeminence of the word *money* which does not refer to cost of vaccines, but to rumors of corruption, or rather several conflicts of interest on the part of the policy makers was mentioned. Rumors of supposedly financial and economic interests at stake refer to the Minister herself in the data; indeed she worked for years with vaccine laboratories and her husband is the head of the INSERM Medical Research Institute[②]. As far as the Head of Government, Emmanuel Macron he is said to also be close to the pharmaceutical companies such as *Sanofi* or *BigPharma* and therefore to be potentially in conflict of interest.

Finally the decision to make vaccines compulsory comes as well at times when penury of some vaccines had been reported, and as consequences profits for the pharmaceutical laboratories; price has been multiplying over the years[③] and mistrust in the *system* that delivers them was also quite high as we can see in comments mentioning the laboratories and their profit.

[①] https://www.cdc.gov/vaccinesafety/concerns/history/narcolepsy-flu.html.
[②] https://www.thelancet.com/action/showPdf? pii=S0140-6736%2818%2931318-7.
[③] https://blogs.mediapart.fr/le-blog-des-associes-par-yannick-et-helene/blog/160617/une-vendue-au-ministere-de-la-sante-agnes-buzyn.

The Health Minister was counting on 'the doctors and the press to do some pedagogy' regarding the compulsory vaccinations. 'Reason prevails' ('C'est la raison qui l'emporte') was the argument of the government representatives (Cf. You Tube program debate). Contempt was also the most frequent emotion we tracked down in our data on the both parties but especially on the pro-vaccine party. Contempt cannot answer the reasons for the fear, anger and mistrust displayed in the comments. Not only this attitude does not answer on the level of the logos but accusing the anti-vaccine to be obscurantists they attack the face of the parents for example, hardening their attitude against the 'opponent'.

Our proposal is that observing and analyzing online argumentation on forums would prove more useful than any other pedagogical scheme in order to develop an understanding of the emotions and argumentation behind resistance and in order to avoid, what some may call, a 'totalitarian health care attitude' (cf. the statement that 'reason prevails').

6.2 Not imposing heath policy, but working on acceptance

Surveys have shown that a majority of citizens in the EU still believe in the importance, effectiveness and safety of vaccines. However as mentioned in our previous sections, reports have also revealed important declines in confidence in certain countries since the year 2000, 'highlighting the need for continuous monitoring, preparedness and response plans'. In a number of EU countries, anti-vaccine groups are gaining power and have started influencing politics and political elections. Reports on the situation in the EU advocate researchers, scientists and health authorities in France to implement a *comprehensive communication strategy*, including public consultations, to improve confidence in and uptake of vaccination in the country. As far as communication strategies are concerned, researchers have identified several communication strategies which have worked in improving vaccination uptake if they are used routinely (Dubé et al., 2015; Mc Donald, 2015; Oku et al., 2016). These strategies include not only 'to inform, educate, remind or recall' but also:

——to enhance community ownership of medical care, i.e. to respect the freedom of the patient in the choice of medical care (which could go against imposing vaccinations);

——to enable communication which we would call 'horizontal', i.e. to answer with arguments to questions asked or problems presented by people doubting vaccination, and answering vertically (i. e. looking down to the other);

—to provide support or facilitate decision-making. (McDonald, 2015: 4162)

For instance a comment such as 13 states first that the person is NOT against vaccination. He/sheexplains three fundamental questions though about vaccine, questions which are most frequent in ours data: the dosage of vaccination, the presence of aluminum and the fact the caution principle ('principe de précaution') is not applied.

> 13) Nous nesommes pas contre les vaccins ... nous sommes contre le sur dosage, l'hydroxide d'aluminium comme adjuvant et l'application systématique du principe de précaution!

If one puts himself/herself in his/her shoes, one could start a discussion with such commentators. This is what we call exhibiting relational sympathy.

6.3 Relational sympathy

Relational sympathy could be developed firstly with respecting the arguments given as well as respecting the feeling expressed. Once this respect is possible one can understand cognitively and affectively the positioning of the other one. This understanding would allow to address firstly the rational level the arguments of the anti-vaccine and secondly on the affective level the emotions implicit or explicit contained in the message.

For that matter empathy can be *deliberate* or spontaneous, making it a kind of disposition (reaction) and also a kind of action. In fact, like most socio-cognitive developments, this emotion develops early in life (e. g. , Hutman & Dapretto, 2009). Since cognitive empathy has been understood as being similar to a *social skill*, to a certain degree it can be *developed with training*. We would advise the communication strategists to develop such attitude and emotion.

The literature also emphasizes the role of social and cultural factors in empathy— why, for whom, where, etc. we might feel or express empathy. These factors may cause variations in development because of socialization, gender, and cultural values. Therefore such training should be contextualized within the social context.

We then conclude that communication regarding health policies should be based on a blend of cognitive and emotional empathy, i. e. a conscious empathy triggered by a fairness perception (Singer et al., 2006). Such an open and understanding attitude on the part of decision makers could therefore affect changes in the social structures (Breithaupt, 2012: 86) such as:

—carrying out more studies on aluminum dosage in vaccine before applying the law;

—organizing more extensive public debates where respect of both parties has to be enforced;

—developing measures to be implemented to respond to some of the discontent;

—undertaking specific research so as to respond to the reticence of the publicand understand the beliefs based system which has a 'strong local and contextual roots'.

7 Concluding remarks

In this paper we have discussed the growing awareness of what is called in medicine 'the increasing vaccine hesitancy' among both members of the public and health professionals in Europe. Indeed a number of European countries have faced important confidence crises in the past 20 years which partly resulted in the measles outbreaks seen today. Medical institutions are aware that understanding the gaining the confidence in vaccines involves 'understanding belief-based factors' (Chen & Fu, 2019; VCP, 2018: 43). Specialists (Dubé et al., 2015; Oku et al., 2016) have also studied the different impact of communication strategies on public confidence in vaccination and advised on the successful ones (VCP, 2018: 8). Previous attempts at applying strategies have been followed by an observable increase in public confidence in the safety and effectiveness of vaccines.

However our study shows that both provider and politicians are not trusted (rumors of corruption on both sides). Indeed observing and analyzing online comments on both sides of the debate helps us to understand the communication gap between parties: instead of insults and contempt expressed on the pro side, understanding the issues of the anti-vaccine side would be more useful as well as developing what we called 'relational empathy'. Understanding the social (here the comments,) context allows the empathizer to reconstruct *why* others have a particular emotion, not only *that they feel a specific emotion.*

However the verticality of the decision on the part of the French minister, her communication strategy relying on the motto that 'reason will prevail', did not take into account research on vaccination resistance and communication strategies. This verticality has also been observed within the pro-vaccine reactions which are the topic of this paper: analysis of these online comments show no attempt to understand *the belief based system* and *the emotion based refusal* of the other side. We will conclude therefore that studying online comments is therefore indeed very useful in deciding on communication strategies:

——to understand the pulse of a nation regarding such health care decision;

——to take into consideration parents unwilling to apply the policy;

——to help constructing a dialogue and develop what we called 'rational empathy' (a blend of cognitive and emotional empathy).

References

[1] Afiong, O. et al., 2016.① Communication strategies to promote the uptake of childhood vaccination in Nigeria: A systematic map[J]. *Global health Action*, 9: 1–10.

[2] Allport, G. W., 1954. *The Nature of Prejudice*[M]. Cambridge, MA: Addison-Wesley Publishing.

[3] Baider, F. & M. Constantinou, 2018, Negotiating empathy in French and Cypriot Greek press: Christian values or social justice in migration discourse? [J] *Studii de lingvistica*, 8: 71–83.

[4] Barsalou, L. W., 1992. Frames, concepts, and conceptual fields[A]. In A. Lehrer & E. F. Kittay (eds.). *Frames, Fields, and Contrasts: New Essays in Semantic and Lexical Organization*[C]. Lawrence Erlbaum, London, 21–74.

[5] Caroline L. E., M. Guay, P. Bramadat, R. Roy, & J. A. Bettinger, 2013. Vaccine hesitancy. An overview [J]. *Human Vaccines & Immunotherapies*, 9(8): 1763–1773.

[6] Charteris-Black, J., 2004. *Corpus approaches to Critical Metaphor Analysis*[M]. Basingstoke: Palgrave Macmillan.

[7] Chismar, D., 1988. Empathy and sympathy: The important difference [J]. *Journal of Value Inquiry*, 22(4): 257–266.

[8] Cohen, L., M. Lawrence, & K. Morrison, 2000. *Research Methods in Education* [M]. London: Routledge.

---

① Angela Oyo-Ita, Claire Glenton, Atle Fretheim, Heather Ames, Artur Muloliwa, Jessica Kaufman, Sophie Hill, Julie Cliff, Yuri Cartier, Xavier Bosch-Capblanch, Gabriel Rada and Simon Lewin, 9: 1–10.

[9] Cravens, R. G., 2015. Morality politics and municipal LGBT policy adoption: A rare event analysis [J]. *State and Local Government Review*, 47(1): 15-25.

[10] Decety, J. & P. L. Jackson, 2004. The functional architecture of human empathy [J]. *Behavioral Cognitive Neurosciences Review*, 3 (2): 71-100.

[11] Dubé, E., D. Gagnon, & N. E. MacDonald., 2015. Strategies intended to address vaccine hesitancy: Review of published reviews [J]. *Vaccine* 33, (34): 4191-4203.

[12] Eisenberg, N. & R. A. Fabes., 1990. Empathy: Conceptualization, measurement, and relation to prosocial behaviour [J]. *Motivation and Emotion* 14, 131-149.

[13] Expert Panel on effective ways of investing in Health (EXPH), Preliminary report on Vaccination Programmes and Health Systems in Europe, 2018. Vaccination programmes and health systems in the European union, Luxembourg: Publications Office of the European Union.

[14] Fagley, N. S. & P. M. Miller., 1997. Framing effects and arenas of choice[J]. *Organizational Behavior and Human Decision Processes*, 71: 355-373.

[15] Fairclough, N., 1989. *Language and Power* [M]. London: Longman.

[16] Fairclough, N., 1995. *Critical Discourse Analysis* [M]. London: Longman.

[17] Fillmore, C. J., 1982. *Frame Semantics. Linguistics in the Morning Calm* [M]. Seoul: Hanshin Publishing Co.

[18] Giora, R., 2003. *On Our Mind: Salience, Context and Figurative Language*[M]. New York: Oxford University Press.

[19] Goffman, E., 1974. *Frame Analysis: An Essay on the Organization of Experience* [M]. Cambridge, MA: Harvard University Press.

[20] Hoffman, M. L., 2000. *Empathy and Moral Development: Implications for Caring and Justice* [M]. New York: Cambridge University Press.

[21] Hoffman, M. L., 1987. The contribution of empathy to justice and moral judgment [A]. In N. Eisenberg & J. Stayer (Eds.). *Empathy and its development* [C]. New York: Cambridge University Press, 47-80.

[22] Hutman, T. & M. Dapretto, 2009. The emergence of empathy during infancy[J]. *Cognition, Brain, Behaviour*, 13 (4): 367-390.

[23] Karafillakis, E., & H. Larson, 2017. The benefit of the doubt or doubts over benefits? A systematic literature review of perceived risks of vaccines in European populations [J]. *Vaccine*, 4840-4850.

[24] Kecskes, I., 2004. The role of salience in processing pragmatic units [J]. *Acta Liinguistica Hungarica*, 51(3-4): 309-324.

[25] Larson, H. J., 2016. The state of vaccine confidence 2016: global insights through a 67-country survey [J]. *EBioMedicine*, 295-301.

[26] MacDonald N. E., 2015. Vaccine hesitancy: Definition, scope and determinants [J]. *Vaccine*, 33, 4161-4164.

[27] Peretti-Watel, P. , P. Verger, J. Raude, A. Constant, A. Gautier, C. Jestin, & F. Beck, 2013. Dramatic change in public attitudes towards vaccination during the 2009 influenza A (H1N1) pandemic in France [J]. *Eurosurveillance*, 20 – 23.

[28] Petrelli, C. M. E. Contratti, & I. Grappasonni, 2018. Vaccine hesitancy, a public health problem [J]. *Ann Ig*, 30(2): 86 – 103.

[29] Sangrigoli S. & S. de Schonen, 2004. Effect of visual experience on face processing: A developmental study of inversion and non-native effects [J]. *Journal of Child Psychology Psychiatry*, 45(7): 1219 – 27.

[30] Sinclair, J. , 2004. *Trust the Text: Language Corpus and Discourse* [M]. London: Routledge.

[31] Stephan, W. G. , O. Ybarra & G. Bachman (1999). Prejudice toward immigrants [J]. *Journal of Applied Social Psychology*, 29: 2221 – 2237.

[32] Strayer, J. , 1987. Affective and cognitive perspectives on empathy [A]. In N. Eisenberg & J. Strayer (Eds.). *Empathy and its Development* [C]. Cambridge: Cambridge University Press, 218 – 245.

[33] Tadlock, B. L. , C. A. Gordon & E. Popp. , 2007. Framing the issue of same-sex marriage: Traditional values versus equal rights [A]. In A. Rimmerman & C. Wilcox (Eds.) *The Politics of Same-Sex Marriage* [C]. Chicago: University of Chicago Press, 193 – 214.

[34] van Dijk, T. , 1993. Analyzing racism through discourse analysis: Some methodological reflections [A]. In J. H. Stanfield II & R. M. Dennis (Eds). *Race and Ethnicity in Research Methods*. London: Sage Publications, 92 – 134.

[35] Wallin A. , C. Paradis, & K. V. Katsikopoulos, 2016. Evaluative polarity words in risky choice framing [J]. *Journal of Pragmatics*, 106: 20 – 38.

[36] Wodak, R. & M. Meyer, 2016. *Methods of Critical Discourse Studies* [M]. London: Sage.

[37] Pan, Z. , G. M. Kosicki, 1993. Framing analysis: An approach to news discourse [J]. *Political Communication*, 10, 55 – 75.

语言学与应用语言学研究

现代汉语副词"相互/互相"联系义用法的涌现*

首都师范大学 郝 琦 北京大学 郭 锐**

摘要: 本文讨论现代汉语相互副词"相互/互相"的一种新用法——联系义用法。相互标记的"相互义—联系义"这一一词多义形式广泛见于世界语言。汉语中相互副词的联系义用法处于萌芽阶段,能产度较低,接受度存在分歧。该用法具有如下四个语义特征:[＋复数事件]和事件参与者[＋同等语义角色]、[＋单一语义角色]、[＋相互联系]。从相互义发展为联系义,其机制是交互关系中交互对象被抑制为非语言成分,从而使事件参与者的相互关系变为隐性的[＋相互联系]特征。

关键词: 相互副词;联系义;复数事件

Title: The emerging of sociative use of Mandarin reciprocal adverbs "xianghu/huxiang（相互/互相）"

Abstract: This study focuses on a new usage of Mandarin reciprocal adverbs "xianghu/huxiang（相互/互相）"—the sociative use. The "reciprocal-sociative" polysemy of reciprocal markers is very common across languages. The sociative use of reciprocal adverbs in Mandarin is in its embryonic stage, with low productivity and divergent acceptability among speakers. There are four semantic features of this usage: [＋Plural Events], event participants [＋Equal Participation], [＋Single Thematic-Role] and [＋Reciprocal Associativity]. The mechanism of the development

---

* 本研究受到国家留学基金委资助。
** 作者简介:郝琦,首都师范大学文学院讲师。研究方向:现代汉语语法、语义。邮箱:6834@cnu.edu.cn。郭锐,北京大学中文系教授,北京大学中国语言学研究中心专职研究员。研究方向:现代汉语语法、语义。邮箱:guoruipku@163.com。

from reciprocal meaning to sociative meaning is that the reciprocees in reciprocal relations are transformed into non-linguistic forms, which makes the reciprocality of event participants change into an implicit [+Reciprocal Associativity] one.

Key words: reciprocal adverbs; sociatives; plural events

1 引言:汉语副词"相互/互相"的新用法

1.1 相互结构

相互结构(reciprocal constructions)是世界语言中普遍存在的一类表达形式。相互结构中往往有至少一个形式标记显示其"相互"意义,如:

(1) a. Yakut 语
  Aγa-m ikki əal öjdö-s̲-t-üler.
  father-my two neighbour understand-REC-PAST – 3PL
  'My father and (his) neighbour understand each other.'
            (我爸爸和他的邻居互相理解。)
 b. John and Bill hit **each other**. (约翰和比尔互相打对方。)
 c. 张三和李四互相攻击。

在上例(1a)Yakut 语例句中,相互结构以动词词缀-s 标记;(1b)英语例句中,相互结构以相互代词(reciprocal pronoun)标记;(1c)汉语例句中,相互结构以相互义副词(reciprocal adverb)"互相"标记。

从语义的角度来看,相互结构表达相互情景(reciprocal situations),即在两个及两个以上的事件参与者中,每一个事件参与者均针对对方做出相同行为,或者说,事件参与者在语义角色上呈对称关系(Nedjalkov,2007a;郭锐,2013)。以汉语为例。

(2) a. 张三和李四互相攻击。 ⇄展开/合并 { b. 张三攻击李四。
                c. 李四攻击张三。}

在该相互情景中,"张三"和"李四"同时具有"攻击"事件的施事(攻击者)和受事(被攻击者)双重角色,(2a)所表达的事件在真值语义上等价于两个子事件(2b)和(2c)的合取。因此,相互情景是复数事件(plural events)的一种(郭锐,2017)。我们把从(2a)到(2b)+(2c)的分解过程称为语义展开,把从(2b)+(2c)到(2a)的概括过程称为语义合并。语义展开和语义合并可以作为相互情景和相互结构的定义,也可以作为二者的测试手段。

1.2 "相互/互相"的新用法

在语料库中,我们发现汉语相互副词"相互"和"互相"的使用存在少量的超出上述定义的用法,举例如下。

(3) 三个和尚互相偷懒不愿意去打水。(CCL)
(4) 一辈子都在相互寻找共同语言,却没寻找到过几次。(梁晓声《冉之父》)
(5) 1997年4月,中国与上述国家签署了《关于在边境地区相互裁减军事力量的协定》。(中国政府白皮书)
(6) 在通电方面,可在厦门和金门相互架起微波天线,或利用卫星建立直达电话电报电路。(1994年报刊精选)

在上述实际语料中,副词"相互/互相"所描述的情景无法被认定为1.1中定义的相互情景,即无法对其进行(2)中所示的语义展开。以例(4)和例(6)(简化)为例,展示如下。

(7) a. 三个和尚互相偷懒不愿意去打水。
$\Longrightarrow$ { b. 和尚 A 偷懒不愿意去打水。
c. 和尚 B 偷懒不愿意去打水。
d. 和尚 C 偷懒不愿意去打水。}

(8) a. 在厦门和金门相互架起微波天线。
$\Longrightarrow$ { b. 在厦门架起微波天线。
c. 在金门架起微波天线。}

在(7b)至(7d)中,"和尚 A"、"和尚 B"和"和尚 C"的语义角色具有等同性,却不具有对称性,即不存在对称的施受关系。在(8b)和(8c)中,"厦门"和"金门"在语义展开式中也无法建立起对称的语义角色。

郭锐(2013,2017)已注意到"相互/互相"的这一类用法,并将这里的"相互/互相"诠释为"共同、一起"或"各自、分别"。本文认为,这些"共同"义副词或"分别"义副词与上述例句中"相互/互相"的意义并不完全等同，分别对比(9a)和(9b)及(10a)和(10b)的语义差别。

  (9) a. 三个和尚相互/互相偷懒不愿意去打水。
    b. 三个和尚共同/一起/各自/分别偷懒不愿意去打水。
  (10) a. 在厦门和金门相互/互相架起微波天线。
    b. 在厦门和金门共同/分别架起微波天线。

  先说(9a)和(9b)的差别。根据我们对该寓言故事的了解，三个和尚处于一种博弈关系中，每个人的偷懒行为都对他人产生影响——没水喝。(9a)中的"相互/互相"在"三个和尚都偷懒"的意义之外，还传达出了"每个和尚的偷懒行为对其余二人产生影响"的隐含意味，符合该寓言故事的情景；而(9b)中的"共同/一起"非但取消了这种"相互影响"的意义，甚至在一定语境下会将博弈关系的解读变为合作关系的解读，而"各自/分别"则传达出三个和尚的偷懒行为各自独立、互不影响的隐含意味。再说(10a)和(10b)的差别。同样地，(10a)中的"相互/互相"传达出了"在厦门和金门架起微波天线"的事件"能够实现这两座城市间的相互通信关系"的隐含意义，符合这句话所处的语境；而"共同/分别"则并不直接带来"实现相互间的通信关系"这一隐含意义。

  我们在其他例句中做类似的替换也能得到这样的语义区别。可见，这里的"相互/互相"和"共同/一起"或"各自/分别"并不等义。

  本文认为，例(3)至例(6)所反映的副词"相互/互相"用法的新发展，应当称为"联系义(sociative meaning)用法"。下文将从跨语言的视角和汉语内部的语义分析两方面给出论证。同时，我们认为这种用法在汉语中尚处于"萌芽"状态。

2 跨语言视角：相互标记的多义模式与联系义用法

2.1 相互标记的多义模式

  从跨语言的视角看世界语言中相互标记的多义性有助于理解汉语相互标记"相互/互相"的新用法。在很多语言中，相互标记都表现出多义性(polysemic)，主要表现为以下三种多义形式："反身义(reflexive)—相互义"、"相互义—联系义"和"重复义(iterative)—相互义"。分别见下述三例(均转引自 Nedjalkov,2007a:17/19)。

(11) Hopi (Kalectaca, 1978: 92, 208; naa-=REFL, REC and PASS, -to-=PL)
  a. tuuhota   'to hurt'（伤害）
  b. Itam naa-tuho-(to)-ta i. 'We hurt each other.'（我们互相伤害）
                  相互义
          ii. 'We hurt ourselves.'（我们伤害自己）
                  反身义

(12) Yakut (Kharitonov, 1963: 46; -s/-h-=REC and SOC)
  a. kör-   'to see, look'（看见/看）
  b. kör-üs- i. 'to see each other'（互相看见） 相互义
       ii. 'to see sth/sb together'（共同看见某物/某人） 联系义

(13) Samoan (Mosel & Hovdhaugen, 1992:180 - 3)
  a. sogi 'to kiss' → fe-sogi 'to kiss each other'（互相亲吻） 相互义
  b. a'a 'to kick' → fe-a'a 'to kick sth again and again'（一次又一次地踢）
                    重复义

  在例(11)中，Hopi 语动词前缀 naa-既可以表达相互义，也可以表达反身义。相互义和反身义共同的语义基础是：事件参与者同时拥有施事角色和受事角色。在例(12)中，Yakut 语动词词缀-s/-h 既可以表达相互义，也可以表达联系义。所谓联系义，可以近似地翻译为"together"，如(12bii)所示。联系义的具体细节及其与"共同"、"一起"等副词的意义的差异见 2.2 中的论述。相互义和联系义共同的语义基础是：二者预设存在两个或两个以上的事件参与者，每个事件参与者拥有相同的语义角色。在例(13)中，Samoan 语动词前缀 fe 既可以表达相互义，也可以表达重复义。相互义和重复义共同的语义基础是：事件参与者或事件本身的复数性。

  根据大量跨语言的语料，四种意义的多义关联模式可以图示为(14)所示的结构(Nedjalkov, 2007b: 248)。

(14) 反身(reflexive)→相互(reciprocal)→联系(sociative)

      重复(iterative)

2.2 联系义用法

  例(3)至例(6)中"相互/互相"的语义，可以用"相互→联系"这一多义形式来分析。所谓联系义(sociatives)，是一种语态(voice)范畴。根据 Nedjalkov(2007a:3)，联系义指的是主语所指涉的一群人参与到同一活动中,即共同地(jointly)、同时地(simultaneously)执行谓词所指涉的动作。典型的联系意义通常包含以下语义成分:空间层面的"一起"(together)、体层面的"同时"(simultaneously)、(主语)数层面的"多数"(all,many,etc.)和情态层面的"共同"(jointly)。除了上文例(12)外,我们还可以举 Tagalog 语例句(15)、Bolivian Quechua 语例句(16)和古汉语例句(17)。

(15) Tagalog(Shkarban & Rachkov,2007:925)
　　Ang　manga tao-ng　　yaon　ay　nag-sa-sayaw-an　at
　　NOM　PL　man-LNK　that　LNK　AG. SOC-IPFV-dance-SOC　and
　　nag-i-imun-an　　　　nang　alak.
　　AG. SOC-IPFV-drink-SOC　　PAT　wine
　　'Those people were dancing together and drinking wine together.'
　　(那些人正在一起跳舞,一起喝酒。)

(16) Bolivian Quechua(van de Kerke,2007:1385)
　　Pedru taṭa-n-wan　　　Cliza-man puri-na-ku-nku.
　　P.　father‑3SG-COM C.‑ALL　walk-REC-REFL‑3PL
　　'Peter and his father walk together toCliza.'
　　(Peter 和他的父亲一起走到了 Cliza。)

(17) 吕氏春秋·务当(解惠全,1984 释"相"为"共同、一起")
　　齐之好勇者,其一人居东郭,其一人居西郭,卒相遇于途。曰:"姑相饮乎!"觞数行,曰"姑求肉乎?"

联系义是相互标记最常见的附加意义。该一词多义形式广泛见于突厥语族、蒙古语族和通古斯语族的语言,也见于日语、Tagalog 语、Indonesian 语、Palauan 语、Kusaiean 语、Halkomelem 语和诸多班图语。

需要重点强调的是,在上文所描述的语义之外,联系义还具有额外的语义特点。Nedjalkov(2007a:33)引 Yakut 语母语者 Kharitonov(1963:24-5)指出,Yakut 语-s/-h-所表达的联系意义,在两个及两个以上事件参与者同等参与同一动作行为这一语义的基础上,还附加了额外的语义——事件参与者通过某种内在纽带(inner bond)联系在一起。这个内在纽带通常是动作行为背后的统一的原因、统一的情景或参与者统一的心理状态,因谓词词汇语义的不同或语境的不同,内在纽带的具体语义内涵也会有所不同。以 Yakut 语例句(18)和日语例句(19)为例。

(18) Yakut(Nedjalkov 2007a: 36)

Oɤo-lor   əta-h-al-lar
child-PL   cry-REC-PRES-PL

'The children are crying (all of them together, as if vying with each other).'

（孩子们在哭泣（所有孩子一同哭泣，仿佛在相互竞赛）。）

(19) Japanese(Alpatov & Nedjalkov 2007: 1043)

Taroo to   Akiko wa   akamboo o   zyunban-ni   daki-at-ta.
T.   and A.   TOP baby   ACC in-turn   embrace-REC-PAST

'Taro and Akiko embraced the baby by turns.'

（Taro 和 Akiko 轮流抱孩子。）

例(18)中，相互—联系标记-h 除了带来"共同、一起"的语义外，还表达"儿童争相哭泣"的附加语义，这里的内在纽带可以解读为儿童的哭泣行为是相互影响的，一个人的哭泣会带动其他人的哭泣，仿佛处于竞赛关系中。例(19)中，相互—联系标记-aw 除了带来"抱孩子的行为是二人共同参与的"语义外，还附带有"二人处于相同的情感状态中"的语义，比如二人是夫妻或亲友，都为新生命的到来感到喜悦，相互间争着迫不及待地要抱小孩(Alpatov & Nedjalkov, 2007: 1043-4)。

综上所述，联系义这一语态范畴可以定义为：两个及两个以上的事件参与者共同地、同时地参与同一动作行为，并且事件参与者之间存在内在的、由词汇语义和语境决定的相互联系性。前一种意义使得联系义标记可以近似地翻译为 together("一起")，后一种意义又表明二者并不完全等义。

3 汉语相互副词联系义用法的涌现

3.1 汉语相互副词新用法的语义分析

郭锐(2013,2017)已注意到如例(3)至例(6)所示的汉语相互副词的新用法，并将该用法诠释为"各自、分别、一起、共同"。正如本文引言部分所指出的，该研究虽然分析出了相互副词新用法的基本意义，但相互副词的新用法与"各自、分别、一起、共同"这类副词并不完全等义。在上节所引述的类型学事实之外，我们将给出汉语内部的分析。

我们将例(3)至例(6)各句的断言义和隐含义分析如下（部分例句有简化及改造）。

(20) 三个和尚互相偷懒不愿意去打水。
    a. 断言义：a1. 和尚 A 偷懒不愿意去打水；
            a2. 和尚 B 偷懒不愿意去打水；
            a3. 和尚 C 偷懒不愿意去打水；
    b. 隐含义：和尚 A、和尚 B 和和尚 C 的偷懒行为产生相互影响(没水喝)。

(21) 张三和李四相互寻找共同语言。
    a. 断言义：a1. 张三寻找共同语言；
            a2. 李四寻找共同语言；
    b. 隐含义：张三和李四通过寻找共同语言而实现相互交流。

(22) 两国在边境地区相互裁减军事力量。
    a. 断言义：a1. A 国在边境地区裁减军事力量；
            a2. B 国在边境地区裁减军事力量；
    b. 隐含义：A 国和 B 国通过裁减军事力量而消除相互间的紧张关系。

(23) 在厦门和金门相互架起微波天线。
    a. 断言义：a1. 在厦门架起微波天线；
            a2. 在金门架起微波天线；
    b. 隐含义：厦门和金门通过架起微波天线而实现相互间的通信联系。

对比我们在第二节中基于类型学事实归纳出的联系语态的语义分析——"两个及两个以上的事件参与者共同地、同时地参与同一动作行为,并且事件参与者之间存在内在的、由词汇语义和语境决定的相互联系性",我们发现,汉语相互副词的上述用法完全符合类型学研究中对于联系语态的定性。我们认为,"相互→联系"这一语义演变已在汉语相互结构中开始发生。

接下来,我们用语义特征分析法刻画相互副词的相互义和联系义的语义异同。对比(20)至(23)中相互副词的用法和相互副词典型的相互义用法(24)。

(24) 张三和李四相互攻击。
    a. 断言义：a1. 张三攻击李四；
            a2. 李四攻击张三；
    b. 隐含义：无。

我们发现,命题(20)至(24)的断言义均由若干子事件构成,整个命题的断言义是这些子事件的合取意义。因此,相互副词的相互义和联系义均具有[＋复数事件]语义特征,这也符合[＋复数事件]特征在副词的语义演变中通常得以保留的一般规律(见郭锐,2017)。

其次,对于(20)至(24)中的每一个复数事件来说,多个事件参与者在各个子事件中的语义角色均相同。(20)至(22)中,事件参与者均具有施事语义角色;(23)中,事件参与者均具有处所语义角色;(24)中,事件参与者均具有施事和受事双重语义角色。因此可以说,相互副词的相互义和联系义都具有事件参与者的[＋同等语义角色]语义特征。

从上述分析中也可以看出,相互义和联系义的差异在于:相互义用法中事件参与者具有"双重语义角色",每个事件参与者在语义角色上呈"对称关系";而联系义用法中事件参与者只具有"单一语义角色",相互间在语义角色上失落了对称关系,但这种对称关系通过隐含的"相互联系"关系残留了下来,而相互联系关系的具体内涵通常只能在具体语境中得以明确。

这种残存的事件参与者[＋相互联系]的语义特征,是相互副词的联系义用法区别于"各自、分别、一起、共同"的最重要特征。

综上,我们可以把相互副词的相互义和联系义的语义异同归纳为(25)中的模式。

(25) 相互副词相互义和联系义的语义异同

	相互义	联系义
事件性质	[＋复数事件]	[＋复数事件]
事件参与者	[＋同等语义角色] [＋双重语义角色] [＋对称关系]	[＋同等语义角色] [＋单一语义角色] [＋相互联系]

3.2 联系义用法涌现的语义机制

如何理解相互副词从相互义到联系义的语义演变机制?我们需要再次回顾(2)中所示的语义展开,重复如下。

(26) a. 张三和李四互相攻击。 $\xrightleftharpoons[\text{合并}]{\text{展开}}$ { b. 张三攻击李四。
c. 李四攻击张三。 }

能够做(2/26)中的语义展开是相互义的本质特征。在该语义展开模式中,展开后的每一个子项均为"施事—动词—受事"形式。这里的施事可称"交互者"(reciprocal participants),受事可称"交互对象"(reciprocees)。此例中"张三"和"李四"互为交互者和交互对象,即[＋对称关系]。典型的交互者—交互对象关系是"施事—受事"关系,在每一个语义展开子项中实现为"主语—宾语"关系。另外,交互者—交互对象关系也可以是"施事—旁格角色"关系或"施事—受事领属者"的关系,在语义展开子项中分别实现为"主语—介词宾语"关系和"主语—宾语领属者"关系(郭锐,2013)。见(27)和(28)中的举例。

(27) a. 我们相互作证。 $\xrightleftharpoons[\text{合并}]{\text{展开}}$ { b. 我为你作证。
c. 你为我作证。 }

(28) a. 我们相互记住生日。 $\xrightleftharpoons[\text{合并}]{\text{展开}}$ { b. 我记住你的生日。
c. 你记住我的生日。 }

根据汉语的语法规则,介词不能悬空,因此在(27b)+(27c)合并为(27a)的过程中,介词"为"被删除。而在(28b)+(28c)合并为(28a)的过程中,为了避免与主语重复,领属结构合并后亦被删除。因此,我们可以说,(27)和(28)所示的相互关系的透明度相比于(2/26)有所降低,因为交互对象从核心论元下降为非核心论元/领属者,在语义展开子项中需要额外补出相应的语言成分(介词、领属结构)才能使其显现,而合并操作会删除这些成分。

上文例(4/21),即"张三和李四相互寻找共同语言",除了分析为联系义用法外,也可以看成是相互义用法经历了两重删除的结果,见(29)。

(29) { a. 张三寻找和李四的共同语言。
b. 李四寻找和张三的共同语言。 } $\xrightarrow{\text{合并}}$
c. 张三和李四相互寻找和对方(沟通)的共同语言。
d. 删除介词和"的"字结构:张三和李四相互寻找共同语言。

因经历两重删除,该句表达的相互关系更为不透明。此例可以视为相互义用法和联系义用法的中间地带。

联系义的出现,在我们看来,实际上是交互对象被进一步抑制为非语言成分,即隐含成分,从而在语义展开子项中完全消失无法恢复的结果。而联系义中附带的语义特征[+相互联系],实际上就是交互者—交互对象间的对称关系被抑制为隐含状态的结果。这一过程可以展示为(30a)到(30d)的变化。

(30) a. 张三和李四相互攻击。→{张三攻击李四,李四攻击张三}
b. 张三和李四相互作证。→{张三为李四作证,李四为张三作证}
c. 张三和李四相互寻找共同语言。→{张三寻找和李四的共同语言,李四寻

找和张三的共同语言}

　　d. 张三和李四相互偷懒。→{张三偷懒(从而影响到李四),李四偷懒(从而影响到张三)}

从相互义到联系义的语义演变可以表格化为(31)。

(31)从相互义到联系义的语义演变机制

	相互义	联系义	
交互对象语法地位	受事论元	旁格/领属者论元	非论元成分
交互者—交互对象关系	施事—受事	施事—旁格/领属者角色	隐含的[＋相互联系]

综合(30)和(31),我们认为从相互义到联系义的语义演变的本质是:交互者和交互对象之间对称的交互关系从直接关系到间接关系再到隐含关系的演变。直接关系是指交互者和交互对象在语义展开子项中可以实现为"施事—受事"关系。间接关系是指,交互者和交互对象在语义展开子项中可以实现为"施事—旁格/领属者角色"关系。上述两种关系的共同点是,交互对象在语义展开子项中实现为显性编码的论元成分,因此二者均归属于相互关系。但在间接关系中,我们需要去"追回"(trace back)特定的介词成分或领属结构才能实现交互对象的论元地位。而当这种追回操作的可能性在语义上被削弱到无法实现时,交互对象在语义展开子项中便无法得到显性编码,于是交互者—交互对象的关系成为了一种隐含的[＋相互联系]关系。这时相互义就发展成了联系义。因此我们说,联系义中事件参与者的[＋相互联系]的语义特征是一种隐含的相互关系(对称关系),是语义演变中的语义残留。

3.3　来自其他语言的佐证

　　相互标记的联系义用法是从"施事—旁格/领属者角色"的间接交互关系发展而来的,我们的这一观点可以得到其他语言的佐证。第一个证据是,从我们目前调查的材料来看,凡是相互标记有联系义用法的语言,其二元不及物动词(带一个主语论元和一个旁格论元的动词)均可以进入相互结构,即我们所认为的相互义和联系义的"过渡地带"均存在于这些语言中。Nedjalkov(2007)编著的五卷本 Reciprocal Constructions 中报道了 15 种拥有"相互标记—联系标记"多义形式的语言[①],在这些语言中均存在建立于

---

① 这 15 种语言是:Tagalog、Udehe、Karachay-Balkar、Japanese、Yakut、Tuvan、Kirghiz、Buryat and Khalkha-Mongol、Bolivian Quechua、Warrungu、Indonesian、East Futunan、Nelemwa、Bamana 和 Ainu。

"施事—旁格角色"交互关系基础上的相互结构。

第二个证据是,在上述语言中,有很多语言联系标记所搭配的动词绝大多数为不及物动词,例如 Karachay-Balkar 语中具有联系义用法的不及物动词和及物动词的比例为 140∶10(Nedjalkov,2007a:35)。这其中较为典型的一类动词是"(动物)发出声音"义动词,这些动词所产生的相互义(A 对 B 发出声音,B 对 A 发出声音)和联系义(A 和 B 一起发出声音)十分接近,可以看成是两种用法的"过渡地带"。

第三个证据是,在有些语言中,联系标记是相互标记和旁格论元标记(施用标记或介词)融合为一的产物。例如 Ainu 语相互标记为动词前缀 u-:

(32) Ainu(Alpatov et al,2007:1754)
　　　[Cokay]　u-koyki-as.
　　　we. EXC　REC-bully – 1PL. EXC
　　　'We bullied each other.'（我们相互欺负。）

Ainu 语的不及物动词不能直接用在相互结构中。在 Ainu 语中有一个施用标记(applicative marker)ko-,为不及物动词引入旁格论元,如(33)(Alpatov et al,2007:1768);不及物动词需要借助于施用标记 ko 来表达相互关系,如(34)所示(Alpatov et al,2007:1769)。

(33) a. apkas　　　　'to go'　　　　　　　　（去）
　　 b. ko-apkas　　'to go on a visit to sb'　（探望（某人））
(34) Kestoankonno　u-ko-uepeker-an.
　　 every. day　　　REC-APPL-tell. stories-IND
　　 'Every day we tell stories to each other.'（每天我们相互给对方讲故事）

在 Ainu 语中,相互标记 u-的联系义用法极其有限,而且很多都带有词汇化意义,不能看成是能产的用法。而 uko-整体发展出了十分能产的联系标记用法。如(Alpatov et al,2007:1790):

(35) Ainu-utar　　uko-horip-pa.
　　 Ainu-PL　　 SOC-dance. PL
　　 'The Ainu danced together.'（Ainu 人一起跳舞。）

Ainu 语联系标记 uko-与不及物动词的相互标记 u-ko 质料相同(materially

identical),这表明联系义发源于不及物动词所在的相互结构。

4 汉语相互副词联系义用法的能产度和接受度

相互标记的联系义用法在不同语言间的能产度存在很大差异。能产度高的语言有:Yakut 语,Tagalog 语,Kusaiean 语,Halkomelem 语,Palauan 语,Rwanda 语,Swahili 语等,在这些语言中,能够与相互标记搭配产生联系义的动词至少在百位这一数量级,例如根据 Nedjalkov & Nedjalkov(2007:1132),Yakut 语中这样的动词有 600 个左右。能产度低的语言有:日语、Kirghiz 语等,在这些语言中,能够与相互标记搭配产生联系义的动词一般只有十几个左右,例如一项针对日语 285 个动词的调查中,只有 19 个动词能够产生联系义(Nedjalkov,2007b:275),并且对于很多日语母语者来说,更容易得到的意义是"竞争义"(competitive)和"轮流义"(alternative)等其他相关意义,而非联系义(Alpatov & Nedjalkov,2007:1042-4)。

汉语相互副词的联系义用法显然属于日语这一类,能产度低,尚处于萌芽状态。我们在 CCL 语料库中爬梳了千余条包含词目"相互"或"互相"的语料,同时搜集相关文献报道,共找到 13 例符合联系义的定义的用例,除去 1.2 中所列 4 例,其余 9 例罗列如下①。

(36) 三相界面也是生物界存在的基础,固体地壳为生物的生存、运动提供了赖以依托的根基,气体的呼吸交换、液体的体内循环,相互构成了生命存在的基本条件。
(37) 这种交往能锻炼自己使对方开口的本领,寻找相互感兴趣话题的本领。
(38) Leech(1983:13)认为语境"就是被认为是交际双方互相明白的内容和各自了解的情况,对于理解说话人的话语意义有很大的作用。"
(39) 不管阶级、集团之间的斗争多么尖锐,斗争的双方都得使用互相懂得的语言。
(40) 根据财政部《会计基础工作规范》第五十五条规定的精神,会计凭证装订时,对于那些重要的原始凭证,比如各种经济合同、存出保证金收据、涉外文件、契约等,为了便于日后查阅,可以不附在记账凭证之后,另编目录,单独保管,然后在相关的记账凭证和原始凭证上相互注明日期和编号,以便日后核对。

---

① 本文所列举的例句中,(3)、(4)、(37)亦见郭锐(2013,2017),(5)、(6)、(36)、(40)、(42)来自北大中文系林恩琦博士 2018 年 3 月 21 日口头报告,特此申明和感谢。其余例句来源于笔者在北大 CCL 语料库中的调查。

(41) 德国现象学哲学家胡塞尔说:"每一个自我——主体和我们所有的人都相互一起地生活在一个共同的世界上,这个世界是我们的世界,它对我们的意识来说是有效存在的,并且是通过这种'共同生活'而明晰地给定着。"

(42) 在怀尔斯讲演结束几分钟之后,这一消息就通过计算机和电波飞遍了全球,全世界的数学家为之欣喜和震惊,数学家们相互警惕地注视着这个发端和这一几乎是完全出人意料的结果。

(43) 我认识他,但从没关系密切到暧昧的地步。就算当时我们互相存过这念头,也从未表现出来,这在当年部队生活的那种气氛中是不能想象的。

(44) "能不能闻味儿啊?"刘书友说。"不都说咱们人有味儿?"大家耸著鼻子互相在各自身上嗅了嗅:"不灵,咱们都没人味儿。"

根据笔者的初步调查,以上各例的接受度存在分歧。可见,汉语相互副词联系义用法的能产度和类推性还十分受限。这一用法的谓词搭配范围以及母语者的接受程度等问题,还需要进一步的调研。

5 结 语

汉语相互副词"相互/互相"表达相互情景,其本质特征是能够做(2)中所示的语义展开,即两个及两个以上的事件参与者具有相同的、对称的语义角色。在语料库中,我们发现"相互/互相"的一些用例不符合上述特征。我们将这种相互副词的新用法认定为"联系义"。

跨语言来看,相互标记"相互义—联系义"的一词多义模式十分常见。联系义除了表达两个及两个以上的事件参与者共同地、同时地参与同一动作行为之外,还附带了事件参与者之间存在内在的、由词汇语义和语境决定的相互联系性的语义。

汉语相互副词的联系义用法是上述一词多义模式在汉语中的表现。不同于以往研究将该用法诠释为"各自、分别、一起、共同",本文认为,"相互/互相"的联系义包含以下语义特征:[＋复数事件]和事件参与者[＋同等语义角色]、[＋单一语义角色]、[＋相互联系]。事件参与者[＋相互联系]是"相互/互相"联系义用法区别于"各自、分别、一起、共同"等副词的重要特征。

从相互义到联系义,其语义演变的本质是交互对象在语义展开子项中被逐渐抑制为非语言成分的结果,换句话说,交互者—交互对象这一交互关系,在语义展开子项中由典型的施事—受事关系(交互对象编码为动词宾语),弱化为施事—旁格/领属者角色关系(交互对象编码为介词宾语或领属者),再进一步弱化为隐含的[＋相互联系]关系

(交互对象无法取得显性编码),从而得到联系义用法。事件参与者[＋相互联系]这一语义特征,可以看作一种隐含的相互关系,是语义演变的语义残留。

汉语相互副词的联系义用法尚处于萌芽阶段,能产度较低,接受度存在分歧,但这一演变具有跨语言的共性,并非语病,很可能在将来扩大为汉语的普遍用法。

参考文献

[1] Alpatov, V. M. & V. P. Nedjalkov. 2007. Reciprocal, sociative and competitive constructions in Japanese[A]. In V. P. Nedjalkov (ed.). *Reciprocal Constructions*, Vol. 3[C]. Amsterdam/Philadelphia: John Benjamins, 1021-1094.

[2] Alpatov, V. M., A. Ju. Bugaeva & V. P. Nedjalkov. 2007. Reciprocals and sociatives in Ainu [A]. In V. P. Nedjalkov (ed.). *Reciprocal Constructions*, Vol. 4[C]. Amsterdam/Philadelphia: John Benjamins, 1751-1822.

[3] Kalectaca, M. 1978. *Lessons in Hopi*[M]. Tucson (Arizona): The University of Arizona Press. Kharitonov, L. N. 1963. *Zalogovye formy glagola v jakutskom jazyke* [Voice forms of the verb in Yakut][M]. Moskva, Leningrad: Izd-vo Akademii Nauk SSSR.

[4] Mosel, U. & E. Hovdhaugen. 1992. *Samoan Reference Grammar*[M]. Oslo: Scandinavian University Press. The Institute for Comparative Research in Human Culture.

[5] Nedjalkov, V. P. 2007a. Overview of the research. Definitions of terms, framework, and related issues[A]. In V. P. Nedjalkov (ed.). *Reciprocal Constructions*, Vol. 1[CM]. Amsterdam/Philadelphia: John Benjamins, 3-114.

[6] Nedjalkov, V. P. 2007b. Polysemy of reciprocal markers[A]. In V. P. Nedjalkov (ed.). *Reciprocal Constructions*, Vol. 1[C]. Amsterdam/Philadelphia: John Benjamins, 231-334.

[7] Nedjalkov, I. V. & V. P. Nedjalkov. 2007. Reciprocals, sociatives, comitatives, and assistives in Yakut[A]. In V. P. Nedjalkov (ed.). *Reciprocal Constructions*, Vol. 3[C]. Amsterdam/Philadelphia: John Benjamins, 1095-1162.

[8] Shkarban, L. I. & G. E. Rachkov. 2007. Reciprocal, sociative, and comitative constructions in Tagalog[A]. In V. P. Nedjalkov (ed.). *Reciprocal Constructions*, Vol. 3[C]. Amsterdam/Philadelphia: John Benjamins, 887-932.

[9] Van de Kerke, S. 2007. Reciprocal constructions in Bolivian Quechua[A]. In V. P. Nedjalkov (ed.). *Reciprocal Constructions*, Vol. 3[C]. Amsterdam/Philadelphia: John Benjamins, 1367-1399.

[10] 郭锐,2013.副词"互相/相互":语义和句法的互动[C].载《中国语文法论丛——木村英树教授还历记念》[C].东京:白帝社,22-37.

[11] 郭锐,2017.复数事件和虚词语义[J].世界汉语教学,(4):435-447.

[12] 解惠全,1984.指代性副词"相"的用法[J].语言教学与研究,(3):124-133.

基于词语法的汉语论元结构阐释*

南京师范大学 张智义**

摘要：词语法是依托依存语法和认知语法构建的语法理论体系，词语法理论的核心内容包括通过网络构建、节点创设和缺省继承形成词的语义网络，通过价位、依存和标界形成词与词间的句法关联。本研究在词语法的架构内分析汉语两类特殊论元结构，一是汉语非标准语序论元结构，二是汉语非标准题元结构。汉语允准非标准语序论元结构的前提是词与词之间不存在依存缠绕；汉语允准非标准题元结构主要因为汉语允准多元缺省继承，词与词之间的语义关联得以建立。生成语法和词语法对汉语特殊论元结构的分析各有优势，且都体现了各自理论的本质特征。

关键词：词语法；依存缠绕；多元缺省继承；汉语特殊论元结构

Title: A Word Grammar Approach to Chinese Argument Structure

Abstract: Word grammar is a theoretical framework of grammar based on dependency grammar and cognitive grammar and its core lies in both the semantic network established through net production, node creation and default inheritance and syntactic relation established through valency, dependency as well as landmark. The present study analyzed the two special argument structures in Chinese, separately non-standard order and non-standard theme structures by taking the word grammar approach. Suppose that the tangled dependency does not exist, non-standard order structure can be allowed. Non-standard theme structure is allowed because the semantic relation can be established through multiple inheritance. The analyses given to the concerning structures by generative grammar and word grammar have their own

---

* 本文是国家社科基金项目"二语对一语的跨语言影响研究"（16BYY069）的阶段性成果。
** 作者简介：张智义，南京师范大学外国语学院教授，博士生导师。研究方向：句法学。联系方式：04359@njnu.edu.cn。

advantages and reflect their individual theoretical essences.

Key words: Word Grammar; tangled dependency; multiple inheritance; special argument structures in Chinese

1 引 言

词语法(word grammar)是英国语言学家 Richard Hudson 于上世纪 80 年代创立的语法学派。其核心要义是以词作为语法建构的基本单位(Hudson,2007)。词语法主要依托依存语法和认知语法建构自己的理论体系,但也约略可见语义网络、神经语言研究甚至生成语法等的影响(Hudson,2010)。词语法自形成以来,主要用于英语句式结构的分析,很少有基于词语法的汉语句式结构分析(Hudson,1992:251-276)。本研究即借助词语法的理论来分析汉语论元结构中的两类特殊现象,非标准语序结构和非标准题元结构,并通过比较生成语法对两类结构的分析,论述两种理论的解释力。

2 词语法的基本理论

词语法的核心思想是:句子的基本也是唯一构成单位是词汇,词汇通过各种关系连接构成句子。在词语法体系中不存在短语结构这一层次,这是词语法和生成语法的最重要区别;也是词语法得以命名的主要依据。关于词是句法构造的唯一单位,Hudson 在《词语法引论》一书中有过生动形象的比喻,"词就好比构成社会的个体人,只有人是社会唯一的,真实的构成要素,人通过各种关系连接起来"(Hudson,2007:262)。

2.1 词语法有关语义网络的思想

除了以词作为句子构造的唯一和基本单位之外,词语法的其他主要思想都围绕词的语义网络和词之间的句法结构关系展开。

在词义网络构造方面,词语法深受认知语言学关于语言是网络结构思想的影响,在这一点上,词语法和认为语言是线性结构的生成语法有很大不同。词语法认为,词和词的属性构成了复杂的命题网络。在这其中,网络构建、节点创设和缺省继承是构成词语法词义网络构造的三个核心概念。从词义网络构建看,生成语法将语义属性通过词库构建的方式排除在生成语法基本操作之外,而单独考察词语的句法属性;与之不同,词语法将词汇的语义属性和句法属性统一纳入词义的网络构建中。我们以一个英语中最具代表性的及物动词 like 为例分析词义网络,其他类型的动词类似。图 1 构建了 likes 集合(写作{likes})的词义网络。通过这张词义网络图示可以清楚的看出,likes 在词义网络中,将类型(category)中作为动词的 like 和第三人称单数特称结合起来实现为 likes 的具体形式。由此可见,词语法将词汇的语义属性和句法属性都纳入词汇的词义网络中,通过网络中上一个层级的类型化特征合并,以词例实现的方式构建词汇在句子中的现实呈现。

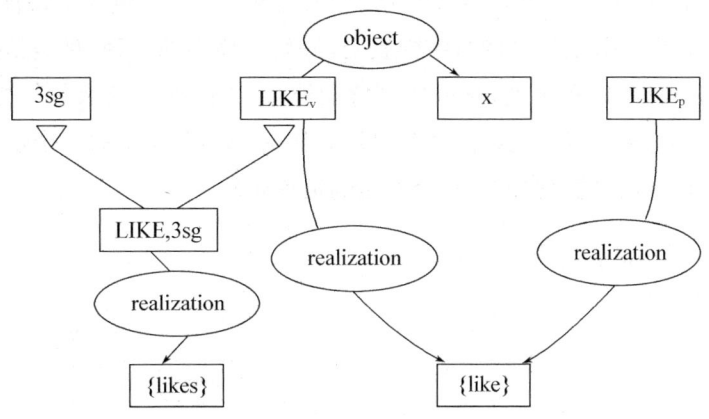

图 1　likes 的词义网络

再看词义网络创造中的节点创设,仍以词例 likes 为例,图 2 显示,一个词例(exemplar)likes 的语义网络有四层节点构成,首先,词例 likes 是集合 likes 的一个词

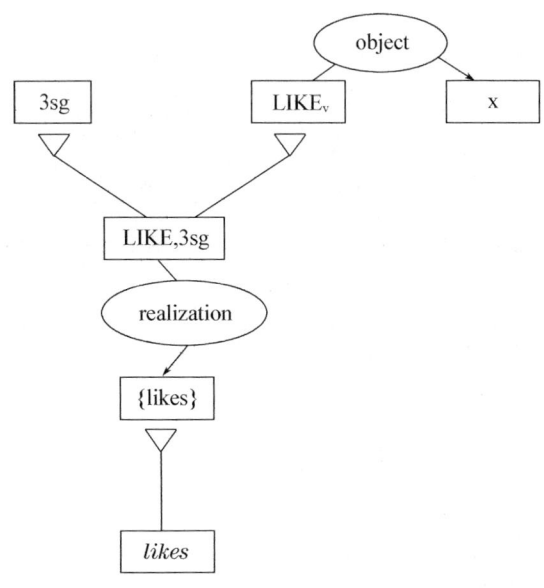

图 2　likes 词义网络的节点创设

例,而集合 likes 是第三人称单数属性和 like 动词属性结合的实现产物,而第三人称单数属性和 like 动词属性构成了语义网络层级的最高节点。这里,为了体现 like 的动词属性,将宾语也纳入这一层级(按照词语法的句法分析,宾语是动词性的直接体现)。

在词语法的词义网络构造中,最基本也是最核心的概念是缺省继承,缺省继承构成了句子语义构建的基本方式。在图 3 中,倒三角和直线组合代表基本的 isA 语义关系,即分类系统中的所属关系。E isA C 表达 E 属于 C,以此类推。每一个下属类型都可以通过搜寻和复制机制,缺省继承上属类型的特征,如 E 可以缺省继承 C、D 和顶层类型的特征 1、2 和 3。图 4 以 sea-thrush(海鸫)词义网络构造为例显示缺省继承的路径。这里所示的 sea-thrush 的语义网络结构表明,海鸫是鸟类的一种,鸟类是生物的一种,海鸫除了自己所具备的有斑点,吃蜗牛等特征外,还依次缺省继承了鸟类和生物的特征。缺省继承还有多元继承的特点,图 5 显示,作为宠物金丝雀的一个示例,通过多元缺省继承,继承了宠物的家庭成员和金丝雀的黄色属性。

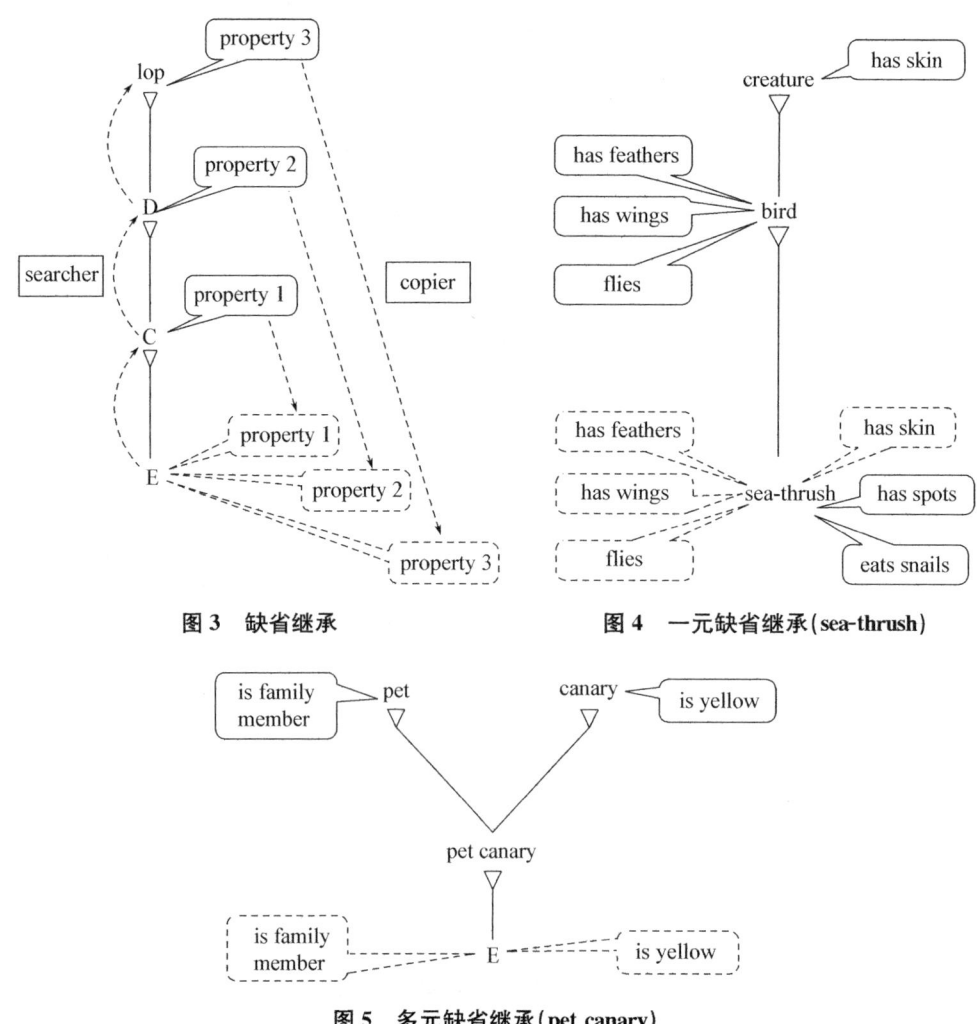

图 3　缺省继承　　　　　图 4　一元缺省继承(sea-thrush)

图 5　多元缺省继承(pet canary)

总之,词语法以词为中心构建词义网络结构,词义网络结构将概念词义和句法词义都纳入词义结构,通过节点创设和网络建构使词语的示例,以缺省继承的方式逐级继承语义特征。

2.2 词语法有关句法构造的思想

在句法维度上,通过词与词的关联,词语法构建相关句法体系。在词语法的句法构建中,有核心意义的概念包括价位、依存和标界(Hudson,2007)。在词语法的句法结构中不存在短语结构,全部句法关系依靠上述三个概念构建。

价位(valency)是价(valent)的数量。而这里的价就是传统语法所界定的论元(Freeman,2011),与价对应的是附加语(adjunct)。一个典型的由价和附加语构成的结构如图6所示。

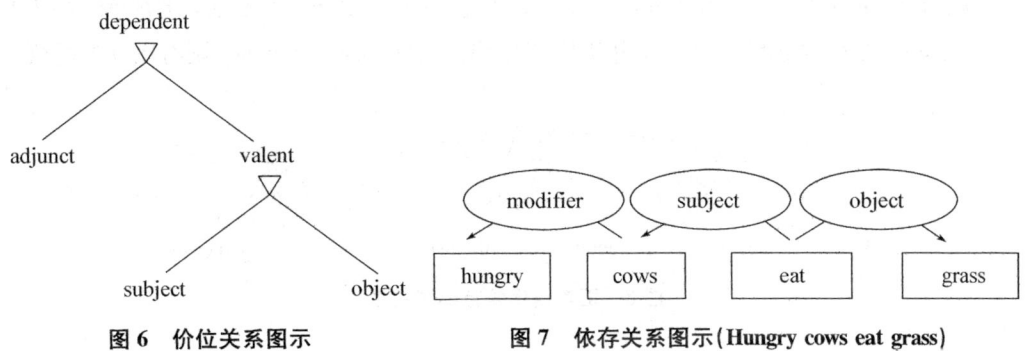

图6　价位关系图示　　　　图7　依存关系图示(Hungry cows eat grass)

图6中,主语和宾语构成价与价之间的关系,而附加语则与价构成依存关系。词语法的依存概念主要来自依存语法,词语法认为句子结构是依存动词谓语建构起来的,因此动词谓语是句子的依存中心。以"Hungry cows eat grass"为例(如图7所示,从图7起,朝下的直线箭头均表示标界,曲线箭头均表示依存关系,曲线箭头所指均表示依存成分),箭头代表依存关系,cows箭头指向hungry,代表hungry作为限定成分对于cows的依存。与此类同,cows作为主语依存动词谓语(具体体现为时体),grass作为宾语也依存动词谓语。因此,动词谓语成为句子的依存中心。和依存相伴的概念包括依存距离和依存缠绕。依存距离指依存子体和母体之间间隔的句法成分数量。众所周知,依存距离会影响句子加工的难度,这也成为当下计算语言学标示句子复杂度的一个核心范畴(陆前、刘海涛,2016)。如:

1. He looked up the word that he wanted to write but wasn't sure he could spell.
2. He looked the girl that he hoped to date but wasn't sure he could name up.

2较1难于理解(本文的英语句例均来自 Hudson,2010,中文句例均来自 Huang, Li, & Li, 2009),主要2中子体附加语 up 和母体动词谓语 look 的依存距离远比1中的依存距离大。依存缠绕由于和标界有关,将在下文介绍。在价和动词谓语的依存关系上,词语法认为作为主语的价依存时体语义成分,而作为宾语的价依存动词,这就说明,词语法虽和生成截然不同,但在某些细部操作上仍然可见生成语法的影响(Chomsky, 1993)。

同生成语法通过短语投射和成分统制将线性句法结构自右向左地投射为层级结构(Chomsky, 2004)并以此标定语序不同,词语法标定语序的方法比较便捷,即通过引入标界概念标定语序。标界就是标识,通过标识可以判定位置。词语法关于标界的基本逻辑为:既然设定动词谓语为句子结构的依存中心,动词谓语就是全句的标界,我们以此来判定句子的语序。图8中竖直向下箭头代表标界,即动词谓语 are 构成全句的标界,以此判定主语(S)"big books about linguistics"在标界之前,述谓成分(P)"expensive"在标界之后。对于特殊语序句如移位句"Grass cows eat"则有图9的呈现。

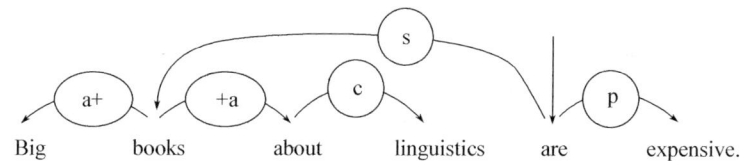

图 8　正常语序依存标界关系

图9中,Grass 是 Grass1 的一个示例,此图表示在语义网络结构中,作为宾语的 grass 在概念层面位于标界之后,但在实现层面位于标界之前。结合标界和依存,词语法提出了依存缠绕的概念,并认为依存缠绕是形成不合法语序的原因(Hudson, 1988)。如:

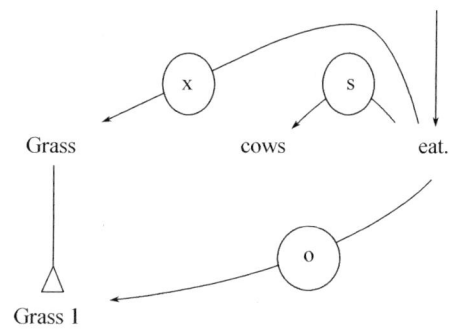

图 9　移位语序依存标界关系

3.　＊Big books are expensive about linguistics.

4.　＊Big books are about linguistics expensive.

均为不合法语序,通过观察两句的标界以及依存关系图示不难发现,两句中均存在提示依存关系的箭头相互缠绕或者和标界箭头缠绕的情况。在第3句中,about linguistics 作为附加语,依存于 books,表示依存关系的箭头线与标界线发生了缠绕;在第4句中,上述缠绕同样存在,另外表示述谓成分 expensive 对于谓语动词 are 依存关系的箭头线也与上述箭头线发生了缠绕,这就意味着 4 句的语序更不能接受(图 10)。

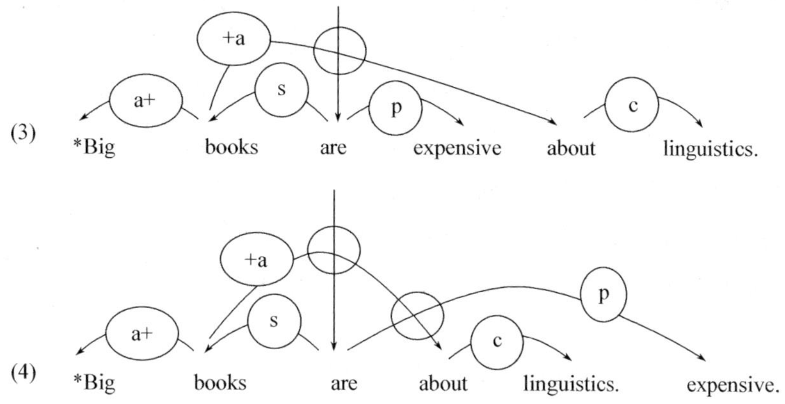

(3) *Big books are expensive about linguistics.

(4) *Big books are about linguistics. expensive.

图 10 依存缠绕关系

上述介绍的是词语法构建语义网络和句法结构的基本概念和范畴,实际上,词语法理论体系涵盖的内容远较上述介绍复杂。词语法理论体系自诞生以来,已经成功的运用于英语复合句、缩略结构、嫁接移位等复杂句法现象的解释上(Hudson,1988:303-342,2006:604-627,2018:1-54)。迄今尚未见利用词语法理论解释汉语句法现象的研究成果,本研究即尝试借助词语法的依存缠绕和缺省继承等基本概念和范畴,提供汉语论元结构中非标准语序结构和非标准题元结构的新阐释。

3 基于词语法的非标准语序论元结构分析

众所周知,汉语允准比较灵活的语序结构,这其中就包括非标准语序的论元结构。按照传统语法的界定,对于一价论元,标准语序论元结构为主语加谓语或者谓语加宾语;对于二价论元,标准语序论元结构为主加谓加宾;对于三价论元,标准语序论元结构为主加谓加间宾加直宾。除此之外的语序都可以界定为非标准语序论元结构。参照《汉语句法学》中关于汉语非标准语序论元结构的分析,本研究主要探讨如下几个类别(Huang, Li, & Li, 2009)。

第一类是动补论元结构,句例如下:

5. 他们打碎了一块玻璃。
6. *他们气喊了那个陌生人。

上述 5 例为可接受动补结构,6 例则为不可接受动补结构。相关合法性可由词语法的依存图示得到说明。通过图示可见,5例中,"打碎"是标准动补短语,补语"碎"和动词"打"存在依存关系。而"打碎"的核心是"打","打"也成为全句的依存中心语。这样,"打"就是标界。主语"他们"依存于"打",宾语"一块玻璃"也依存于"打"。全句标界线和依存线不存在依存缠绕,因此结构被允准。6例不同,"气喊"在语义网络结构中并非标准的动补语义关系,"气"和"喊"之间不存在依存关系,都是谓语动词,都可做标界。主语"他们"和宾语"那个陌生人"之间存在依存关系,"那个陌生人"和"喊"也存在依存关系,存在缠绕,因此6例不可以接受(图11)。

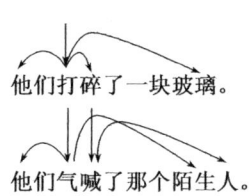

图 11 汉语动补论元结构依存关系图示

第二类是复合型谓语动词论元结构,句例如下:

7. 他生吃过很多蔬菜。
8. *他生着吃过很多蔬菜。
9. 他哭诉了侵略者的暴行。
10. 他哭着诉说了侵略者的暴行。

在例7中,"生"是动词附加语,依存于"吃"。"吃"是标界,主语"他"依存于"吃",宾语"很多蔬菜"也依存于"吃",图中不存在依存缠绕,因此句子可以接受。例8不同,"生"添加了时态助词"着",这表明"生"在例8中是动词,因此8有两个标界。"他"依存于"吃","很多蔬菜"也依存于"吃",同时"生着"是"很多蔬菜"的述谓成分,因此"很多蔬菜"又依存于"生着"。这样"很多蔬菜"与"生着"之间的依存线发生了与"吃"上标界线之间的缠绕,导致例8不可以接受。例9图示与例7相同。例10和例8又有不同。"哭着"和"诉说"同为谓语动词,同为标界。主语"他"依存于"哭着",也依存于"诉说",词语法设定这样的结构中存在两个主语,即可以参照上面移位句的图示,设定"哭着"之前是示例的"他","诉说"之前存留提示概念语义的"他1","他"和"他1"之间存在 isA 关系(如图12中的倒三角)。这样,"他"依存于"哭着","他1"依存于"诉说","侵略者的暴行"也依存于"诉说",图12不存在依存缠绕。

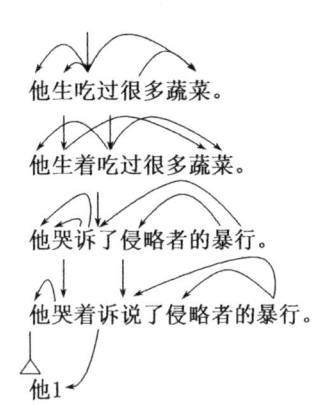

图 12 汉语复合型谓语动词论元结构依存关系图示

第三类是添加"得"字的非标准语序论元结构,如:

11. 那瓶酒喝得他醉了三天三夜。
12. *刚来的教练跑得他流了一身汗。

上述 11 例典型地体现了汉语论元结构在语序上的灵活性(Babby,2013)。"那瓶酒"本是"喝"的宾语却被置于谓语动词"喝"之前,"他"本是施事,却因为使役结构的原因被置于"得"字之后,在"他"之后又接续一个述谓成分"醉了三天三夜"。由 11 句的依存图示和标界图示可知,参照移位结构,作为宾语的示例"那瓶酒"依存于标界谓词"喝";提示概念语义的"那瓶酒 1"位于标界谓词"喝"之后。这里再借鉴既往文献的做法(黄锦章,2004:100-105),将得字结构的"得"也当做一个表示致使语义的谓词,因此"喝"和"得"均为标界。"他"作为使役结构的宾语依存于"得",又依存于后面的述谓"醉了"。整个结构图示不存在依存缠绕。12 则不同,"跑"和"得"均为标界,"刚来的教练"既成分依存"跑",也成分依存"得",因为它既是谓词"跑"的主语,也是使役结构的主语。这里就存在依存缠绕,进而导致结构不能成立(图 13)。

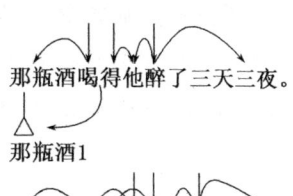

图 13 汉语"得"字特殊论元结构依存关系图示

综上,利用词语法依存和标界结构图示中是否存在依存缠绕判定句子中的非标准语序论元结构,能够合理有效的解释汉语非标准语序论元结构的可接受性问题。

4 基于词语法的非标准题元结构分析

汉语论元结构的特殊性,除了有横向语序上的特殊性以外,还有一类纵向题元选择上的特殊性。这一类构成类似"吃食堂"这样的非标准题元结构。汉语中非标准题元结构较多,这也构成汉语和英语的主要区别。如:

13. 他吃食堂。
14. * He eats the dining hall.

既往研究结合不同的理论视角对汉语的非标准题元结构进行了多种解读。如生成语法认为,构成这一结构特殊性的主因是动词具备不同的词汇语义表征或汉语中部分动词可以不选择标准题元解读而获得句法实现(Huang,1997);构式语法则认为"吃食堂"是单宾语句的基本构式之一(张建理,2008:182-189);认知语法研究认为,"吃食堂"结构中的"食堂"是受事宾语的转喻形式(孙天琦、李亚非,2010:21-33);计算语言学则认为"吃食堂"这一结构属于汉语语义表达框架中的广义配价模式(姚旭晨,2009)。尽管各种理论在汉语非标准题元的解释上都具备一定的解释力,但仍有诸多难题,如同为吃饭的场所,因何汉语允准"吃食堂",却不允准"吃家"。

本研究借助词语法理论,特别是词语法理论中的缺省继承研究汉语非标准题元的允准条件,主要涉及"吃食堂"因何得以允准,"吃家"为何不行,英汉语在题元允准上的差别如何解释,其他非标准题元结构(工具类、方式类、结果类、杂类)如何允准等诸多方面,最后还涉及汉语论元结构中语序和题元选择均存在特殊性的结构。

本研究认为,英汉题元选择的差异可能和词语法所界定的两种不同缺省继承模式有关,一类是一元缺省继承,另一类是多元缺省继承。英语主要采用一元缺省继承模式,汉语主要采用多元缺省继承模式,这可以解释为什么汉语允准"吃食堂",英语的"eating the dinning hall"不被允准。如图14所示:

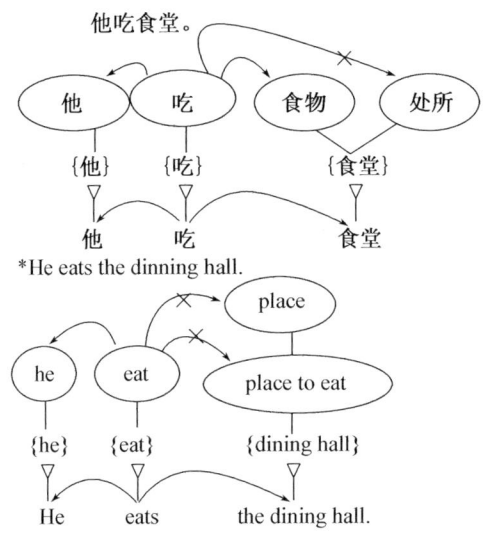

图14 汉语非标准题元结构依存关系及与英语类似句例依存关系图示

以上图示不仅反映"他吃食堂"和"He eats the dining hall"在句子结构层面的依存关系和标界关系,也反映句子组成成分间的语义关系。汉语和英语的差别在于,汉语宾语"食堂"在语义上采用了多元缺省继承的模式,一如前文所列 pet canary 例,即"食堂"既缺省继承了"食物"的语义特征,也缺省继承了"处所"的语义特征。这样,"吃"的动词语义就能和"食堂"中的食物语义建立起语义联系。英语宾语"the dining hall"在语义上采用了一元缺省继承的模式,即在语义的第一层级提示"place to eat",第二层级提示"place",但是这两个层级均不能与句子的谓语动词"eat"建立起语义联系,因为"eat"的受事宾语不可能是"place"。

汉语非标准题元的多元缺省继承模式,既可以解释汉语为什么允准"吃食堂",也可以解释"吃家"这样的表达为什么不能接受。过去基于隐喻的认知研究认为,主体心理关照方式的改变所带来的认知域切换,即食物的去焦化和环境的核心化,是导致"吃食堂"结构成立的主因(董粤章,2011:2-12);但是像"吃家"这样的表达也可以理解为认知域的切换,结构却不能成立。这就表明对非标准题元结构,简单的认知域切换解释力不足。但是结合词语法的缺省继承就不难发现,"家"的语义特征不能认定为多元缺省继承了"食物"和"处所"的语义特征,因为"食物"并非"家"概念语义网络中的应有之义。这样,"吃"的概念语义无法顺利地建立起同"家"的语义联系,"吃家"结构因而不被允准。

除了处所类非标准题元结构,汉语的其他类型非标准题元结构如工具类、方式类、结果类、杂类等都可在词语法概念语义网络的多元缺省继承模式中求得允准条件。如:

15. 写毛笔
16. 唱A调
17. 揉馒头
18. 插嘴

上面15～18例分别代表工具类、方式类、结果类、杂类非标准题元受事宾语。对于"写毛笔","毛笔"通过多元缺省继承,继承了概念语义网络中的字的语义特征,这样写的概念语义和字的概念语义能够形成关联,表达成立。"唱A调"与之类似,"A调"的概念语义网络中有曲子的语义特征,否则A调无法凭空界定,因此唱的概念语义和曲子的概念语义形成关联。17例有所不同,这是典型的结果类非标准题元,表示揉成馒头,这里动词"揉"多元缺省继承了揉成一定形状的语义特征,因为揉必然关联行为的结果,因此和馒头形成语义关联。18例又有不同,"插"多元缺省继承有形或无形进入的语义特征,"嘴"多元缺省继承身体器官和语言的语义特征,无形进入和语言形成语义关联,表达以话语的形式无形进入,因此结构允准。尽管汉语非标准题元结构各个类型间语义特征继承有差别,但无疑都采取了与英语不同的多元缺省继承模式。

最后,还要涉及一类汉语论元结构中语序和题元选择均存在特殊性的结构,如:

19. 这条河能开千吨级货轮。

19例所表达的含义是"千吨级货轮能开在这条河上",在这一句中涉及题元和语序的特殊性。在题元选择上,原来表处所的状语省略了"在"形成非标准题元的处所宾语,然后这一非标准处所宾语发生移位形成非标准的处所主语。结合词语法的理论框架,这里同步运用了多元缺省继承和语序变化,并且不存在依存缠绕,因此句子得以成立(图15)。

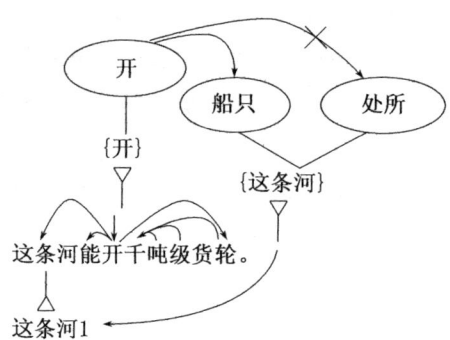

图 15　汉语同时存在特殊语序和非标准题元论元结构依存关系图示

综上,汉语各类非标准题元结构也可以在词语法语义概念网络的多元缺省继承框架内求得解释。

5　与生成语法的比较

词语法强调结合语义网络分析句法结构,这和强调脱离语义分析句法自足性的生成语法有很大差别。由于既往生成语法对汉语论元结构的语序和非标准题元多有研究,因此有必要将两者进行对比,以进一步明晰两种理论的方法论特征。

对于汉语特殊的论元和论元语序,生成语法多从设定轻动词语类出发或从词库出发。例如,对于下面的论元语序问题:

20. 他哭着说。
21. 张三气哭了李四。

20 句中哭不能后续宾语,21 句中哭却可以。按照生成语法的解释,两者的差别主要是因为动词哭所带的轻动词不同。如 Huang、Li & Li(2009)的研究认为,词库内的动词是由词根$\sqrt{}$和少量标明事件类型的轻动词(Lv)组成。词根$\sqrt{}$将动词所对应的事件概念化(conceptualize),轻动词负责筛选出与事件类型直接相关的参与者信息,供句法操作使用。其具体内容包括:

$$V \in \{(\sqrt{}),[Lv1\sqrt{}],[Lv2\sqrt{}],[Lv2[Lv1\sqrt{}]]\}$$

其中 Lv1 标明没有外部使因的自发性事件类型,Lv2 标明有外部使因的事件类型。结合汉语哭的论元语序不难发现,哭既可以选择 Lv1,也可以选择 Lv2,其选择 Lv1 则生成20句的语序结构;其选择Lv2则生成21句的语序结构(转引自杨大然,2015)。对于非标准题元结构,生成语法也有类似的结合轻动词成分的解释,即英汉语在非标准题元选择上的参数差异,主要由轻动词决定。如Huang的研究认为,词根中的参与者经过轻动词审查,与自发性事件和外部使因事件直接相关的参与者,即受事和施事获得句法实现。但是不同语言在动词语义表征的参数设定上存在差异。以英汉语为例,英语属于动词必包含词根和轻动词类语言,因此在事件所有参与者中最终获得句法实现的是事件的受事和施事,这一句法现实进一步决定了英语语言为标准题元结构语言。相反,汉语动词则不同,在语义表征方面,其既可涵盖词根和轻动词构建标准题元结构;也可以不包含轻动词而使事件参与者无需审查均可获得句法实现,这样动词可以建构非标准题元结构(黄正德,2007:3-21)。当然,也有研究如Zhang将事件结构语法和词库融为一体,认为汉语非标准题元结构的允准,主要是汉语在词库阶段已将处所等事件结构成分融入词库中(Zhang,1998)。

而结合词语法对汉语特殊语序论元结构和非标准题元结构进行分析,则不依赖词库、轻动词等句法要素,词语法主要依赖的是概念语义网络和构成句子要素的相互依存和标界。只要概念语义网络中的缺省继承模式允准继承局部的语义特征,语义关联能够建立,非标准题元结构就能够允准。另外,只要构成句子的要素通过标界后,相互依存关系不形成依存缠绕,特殊语序论元结构就能够成立。简言之,在句法和语义所形成的认知网络结构中,只要连接语义特征和句法要素的连接线不交错,语义特征能够通达,句法就能够实现。这更体现了词语法的认知基础。

这里很难对两种理论做简单的评判,两种理论在解释汉语论元结构上各有优劣。生成语法的优势在于其通过设定轻动词成分,使以线性结构为基础的生成推导更加清晰可解,但其不足是轻动词以及词库往往饱受无认知语义基础的诟病;词语法的优势在于牢牢建立在认知网络基础上,更加符合我们对认知模式的理解,不足在于结构描写复杂难辨。这也反映了生成语法的数理逻辑和词语法的认知本质。

6 结 论

本研究是结合词语法对汉语特殊语序论元结构和非标准题元结构的分析。与生成语法不同,词语法在认知语法和依存语法的基础上,通过构建概念语义网络,确定句法成分间的依存关系和标界关系来解释句子的语义和结构现象。本研究认为,汉语论元结构的语序相对灵活,但是这种灵活性也有一定的规约。当句子的标界确立以后,只要句子成分间依存线、标界线之间不存在依存缠绕,句子都可以成立。这种界定可以广泛应用于汉语动补型、复合型以及添加"得"字型特殊论元结构的阐释中。对于汉语非标准题元结构,本研究认为,借助词语法理论的多元缺省继承,汉语之所以允准"吃食堂"类结构,主要是因为在概念语义网络结构中,"食堂"多元缺省继承了食物的语义特征,吃和食物之间能够建立语义关联,结构因而允准。而英语的一元缺省继承则不允准这种语义关联。

结合词语法对汉语句法结构进行分析是句法研究领域的新课题,期待今后能够有更多相关研究为进一步深入探究汉语句法做贡献。

参考文献

[1] Babby, L. H. 2013. *Enriched Composition and Inference in the Argument Structure of Chinese*[M]. Cambridge: Cambridge University Press.

[2] Chomsky, N. 1993. *A Minimalist Program for Linguistic Theory*[M]. Cambridge, MA: The MIT Press.

[3] Chomsky, N. 2001. Beyond Explanatory Adequacy. *MIT Occasional Papers in Linguistics*, (20): 131-137.

[4] Chomsky, N. 2004. Beyond Explanatory Adequacy. *Structures and Beyond: The Cartography of Syntactic Structures*[M]. Oxford: Oxford University Press.

[5] Freeman, J. B. 2011. *Argument Structure*[M]. Netherlands: Springer Netherlands.

[6] Huang, C.-T. J. 1997. On lexical structure and syntactic projection[J]. *Chinese Language and Linguistics*, (3): 45-89.

[7] Huang, C. T. J., Y. H. A. Li, & Y, Li. 2009. *The Syntax of Chinese*[M]. Cambridge: Cambridge University Press.

[8] Hudson, R. 1988. Coordination and grammatical relations[J]. *Journal of Linguistics*, 24(2): 303-342.

[9] Hudson, R. 1992. So-called 'Double Objects' and grammatical relations[J]. *Language*, 68(2): 251-276.

[10] Hudson, R. 2006. Wanna revisited[J]. *Language*, 82(3): 604-627.

[11] Hudson, R. 2007. *Language Networks: The New Word Grammar*[M]. Oxford: Oxford University Press.

[12] Hudson, R. 2010. *An Introduction to Word Grammar*[M]. Cambridge: Cambridge University Press.

[13] Hudson, R. 2018. Pied-piping in Cognition[J]. *Journal of Linguistics*, 54(1): 1-54.

[14] Zhang, N. N. 1998. Argument Interpretations in the Ditransitive Construction[J]. *Nordic Journal of Linguistics*, 21(2): 179-209.

[15] 董粤章,2011.构式、域矩阵与心理观照——认知语法视角下的"吃食堂"[J].外国语(上海外国语大学学报),(3):2-12.

[16] 黄锦章,2004.汉语中的使役连续统及其形式紧密度问题[J].华东师范大学学报(哲学社会科学版),(5):100-105.

[17] 黄正德,2007.汉语动词的题元结构与其句法表现[J].语言科学,(4):3-21.

[18] 陆前、刘海涛,2016.依存距离分布有规律吗?[J].浙江大学学报(人文社会科学版),(4):63-76.

[19] 孙天琦、李亚非,2010.汉语非核心论元允准结构初探[J].中国语文,(1):21-33+95.

[20] 杨大然,2015.基于事件轻动词理论的致使性交替现象研究[J].解放军外国语学院学报,(3):40-48.

[21] 姚旭晨,2009.几个汉语典型语言现象的范畴语法分析[J].中国中文信息学会,(6):13-21.

[22] 张建理,2008.单宾语句的认知构式语法研究[J].浙江大学学报(人文社会科学版),(4):182-189.

哈尔滨市中心与郊区楼盘名称的语音、语用研究

北京理工大学 郭思文 柳君丽*

摘要:楼盘名称作为符号是城市内在文化的载体。本文通过对哈尔滨楼盘名称进行音节数、修辞手法以及通名的比较,研究哈尔滨市中心与郊区楼盘名称的特点及其承载的文化内涵。研究发现郊区的楼盘名音节数与修辞手法的种类多于中心区楼盘,呈现多样化的趋势。郊区楼盘因坐落于城市周边,自然风景与优雅的环境为主要吸引力。其命名更加注重山、水等自然事物。而市中心的楼盘命通常呈现出繁荣富贵的特点,这一特性与其地理位置和楼盘价格关系紧密。通过对楼盘名称的研究分析区域发展差异和文化变迁,探寻名称背后的语用内涵。

关键词:音节数;修辞手法;通名;中心区与郊区;楼盘名

Title: The Phonetic and Pragmatic Analysis of Real Estate Names in Harbin Downtown and Suburban Areas

Abstract: The real estate name as a symbol embodies the culture of a city. This paper analyzes features of real estate names in Harbin downtown and suburban areas from the perspectives of syllables, rhetorical devices and common names. We find that the number of syllables and rhetoric devices of suburban real estate names is more than that of downtown, showing a trend of diversification. As suburban real estates are located in the periphery of the city, the natural scenery and elegant environment become its main attraction. Suburban real estate names emphasize beautiful scenery with mountains and water, while downtown real estate names possess features of prosperity and wealth due to its geographical location and real estate prices. By

---

* 作者简介:郭思文,北京理工大学外国语学院硕士研究生。研究方向:语用学、专门用途英语。电子邮箱:ninagreen818@163.com。柳君丽,北京理工大学外国语学院副教授。研究方向:语用学、会话分析、学术英语。邮箱:liujunli@bit.edu.cn。

analyzing real estate names, this paper explores the regional development differences and cultural changes in the suburban and downtown areas of Harbin.

Key words: syllables; rhetorical devices; common names; downtown and suburban areas; real estate names

1 引 言

名称作为一种符号,除指称作用外,具有一定的语用功能。名称往往会给人不同的第一印象,因为人们根据经验判断和推理出名称多重的社会语义和内涵。"楼盘名称能够反映出人们的社会心理,同时人们的社会心理也同样会影响到楼盘的命名。"(曾舟、刘颖群,2011:120)楼盘的名称会给住房者、买房者以及建房者多方面的暗示或影响,因此,关于楼盘命名的研究可以为不同的房产需求者提供多方面的、可以用于比较和衡量的有效信息。在一所城市中,市中心的楼盘和郊区的楼盘,由于地理位置、房价、交通等多方面的影响因素,呈现出不同的命名特点,可吸引有不同购房需求的群体。买房者在购房时,除了关注楼盘的硬性条件外,还会对楼盘的名称进行考虑和思量。因为楼盘名背后的寓意,与中国人从古至今注重姓名的历史传统有着千丝万缕的联系。

有鉴于此,本研究以哈尔滨市为例,尝试比较城市中不同区域楼盘命名的异同,以探究地理环境和区域发展对楼盘命名的影响,明晰楼盘命名背后的语音和语用内涵。本研究尝试解决如下研究问题:

(1) 哈尔滨中心区与郊区楼盘名在音节上具有怎样的异同?

(2) 哈尔滨中心区与郊区楼盘名在修辞手法的应用上具有怎样的异同?

(3) 哈尔滨中心区与郊区楼盘名在通名上具有怎样的异同?

楼盘名作为一种语言现象,承载着地区的文化底蕴,反映人们的社会心理和区域的经济发展情况。在理论层面,对比哈尔滨市不同区域(中心区与郊区)的楼盘名可以丰富语言学的研究对象,在一定程度上填补楼盘名区域对比研究的空白。在实践层面,城市内部不同区域的楼盘名对比可以促进楼盘命名的规范化,为开发商和购房者等提供一定的参考。

2 楼盘名的相关研究

有关楼盘名称的研究,很多学者已经从社会语言学、语用学、语音学等不同角度进行了分析。一些学者从文化语言学与社会语言学的角度展开,试图分析楼盘名所反映的历史文化以及传播的社会价值(姜淑珍,2009;李葵,2010;刘芳,2018;吕洁丽,2014;谭汝为,2004)。一些学者从认知语言学视角研究楼盘名中的隐喻现象(邓统湘,2012;田新柳,2015)。可见,楼盘名蕴含着丰富的文化内涵,具有一定的研究价值。

在楼盘名的语音研究上,一些学者从语音修辞的角度分析楼盘名的语音效果(冯苗苗,2014;胡蓉,2013;吴泓,2013),研究发现楼盘名"在语音形式上大多简短上口、富有韵味"(薛健,2008:54)。从楼盘名语料的来源看,多数学者通常是以某一城市为样本采集地(龚韶,2013;姜淑珍,2009;米幼萍,2011),将楼盘命名现状与城市发展联系,分析楼盘名反映的社会变迁及其语用价值。在楼盘通名的研究上,有学者通过大量的对比分析,解读不同城市间的发展差异(王洁,2017)。还有学者将国内城市与美国城市的楼盘名进行对比,得出命名背后不同的文化特点和命名侧重角度,发现"美国文化强调实用主义,倾向于突出案名的辨识作用"(刘奕男,2011:48)。

可见,目前关于楼盘名称的研究多集中于楼盘名背后的含义,以及楼盘名音律上的特点。同时,多数学者通过对比研究分析国家间、城市内甚至区域间的发展差异和文化差异。其中,大多学者是以某一城市为例,把城市内所有的楼盘名称作为一个总体进行研究。然而,少有学者对城市内部楼盘名称的区域异同进行比较。一座城市内,区域发展或多或少存在着不平衡的现象。经济发展的不平衡以及地理环境差异会影响人们的购房需求和楼盘命名,所以横向比较区域内的楼盘命名的异同点具有一定的研究价值。

哈尔滨作为市区面积和辖区面积较大的省会城市,下属各区的楼盘名称具有显著的特点。同时,其郊区与市中心的界限明晰,中心区域与郊区的楼盘名称各具特色,因此其楼盘名称的区域异同点值得深入探究。

3 研究设计

3.1 语料搜集

通过查阅哈尔滨城市区域的全图和二环区域(中心区)的地图,作者共整理出 406 个楼盘名称。其中,中心区域内的楼盘名称 76 个,市郊楼盘名称 330 个。根据哈尔滨不同分区,道里区楼盘名称68个,南岗区101个,道外区38个,松北区62个,香坊区56个,呼兰区47个,平房区与阿城区合计33个。

第一,土地面积是房地产投资,楼盘建设以及人口居住的前提之一。选取的这八个市辖区为哈尔滨下属面积前八名的市辖区。统计这八个面积较大的市辖区内的楼盘名,可以扩大样本的广泛度和多样性,为研究提供多元化的样本和案例。

第二,这八个市辖区各具代表性。南岗区、道里区、道外区和香坊区是哈尔滨城市的中心区域,这四个市辖区的楼盘名可以体现城市中心区域楼盘的命名特点。松北区、呼兰区、平房区和阿城区是哈尔滨市近年来向外扩展或者大力发展的新区;因此,这四个市辖区的楼盘名可以体现哈尔滨郊区楼盘的命名特点。

第三,位于哈尔滨市中心的四个市辖区,面积较大,其中包含二环以外、属于郊区的楼盘,因此南岗区、道里区、道外区和香坊区的楼盘既包括市中心区域,也含有郊外区域的楼盘。

3.2 研究方法

本文主要采用定量和定性相结合的分析方法,同时结合统计学检验方法对比哈尔滨市中心区与郊区楼盘名称的异同。首先,作者通过Excel对楼盘名的数据进行整理,对楼盘名称字数、楼盘名称音节数和楼盘通名进行识别和分类。然后,作者分别从音节数、修辞手法和通名三个角度对楼盘名进行分析。其中,音节数的分析采取了T-test方法,通过p值(T检验的概率值)比较楼盘名称在音节数上的异同。其他两个方面则主要通过列举和数量统计进行对比分析。

4 结果与讨论

4.1 中心区与郊区楼盘名音节数比较

从表1中可以看出,中心区的楼盘总数明显少于郊区(中心区为76,郊区为301)。原因在于中心区域作为一座城市的商业、政治和经济的主要发展区域,更多的建筑被用于建设商场、办公场所、行政楼、商业公司以及学校等带动经济发展或者促进政治稳定的商用和公用建筑。中心区域寸土寸金,商用和公用建筑较普通居民楼可以带来更多的经济价值。随着哈尔滨市的发展,中心区的人口容纳量有限,面积广阔的郊区得以开发。政府和房地产商投资郊区,建造居民住宅以带动城市整体发展。因此中心区域的楼盘名总量小于郊区的楼盘名总量。

表 1　中心区与郊区的楼盘名音节数

	中心区/个	比重	郊区/个	比重
2 音节	3	3.95%	18	5.98%
3 音节	3	3.95%	15	4.98%
4 音节	63	82.89%	196	65.12%
5 音节	4	5.26%	42	13.95%
6 音节	3	3.95%	27	8.97%
7 音节	0	0.00%	1	0.33%
8 音节	0	0.00%	2	0.66%
总数	76	100%	301	100%

在楼盘名音节的数量上，中心区楼盘除四音节外，其余各音节的楼盘名占比明显少于郊区。从表 1 中还可以看出，四音节的楼盘名在郊区和中心区的占比都是最大的。这表明四音节的楼盘名较其他音节(二、三音节等)普及性更高。四音节的普遍性体现了四音节更受大众欢迎。原因在于四音节楼盘名如"文君花园""先锋小区""药六嘉园"等发音朗朗上口、韵律性较强。这一发现在以往的研究中也得到了证实(程宏，2011；龚韶，2013；吴锋文、张秋雯，2013)。四音节的楼盘名短小精悍、极具韵律，容易被人记住。与音节数较长的楼盘名(六、七、八音节如"辰能溪树庭院""欧美亚世界阳光""盛高国际望江花园")相比，四音节在提供必要信息的基础上，更为简洁有力。四音节楼盘名在中心区的占比高于其在郊区的占比，体现出中心城区的楼盘命名强调实用性和易读性。

四音节的楼盘名分为两大类：一类是"专名+通名"的组合，如"陶瓷小区""迎宾家园"和"天悦国际"；另一类是应用隐喻等修辞手法的名称，如"碧水庄园""盛世江南"和"金色莱茵"。其中市中心的楼盘多以"××小区"等"专名+通名"的形式命名；郊区楼盘多含有隐喻等修辞用法。由此可见，市中心的楼盘名更加注重楼盘的建筑标识作用，因此更多应用"小区"的命名方式。由于郊区的楼盘开发时间相对更晚，其命名呈现多样化趋势。同时郊区楼盘的四音节名称搭配方式也更加灵活，如"春天故事""幸福港湾""水韵长滩""湖滨绿茵"等，不再遵从原来的通名与专名的组合形式，而是变得更加婉转、优雅和间接。

在不同音节楼盘名的分布上，郊区楼盘名的音节数更加多样化。由表 2 可以看出，两区的音节数平均值都在四左右，郊区楼盘名音节数的标准差远远大于中心区的标准差，表明郊区的楼盘音节数与平均音节数四相差较大，楼盘音节数分布更加离散，楼盘名称更加多样。相反，中心区的标准差较小，表明中心区的楼盘音节数与郊区相比主要集中在四音节。同时，T 检验的概率值 $p>0.05$，表明中心区与郊区的楼盘音节数存在共性,二者四音节楼盘名比重均为最高。但是郊区楼盘名的音节数更加多样,从二音节到八音节均有分布,如"上院""睿城""盛高国际望江花园""欧美亚世界阳光"等,而中心区并没有七音节与八音节的楼盘名。从楼盘建造时间和区域开发时间可以解释这一现象:开发较早的中心区楼盘(如"红旗小区"始建于1995年)命名较为保守,强调实用性;开发较晚的郊区楼盘(如"上院"始建于2010年)命名在音节数量上更具有时代性和创新性。

表2　中心区与郊区的楼盘音节数差异性对比

	中心区		郊区		p
	平均值	标准差	平均值	标准差	
音节数	4.013158	21.33695	4.186047	63.83013	0.26477

4.2　中心区与郊区楼盘名修辞手法比较

在修辞手法上,中心区使用修辞手法的楼盘名比重高于郊区,但郊区楼盘名较中心区楼盘名使用的修辞手法种类更加丰富(见表3)。经统计,哈尔滨中心区楼盘名主要应用的修辞手法有比喻、象征、仿词和引用四类;郊区楼盘名主要应用的修辞手法有比喻、象征、仿词、引用、借代和双关六类。其中,中心区域应用比喻手法楼盘名的比重高于郊区,应用象征和仿词手法楼的盘名比重低于郊区。

表3　中心区与郊区的修辞手法

	中心区		郊区	
	数量	比重	数量	比重
比喻	18	56.25%	25	20.16%
象征	10	31.25%	65	52.42%
仿词	2	6.25%	18	14.52%
引用	2	6.25%	13	10.48%
双关	0	0.00%	1	0.81%
借代	0	0.00%	2	1.61%
修辞手法楼盘名	32	42.11%	124	37.58%

在象征手法的应用上,郊区的楼盘命名更倾向于选取大自然中的花草树木、山川河流作为象征物,以体现楼盘的地理位置属性,如环境优美、气质高雅等特点。如"宏润翠湖天地""玫瑰湾""涧桥西畔"等使用象征手法(表4)将自然景物和颜色应用于楼盘名中。由于楼盘命名的重要参考依据为"地理位置、周边环境、楼盘特色"等(姜淑珍,2009:119),因此郊区楼盘呈现的这一特点也是由其地理位置决定的。郊区楼盘通常没

有市区的高楼大厦鳞次栉比,而是湖光山色、风景秀丽。因此,象征手法的应用可以更好地表达郊区楼盘的主要特色。

表 4 中心与郊区楼盘名修辞手法案例

	中心区	郊区
比喻	盛世江南、聚贤花园、公园丽景	天合俊景、涧桥西畔、中央公园壹号
引用	轩辕花园、昆仑小区	盛和·天地人和、雍景熙岸
仿词	青年城邦、紫金城	巴黎第五区、唐宁郡、东方哥德堡
象征	紫园、富达·蓝山、四季上东	世茂·翡冷翠、金域蓝城、春天故事

在比喻修辞手法的应用上,中心区楼盘名强调楼盘位置繁华,而郊区楼盘名强调楼盘环境宁静、安逸。在中心区域,应用比喻手法的楼盘名如"盛世江南"将楼盘周围的热闹比喻为江南盛世的景象,体现了城市中心区的繁华热闹。但也不乏中心区的楼盘强调环境优雅,如"公园丽景"等,体现出中心区楼盘不仅强调其雍容华贵,尊贵气阔的特点,也重视环境的优美和宜居。而郊区的楼盘名称,如"世茂·翡冷翠""涧桥西畔""盛和·天地人和"等,则主要体现其风光自然、环境秀美的特点,不强调繁华热闹的环境。

在仿词手法的应用上,郊区楼盘名较中心区楼盘名比重更高,但二者侧重不同。郊区楼盘名如"纳帕英郡""华润·凯旋门""您好荷兰城""世茂都柏林""地中海阳光"等具有的共同特点是仿照欧洲国家的名称或地标进行命名。这样的命名使楼盘听起来洋气、摩登、现代化,这类"展现异国建筑风情"的楼盘名体现人们"对西方有强烈的崇尚感和追随欲"(黄玉淑,2009:73)。因此,郊区楼盘名顺应了城市国际化发展下年轻一代购房的心理需求。中心区的仿词手法如"紫金城",则是仿照古代皇帝居所命名,表现楼盘的富贵和入住人的尊贵。相比之下,中心区的楼盘名很少使用仿词手法,也很少借鉴欧洲地名和地标建筑命名。二者差异主要在于郊区的楼盘开发时间较晚,而且地广人稀,与一些欧洲国家的人口和地理特点具有相似性,从而借鉴欧洲的地名进行命名,侧面表现出楼盘环境的宽阔、宁静,与闹市的熙熙攘攘形成对比,这也是郊区楼盘的主要卖点之一。同时,这样命名会吸引一些向往海外生活的购房人群,符合其对生活的憧憬与心理需求。

4.3 中心区与郊区楼盘通名比较

中心区的通名使用种类少于郊区的通名种类。如图 1 所示,其中"别墅"和"城"这两个通名的差异最为明显。"别墅"在中心区没有使用。原因在于别墅的建筑面积较大,而且价格昂贵,其需求量相对少于普通楼房的需求,不符合房地产开发商利益最大化的需要,因此很少在城市中心区建设别墅。其次,别墅对于生活环境的要求较高,尤其是自然环境,哈尔滨的别墅通常建设在人流较少,噪音和污染较少的郊区。所以,哈尔滨中心区与郊区的楼盘在"别墅"这个通名的使用上差异显著。

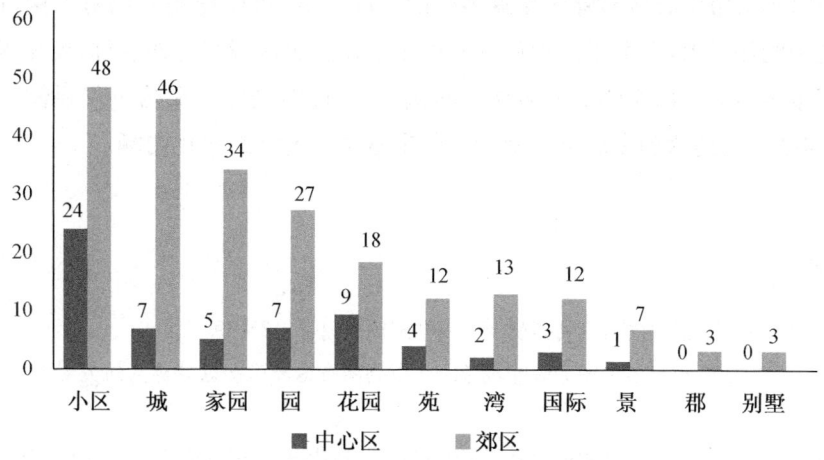

图1　中心区与郊区通名使用数量统计

其次,"城"这一通名使用差异在于对于地理面积的要求。"城"突出了住房区面积之大,而城市中心区很难满足这一需求。因此,"城"在中心区楼盘的应用尤其少。此外,中心区楼盘多使用"小区"这一通名(中心区31.58% vs. 郊区15.95%)。"小区"这一通名在其他城市的楼盘中也广为使用,但在哈尔滨中心区的比重明显高于其他城市,如天津以"小区"作为通名的楼盘占比仅为"14.18%"(谭汝为,2004:37)。因此,哈尔滨中心区的楼盘在通名上呈现出种类少,且多以"小区"作为通名的特点。相比之下,郊区通名种类更加多样,体现郊区文化发展的多样性。随着人们视野的开阔、思想的开放,其对楼盘的命名也呈现多元包容的特点。结合哈尔滨的发展,随着政府、企业向郊区的迁移,郊区的发展速度加快,郊区的楼盘名在发展的大势下呈现出较市中心更为多样化、开放化的命名特征。

5　结　论

通过比较哈尔滨市中心区与郊区楼盘名称的音节数、修辞手法和通名的使用情况,得出以下三点异同:1)郊区楼盘和中心区楼盘名称的音节数均以四音节为主。郊区楼盘的命名方式更为多样;中心区的楼盘除四音节外,其他音节数的楼盘名称鲜少出现;2)郊区楼盘由于地理环境为主要吸引力并且开发时间较晚,其楼盘命名更加注重自然风光和景色;而中心区的楼盘多强调繁荣热闹、尊贵富华的特点。这样的差异主要取决于中心区与郊区的经济发展水平不同和地理环境差异;3)在通名的使用上,郊区楼盘的通名种类更丰富,体现随着经济的发展城市文化呈现出的开放、多元的特点。

哈尔滨市中心区和郊区楼盘名称的异同反映出其背后的经济发展和文化发展差异。分析哈尔滨市中心区与郊区楼盘名称的不同特点,可以挖掘人们对于楼盘名称的关注侧重和购房需求,有助于房地产开发商赋予楼盘更具吸引力的名称,突显楼盘的特性。由于楼盘名称会影响购房者对楼盘的认知,因此对楼盘的命名不仅要体现其地缘优势,还需结合人们的购房需求和地区文化丰富楼盘名称的文化内涵。

参考文献

[1] 程宏,2011.武汉楼盘名的语言特点研究[J].中国校外教育,(2):39.

[2] 邓统湘,2012.解析楼盘名称中的隐喻现象——以湖南省株洲市楼盘名称为研究对象[J].语文学刊,(17):55-57.

[3] 冯苗苗,2014.秦皇岛楼盘名称的语音、语用分析[J].现代语文(语言研究版),(10):110-113.

[4] 龚韶,2013.三亚市楼盘名称的语言学分析[J].现代语文(语言研究版),(12):114-116.

[5] 胡蓉,2013.南充市住宅楼盘名称的语音修辞分析——中小城市住宅楼盘名称分析一例[J].语文学刊,(11):39-41.

[6] 黄玉淑,2009.桂林市楼盘名称命名的语言文化分析[J].广州广播电视大学学报,9(6):69-74+111.

[7] 姜淑珍,2009.新楼盘命名研究[J].河北理工大学学报(社会科学版),9(4):117-120.

[8] 李葵,2010.武汉楼盘命名的社会语言学分析[J].语文学刊,(14):39-41.

[9] 刘芳,2018.文化语言学视角下城市形象传播之楼盘名称研究——以南宁市为例[J].传播与版权,(2):163-165。

[10] 刘奕男,2011.中美楼盘案名比较与分析[J].中外企业家,(1):45-49.

[11] 吕洁丽,2014.杭州市楼盘名的社会语言学分析[J].现代交际,(6):29-31.

[12] 米幼萍,2011.长沙楼盘名的语用分析及其经济内涵[J].邵阳学院学报(社会科学版),10(4):71-74.

[13] 谭汝为,2004.楼盘命名的社会语言学分析[J].修辞学习,(1):37-40.

[14] 田新柳,2015.隐喻转喻视角下上海市楼盘名称研究[J].现代语文(语言研究版),(12):117-120.

[15] 王洁,2017.关于"公馆"作为楼盘通名的思考[J].中国地名,(8):8-9.

[16] 吴锋文、张秋雯,2013.南阳市楼盘名称的语言学分析[J].语文学刊,(7):71-72+77.

[17] 吴泓,2013.以哈尔滨为例谈楼盘名称的语音修辞特点[J].边疆经济与文化,(8):142-143.

[18] 薛健,2008.南京楼盘名称的语音修辞分析[J].南京广播电视大学学报,(3):54-57.

[19] 曾舟、刘颖群,2011.从模因论角度看楼盘命名——以南昌市楼盘名为研究对象[J].江西教育学院学报,32(2):117-120.

中英文社交媒体不礼貌话语的同异性探究：
以微博、Twitter 为例*

兰开斯特大学　刘胜男　太原理工大学　侯　涛**

摘要： 本文探究中文微博、英文 Twitter 两种社交媒体中同一热点话题引发的在线反馈话语中的言语行为不礼貌现象。基于实时收集的中英文博客话语真实语料，研究两语种网络话语不礼貌语言的同异。结果表明：首先，在相似的网络交际语境下，微博和 Twitter 用户在使用不礼貌话语的策略上具有类似点；其次，微博和 Twitter 用户在一些不礼貌话语的输出策略方面表现出明显差异性；最后，两种语料整体上语用特点和局部区别性特点之形成源于动态性、多样性的网络交际语境及交际资源以及不同语言文化语境的共同作用。研究为社交媒体网络话语特征研究提供了宝贵的新发现，启迪人们对网络语言和功能等的全面认识。

关键词： 社交媒体；网络语言；不礼貌话语；语用研究

Title: A Comparative Study of Chinese and English Social Media Impolite Discourse: *Weibo* vs. *Twitter*

Abstract: The research explores the impoliteness discourse produced by Chinese *Weibo* and the English *Twitter* users under the same hot topic discussion. By applying Culpeper's impoliteness theory to the comparative data sets, a thorough comparative study adopting both qualitative and quantitative methods on the impoliteness of the online discourse has been undertaken. It is concluded that: a. under similar social media communication contexts, the Chinese *Weibo* and the English *Twitter* users

---

* 本文系"'微言''微文'之语言时代化规范化研究"项目（2018 年山西省哲学社会科学规划课题）部分成果。

** 作者简介：刘胜男，英国兰开斯特大学博士，研究方向：话语分析、语用学。邮箱：s.liu26@lancaster.ac.uk。侯涛，太原理工大学教授，研究方向：语用学、文体学、应用语言学。邮箱：houtao@tyut.edu.cn。

show similar discursive characteristics in using impoliteness superstrategies; b. the *Weibo and Twitter* users, respectively, show significant differences in certain impolite output strategies; c. both the overall pragmatic features and the distinctive characteristics of local discourse are influenced by the dynamics of online communication context and different cultural contexts of the language communities. This study provides new findings on the comparative uses of impoliteness strategies in Chinese and English social media discourse, shedding light on people's knowledge of the hidden forms and neglected functions in CMC (computer mediated communication).

Key words: social media; network language; impolite discourse; pragmatics

1　引　言

近年来网络语言经历了从无到有的发展历程,学者对网络语言研究的态度也经历了从质疑与反思到承认与接受的转变历程(胡凌、刘云、杨传丽,2014)。网络语言也在经历着巨大的变化,网络语言文本数量激增、网络语言变体日益增多,新的语言特征不断涌现,这些现象蕴含着巨大的语言价值及语言学价值。随着网络服务升级和智慧化生活的到来,网络语言呈现强大的创造性与生命力,吸引学者们从词汇、语法、修辞、语体、语用等角度研究网络语言的性质及特征(冯薇、王立非,2017;黄国文,2005;左海霞、姚喜明,2006),越来越多的学者不止局限于对网络语言的特征描述,而是尝试从认知语言学、语言顺应理论的角度来探讨解释网络语言的传播特征,以及研究网络语言与社会文化的关系(王彦彦,2010;李国防,2006;程伟,2013)。《2006—2020年国家信息化发展战略》明确我国信息化发展的战略重点:在中国"建设先进网络文化"。国家更需加强对自媒体的语言舆情等的引导(张挺、武超,2017)。加强关于网络语言文本语言动态使用的考察研究,多方面运用机制及效果的考察,对社会生活在网络时代健康发展和繁荣进步意义重大。面对新媒体、自媒体语境下网络语言时而有失规范、时而鱼龙混杂的局面,借鉴中外学术思想研究方法及时考察"网络语言不礼貌"现象当有助于对网络语言规范的理解。

2　文献综述

语言不礼貌(linguistic impoliteness)现象因其字表的"负面"映像和初期研究中的

的"礼貌研究"附属性,在理论和实践研究方面的受重视程度较弱(Leech,1983)。随着日常语言研究的不断深入,近年来人们越来越注意到,语言不礼貌与语言交际的欠规范和不文明并非偶发的、变异的,而是频频出现、现象内容庞杂、发挥重要功能的,应予专项专门研究(Blitvich & Sifianou,2019;Chen,2019;Culpeper,1996,2005,2015;Eelen,2001;Kienpointner,1997;Mills,2009;毛延生,2014)。事实上,言语不礼貌是有目的发出的、故意的行为(Bousfield,2008:72),它有意性地交流话语的争论性的意图,在人际关系的构建过程中作用不可小觑。二十世纪八十年代以来,许多相关领域的学者不仅在礼貌研究理论的基础上发展不礼貌研究(第一浪潮),更有第二浪潮、第三浪潮研究积极发展理论视野、上升理论研究层次,努力从微观—宏观—中观联系的视角阐述解释各种语言不礼貌现象及其语用—社会交际话语机理(Blitvich & Sifianou,2019:92)。Lachenicht(1980)、Austin(1990)、Culpeper(1996)及Kienpointner(1997)等学者最先对话语不礼貌现象进行了理论解释。其中,Culpeper(1996,2005)基于Brown和Levinson(1987)的礼貌策略研究之上的不礼貌模式受到了学界广泛的认可,在实际应用研究中广为参照。之后不少实证研究将语言不礼貌的理论模式应用到具体语境的研究中,如军事训练话语、法律话语、课堂话语、工场对话、机构对话、政宣语篇、电视节目对话、影视剧人物对话以及文学语篇(Cashman,2006;Chen,2019;Culpeper,1996,1998,2001,2005;Culpeper & Holmes,2013;Dobs & Garces-Conejos Blitvich,2013;Dynel,2015,2016;Harris,2001,2011;Holmes 等,2012;Lorenzo-Dus 等,2013;Marquez Reiter & Bou-Franch,2017;Mathias,2011;Rudanko,2006;Taylor,2011;Tracy,2008,2017)。

相对于面对面交际中的不礼貌现象,在网络环境下的不礼貌呈现出超量运用的倾向,因此计算机中介交际(CMC)成为不礼貌现象的研究聚焦(Angouri & Tesliga,2010;Haugh,2010;Locher,2010;Nishimura,2010;等)。2010 年《礼貌研究》(Journal of Politeness Research)刊发计算机中介交际语境中的(不)礼貌研究专刊。尽管一些研究尚在起步阶段,CMC 语境下不礼貌研究的实践及学术价值(Locher,2010)显而易见。现有研究涉及的语料来源包括网络报刊(Upadhyay,2010)、电子邮件(Haugh,2010)、网络论坛(毛延生,2014;Nishimura,2008,2010;Angouri & Tseliga,2010;Shum & Lee,2013;Lorenzo-Dus 等,2011,etc.)及机构的网络话语(周树江,2016)和商务话语(孙亚、赵彬楠,2015)不礼貌和言语冲突现象。具体研究涉及希腊语、日语、西班牙语、英语、汉语及粤语方言等。相对而言,汉语中不礼貌现象的研究数量明显不足;此外,现有国内外研究大多专注于一种语言的不礼貌,跨语言、跨文化的不礼貌对比研究较为少见——我们认为,由于不礼貌研究的理论多是建立在英语基础上,其对各种语言的适用性仍有待于进一步验证。

因此,本研究聚焦网络社交媒体语言,选择中文、英文社交网络微博和 Twitter 用户在"美联航暴力事件"发生后同一话题下微贴话语的不礼貌策略使用情况,其同异性及驱动语境因素进行对比研究,旨在对中英文社交媒体网络语言不礼貌现象进行细致的语用分析,在动态性语境观和跨文化比较的视角下系统呈现和梳理问题。本研究是对公共危机事件舆情下的网络争论性语言的对比性发现研究,有助于了解和掌握中外网络语言使用的现状及预测今后网络话语使用的影响范围和发展趋势。

3 理论框架

本研究的理论框架基于 Culpeper(1996,2005)的不礼貌策略,同时借鉴了 Herring 的用于计算机中介交际模式的多面分类系统。Culpeper (1996,2005)为分析不礼貌策略提供理论及方法论的指导。在此基础上,Herring(2007)的多面分类系统为语料的筛选和收集提供科学依据,从而确保了中文、英文语料的可比性,使研究更加严谨准确。本研究旨在回答三个相关问题:(1) 中文、英文交际者(相应社交媒体用户)使用何种不礼貌策略来表达不礼貌?(2) 中文、英文两种社交媒体网络交际中,不礼貌策略的使用是否有区别?如果有区别,两种使用的区别性特征是什么?(3) 上述共同点和不同点的驱动语境因素是什么?

3.1 不礼貌策略

Culpeper 参照 Brown & Levinson(1987)的框架提出不礼貌策略(Culpeper, 1996),并在理论和应用实践中不断修改发展。按照 Culpeper(2005:41-44)的不礼貌策略模式,不礼貌策略分为如下五类:直接不礼貌、积极不礼貌、消极不礼貌、间接不礼貌和抑制不礼貌。

表 1　Culpeper 的不礼貌策略模式

直接不礼貌	以最清晰的、无掩饰的方式威胁对方面子(在面子并非无所谓的场合)
积极不礼貌	故意损害对方的积极面子需要
消极不礼貌	故意损害对方的消极面子需要
间接不礼貌	具有"超意图"、以含义方式("越间接越挑衅"地)威胁面子
抑制不礼貌	故意忽略应有的礼貌

Culpeper(2005)将这些策略定义为高级策略(superstrategy),其中,积极不礼貌与消极不礼貌各包含一系列特殊的输出策略(output strategies)或高级策略的具体实现方式。如,积极不礼貌策略包括:忽视对方存在、将对方从活动中驱逐、割裂对方与周围、冷漠、使用隐晦语言、找茬、用禁忌语等。消极不礼貌包括:威胁、蔑视嘲弄、入侵"领

地"、负面化联系、使担责等。此外,该分类模式也还包含讽刺和虚假礼貌的元策略(meta-strategy)。

通过对英国电视节目《智者为王》中有时"爆炸性"的不礼貌而引人入胜的参与者对话分析,Culpeper(2005)结合了语用微观(micro-level)与语用社会心理过程,改进了前期不礼貌策略理论的框架。

3.2 多向分类模式

多向分类模式(faceted classification scheme)假设计算机中介交际(CMC)受多种向度因素的影响,包括媒介因素(medium factors)和情境因素(situation factors)(Herring,2007),它们的具体内容如表2及表3所示:

表2 多向分类模式之媒介因素

媒介模式因素
实时性(是/否)
信息传输(单向/双向)
文本留存(永久性/暂时性)
单次信息容量
交际渠道(文字/图像/声音)
匿名性(是/否)
私信(是/否)
信息过滤(有/无)
信息引用/转发(有/无)
信息格式

表3 多向分类模式之情境因素

情境模式因素
交际参与结构(参与人、参与量等)
交际参与者特征(生理特征、行业经验、交际习惯、态度动机等)
对话目的性(专业组群/社交组群、具体参与交际目的)
对话话题/对话主题(组群一般性话题、小组事务性交流话题)
对话语气(严肃性/戏谑性、正式性/随意性、争议性/友好性、合作性/讽刺性等)
交际活动(辩论、交流信息、寒暄、解决问题、互贬、谈情等)
交际规范(机构组织规范、社交合适性规范、语言规范等)
使用语码(语种、方言、字体/符码等)

依据该分类模式,可以将交际话语样本在数个变量向度上进行分类,既看到样本的复杂性,又有利于研究者在"参数"一定的情况下进行样本内与样本间的分析比较(Herring,2007)。因此,模式适用于本文的中文、英文网络社交媒体中不礼貌策略使用的对比研究。

目前，以单片言语为据(utterance-based)的不礼貌研究应时代潮流需要，正转向不礼貌话语语用学，即与该现象有关的"d"(discourse 话语)层面的研究(Blitvich & Sifianou, 2019)，以逐步实现从(不)礼貌研究的经典路径向宏观话语路径的研究范式更新。实际上，Herring 多向分类模式提示社交媒体网络交际研究的形式—功能体裁配置语境化因素，是一种网络交际"中观"(meso-level)方法。

在本研究中，多项分类模式确保了中文、英文语料在以上媒介因素和情境因素上有较高的可比性，而 Culpeper (2005) 的不礼貌策略则运用在对语料的定性、定量分析中，共同达到回答本研究问题的目的。

4 研究语料和路径

4.1 研究语料

本研究选取了具有代表性的中文、英文两种社交媒体，微博（新浪微博 Sina Weibo）与 Twitter。就媒介因素而言，微博和 Twitter 在多个方面具有较高的相似性，尤其是在实时性、信息传输模式、文本留存模式、一次性信息容量、匿名性和信息格式方面——Twitter 与微博都向用户提供实时性的双向信息传送模式，文本留存模式均为永久型，信息容量相近（140~160 字节），所有信息都可以由用户匿名发布，信息格式均为按热度或用户相关度排列。其余的媒介模式因素也同理，因此通过排除媒介因素的影响，本研究可以关注社交媒体不礼貌交际及及语境模式因素的相关影响。

在情境模式的一般因素方面，微博和 Twitter 这两种社交媒体用户使用交际语码虽然有不同，但交际参与结构与交际目的相似；信息发布均为匿名，交际参与者特征不可控；交际语气、交际活动与交际规范这三个变量也较自由和普遍，取决于交际参与者的个人选择。

研究者在两种社交媒体的中选择了相似的交际话题——2017 年 4 月 9 日，美国联合航空公司一航班上几名员工将一名亚裔乘客暴力拖拽下机，造成该乘客面部瘀伤与出血；航班上乘客将这一过程录制成视频发布，激起了大量的用户讨论，纷纷对这一事件表示愤慨和谴责美联航。与此同时，这一事件在微博上也引起了热烈的讨论。相似话题的语境非常适宜于研究中文、英文网络交际中的不礼貌现象对比研究。

在微博与 Twitter 同一话题下，研究选取了两种用户各 200 条回复，在删除不适宜研究不礼貌策略的回复（如微博中的非中文评论与 Twitter 中的非英文回复、表达有歧义的回复和与话题无关的回复等）后，本文的研究语料确定为微博语料（包含 128 条回复）和 Twitter 语料（包含 161 条回复），并分别按照顺序标记为 W1-128 和 T1-161。

4.2 研究路径

本研究采用定性研究与定量考察相结合的方法,在对语料详细分析的基础上,归纳总结推理并作出发现。首先对语料中的言语行为进行语境化考察辨认,根据 Culpeper(2005)不礼貌策略以及新出现的策略,对语料加以标记、分类和分析,进行定性研究,并在此基础上进行统计对比的定量研究。然后根据定性分析与定量研究的结果,对微博语料与 Twitter 语料结合语境因素进行对比分析与讨论。本研究不仅分析对比中文、英文社交媒体用户回复中不礼貌话语、不礼貌策略使用以及各类策略形式、功能与使用情形和频率等的差异,而且检验不礼貌策略分析"工具库"(量表)在两种语料中的适用性,基于真实语料检验发展相关理论模式对网络交际的解释力。

5 结果与分析

5.1 研究结果

首先,通过对两类语料中不礼貌语用的辨认标记,发现了 3 种新的不礼貌输出策略,在 Culpeper(2015)的输出策略列表中十类积极不礼貌策略和六类消极不礼貌策略未予包括,它们分别是:a 批评/抱怨、b 挑战/质疑、c 消极情绪表达(诅咒)(在表 3 中标有"ⓧ")。其中,批评/抱怨攻击网络评论目标的积极面子,属于积极不礼貌策略;挑战/质疑与消极情绪表达(诅咒)攻击网络评论目标的消极面子,属于消极不礼貌策略。此外,研究者还发现有若干策略没有出现在收集的研究语料中,如抑制礼貌语不礼貌、使用不恰当的身份标记语不礼貌、侵入他人空间不礼貌等。研究语料中出现的策略及分类如表 4:

表 4 中文、英文社交媒体不礼貌策略使用语例及类别

不礼貌策略		语料实例
1. 直接不礼貌		W37:投诉！赔偿！
2. 积极不礼貌	排除对方	T37：… ♯neveragainthefriendlyskies …
	否认联系	T23：… Boycott United would be my response to this appalling behaviour.
	冷漠/不关心	W70:此时此刻,想说一句,去美国干嘛哦……
	强调分歧(提出敏感话题)	T13：… An "Asian" man, that's what the headline should say! It's a racist incident that what it is
	使用禁忌语	T49：… what the actual fuck …

(续表)

不礼貌策略		语料实例
	辱骂	W27：……坐过 UA 的都会觉得 UA 就是个垃圾
	批评/抱怨*	T114：... This is absolutely barbaric!!!
3. 消极不礼貌	威胁	T56：... Passenger was a doctor that needed to see patients. You could be next.
	轻视/鄙视/取笑	T100：……而且更恶心的是这个航空公司的 ceo。
	将负面形象与对方联系	T153：How do those freaking NAZIS look at themselves in the mirror? (also an example of [CQP] and [CON])
	揭短	W23：美联航就是这样的垃圾，上次和老公带宝宝回国，两个人只有一个小手提箱和一个妈咪包，死活让我们托运，前提是已经在安检那里量了箱子的大小，走到机舱门口才说，而且我们都是商。务。仓。一路上 10 几个小时，三个月的宝宝要用多少东西！垃圾乘务员坚持没有行李位了，不托运就坐下班飞机。(also in [con])
	挑战/质疑*	T55：... why would customers use your service after seeing this?
	消极情绪表达*	W120：UA 凭什么把买了票已登机的乘客拖下去，还是医生…最好死了都没人救他
4. 讽刺		T50：... Fly United for an exciting, dangerous adventure.
5. 间接不礼貌		T48：North Korea?

根据上表所展示的标记与分类结果，研究者进一步统计了中文、英文两种社交媒体中不礼貌策略使用的频率与比例，结果如下表 5 所示：

表 5 两种语料中不礼貌策略使用的频次与比例

不礼貌策略	微博语料		Twitter 语料	
	频次	百分比	频次	百分比
直接不礼貌	5	2.9%	8	3.3%
积极不礼貌	86	49.4%	117	49.0%
消极不礼貌	58	33.3%	75	31.3%
讽刺	24	13.8%	36	15.0%
间接不礼貌	1	0.6%	3	1.2%
总计	174	100%	239	100%

从表 5 可以看出，中文与英文语料中，交际者使用的不礼貌策略频次与比例结构相似：使用最多的策略为积极不礼貌策略，其次是消极不礼貌策略，讽刺、直接不礼貌及简介不礼貌的策略依次较少。Garces-Conejos Blitvich(2010)、Lorenzo-Dus(2009)、Lorenzo-Dus 等(2011)以及毛延生(2014)的研究结果也显示网络交际积极不礼貌策略

的使用多于消极不礼貌策略的使用。作为验证,中文、英文语料中不礼貌策略的对比卡方检验结果(X2=0.798,df=4,sig=0.940)显示两种网络语言交际不存在显著差异,说明中文、英文语料中此处不礼貌策略的使用结果相似。换言之,在相似语境下,使用中文的交际者与使用英文的交际者倾向于使用相似的不礼貌策略(如高级策略与其他层面的)来实现交际目的。

在不礼貌策略的使用中,积极不礼貌策略与消极不礼貌策略占比最大,而这两种高级策略中又包含许多具体输出策略,因此,需进一步比较中文、英文语料不礼貌策略在输出策略使用层面上的差异。对比微博语料与Twitter语料可以看出(图1),在两者使用的7类积极不礼貌策略中,各类输出策略的使用频率异大于同:

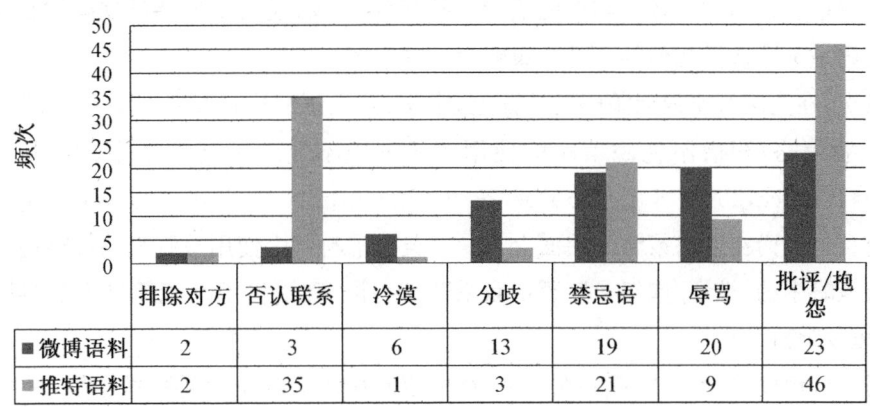

图1　微博、Twitter语料中积极不礼貌输出策略使用频次对比

从图1可以清晰看出,虽然中文、英文语料中积极不礼貌策略在所有不礼貌策略中所占比例相似,但是具体输出策略上,两种语言在网络交际中实际使用的具体策略频率上有明显不同。卡方检验结果(X2=45.024,df=6,sig=0.000)也显示两组数据有显著差异——使用中文的交际者与使用英文的交际者在相似的网络语境下会使用不同的积极不礼貌输出策略。

在中文、英文语料中消极不礼貌的输出策略分别使用频率统计如图2:

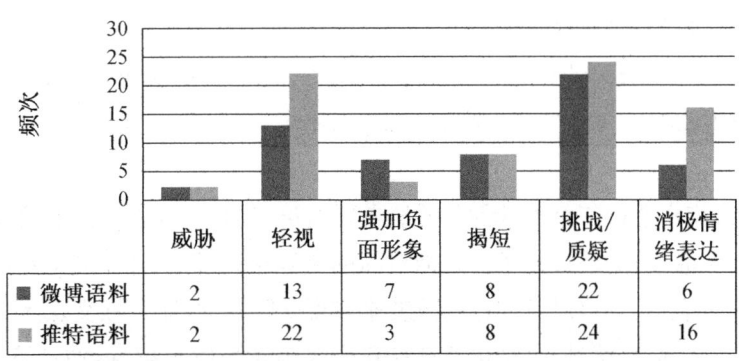

图2　微博、Twitter语料中消极不礼貌策略使用频次对比

从图 2 可以看出,消极不礼貌策略的输出策略使用频率方面,中文语料与英文语料也有差别,例如 Twitter 语料中"轻视""挑战/质疑""消极情绪表达"的策略的使用频率较微博语料更高,而微博语料中"强加负面形象"这一策略的使用频率较 Twitter 语料更高。

5.2 "相似性"的不礼貌策略使用

首先,根据上述研究发现,中文、英文社交媒体用户都使用了相似的不礼貌策略(图 3),而在一些在其他语境中出现的不礼貌策略,如"使用不恰当的身份标记语""使用晦涩语""打断会话结构"等策略在两种语料中均无出现。考虑到本研究在收集语料时在两种社交媒体中选择了相似的语境,说明使用中文、英文的网络社交媒体交际者在相似的语境下会选择相似的不礼貌策略表达其意图。

其次,在高级策略或元策略的层面上,中文、英文语料中使用最频繁的策略均是积极不礼貌策略,积极不礼貌策略的使用多于消极不礼貌策略的使用,形同 Garces-Conejos Blitvich(2010)、Lorenzo-Dus(2009)、Lorenzo-Dus 等(2011)以及毛延生(2014)的研究结果。而在输出策略的层面上,中文、英文语料库中使用最频繁的策略均为积极不礼貌策略中的"批评/抱怨*""否认联系""禁忌语"和消极不礼貌策略中的"挑战/质疑*"以及"轻视"。

另一个角度看,不礼貌策略在中文、英文语料中均呈现出两种模式:某一策略的重复使用及多种策略混合使用,Culpeper(1998)对电视记录片 *The Clampers* 的研究中也指出了这两种模式。试比较以下两例社交媒体用户回复:

(例 1、例 2 分别选自微博、Twitter 中美联航拖拽打人这一话题下的回复)
例 1
W12:他们做这件事情之前难道就没有考虑过人权考虑过后果吗?真的是随机选了"超额"的吗?还是到底是要给谁让座啊(挑战/质疑*)
例 2
T40:@BuzzFeedNews　　　　　　　　　　　　　　　@JayseDavid
#Never fly @UnitedAirlines　　　　　　　　ever again! #neverflyunited
#neverflyunited　　　　　　#neverflyunited　　　　　(否认联系)

例 1 中该用户通过三个连续问句质疑美联航员工的行为,表达强烈的挑战与质疑,以威胁目标(美联航)的消极面子。在面对面的交际中,交际者不可能(重复)使用标点符号,而是通过表情、手势以及韵律的改变来实现交际目的,而在社交媒体交际中,交际者可以通过文字、标点符号、表情以及话题符号来表达情感。可见,在计算机中介交际

(CMC)中,由技术载体带来的交际模式的变化,使得不礼貌策略的语言形式的实现呈现出全新的方式。

例2中话题标签符号"♯"的重复使用也是CMC交际中的特有表达,在文本前加上话题标签符号,可以使其后的文本成为一个超链接,用户可以点击这一超链接,从而搜索到这一话题下的更多讨论。因此,新话题"♯neverflyunited"(♯再也不坐美联航)的重复使用不仅通过"否认联系"的不礼貌策略来威胁美联航的积极面子,同时也是邀请其他用户加入到谴责美联航的行列当中,从而进一步增加了威胁面子的力度。Holmes(1984)指出重复作为一种修辞手段可以增加言语行为的力度。Culpeper(2005)也认可不礼貌策略的重复使用能够增加对交际目标的强加程度,并强调说话人对目标的消极态度,从而增强不礼貌的力度。

除重复使用不礼貌策略的模式外,还有多种不礼貌策略混合使用的模式。本研究经统计发现,微博语料中有36条回复混合使用了多种策略,占微博语料总数的28%;Twitter语料中有66条回复混合使用了多种策略,占Twitter语料总数的41%,可见多种不礼貌策略的混合使用在网络社交媒体热点话题讨论活动中也是一种普遍现象。

进一步分析多种策略混合使用的具体情况发现,不礼貌策略混合使用的具体情况可以分为三类:即使用两种、使用三种以及使用四种的策略,通过统计各种情况的回复,可以得到以下结果:

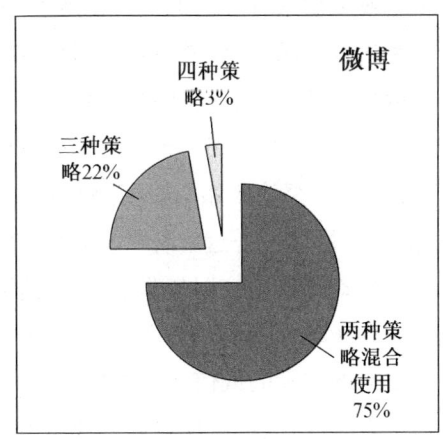 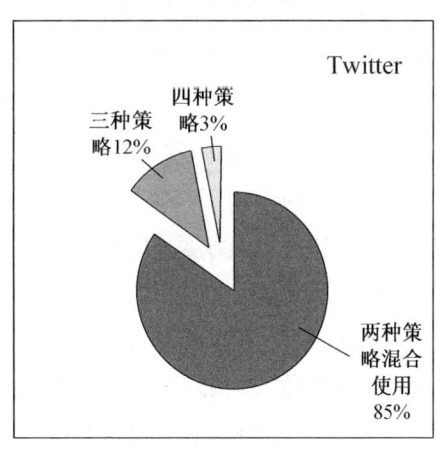

图3 微博语料中多种不礼貌策略
使用的分布情况

图4 Twitter语料中多种不礼貌策略
使用的分布情况

从图3、图4可以看出,多种不礼貌策略混合使用的模式中,两种策略混合使用的情况最为普遍,四种策略混合使用的情况最少,中文与英文语料中不礼貌策略混合使用的模式相似。

5.3 "差异性"的不礼貌策略使用

研究结果可以看出,中文、英文社交媒体中不礼貌策略的使用中,在积极不礼貌策略这一类别方面有显著差异(图2),主要体现在否认联系、辱骂和批评/抱怨三种策略的使用上。

英文语料中"否认联系"这一策略的使用频率高于在中文语料的使用频率,使用这一策略的输出差异主要体现于话题标签符"♯"的运用,如:

例3

W49:还是 delta 好……幸好不坐 Ua 这种没良心的廉价航空……(否认联系)(轻视)

例4

T132:@BuzzFeedNews　　　　　　@EmptySeatsPics
@JayseDavid　　　　　　　　　♯BoycottUnited　　　　　(否认联系)

话题标签符号"♯"最初被设计为一种搜索方式,然而在广泛的使用中,"♯"被赋予了新的网络语用功能,"话题标签符号可以使 Twitter 用户在不改变语气的前提下使读者做出一定的语境设想",还可以"强调推文的主题或主位"(Scott 2015)。实际上,大量用户使用同一个话题标签,那么这个话题就会成为热点话题,从而进一步吸引更多的用户加入讨论,并且用户为了增加朝向自己的访问量与互动量,网评发帖也会积极地使用热点话题标签——话题标签符号的使用具有煽动功能。在"♯"的"语境预设"和"话题强调"功能的共同作用下,例4的用户不仅突出强调了"否认联系"这一策略的言语行为,增强了攻击面子的力度,还煽动更多用户效仿这一行为——这解释了 Twitter 语料中这一策略大量使用的原因。而中文语料中,话题标签符号的使用却非常少见,这可能与用户习惯有关,也有可能与文化差异有关(Fang & Faure 2011:326):由于传统中国文化影响下的中文交际推崇含蓄内敛,尤其在社交网络交际的低信任度语境下,中文用户不愿意强调不礼貌的表达、呼吁他人加入这类讨论,以凸显针对反对方的贬损面子的意图。

相对而言,"辱骂"这一策略在中文语料的使用频率高于在英文语料中的使用频率。值得注意的是,这一策略在英文语料中常与其他策略共同使用,而在中文语料中单独使用,例如:

例5

W77:野蛮的土匪,(辱骂)

例 6

T76：@BuzzFeedNews so we can expect this the next time we fly @united anyone is fair game for getting physically assaulted by [emotion：pig] due to overbook（辱骂＋讽刺）

在中文语料中，"辱骂"这一策略的使用多通过"贬义形容词＋贬义名词"的结构来表达（如例 5），这种形式短促有力，可以表达对交际目标的强烈不满；而在英文语料中，"辱骂"的策略多与其他策略混合使用，并且这一策略的表现形式也呈现出计算机中介交际（CMC）的特有方式。在例 6 中，交际者使用了"猪"的表情符号（emotion）来指称犯错的美联航雇员，攻击了他们的积极面子。可以看出，在计算机中介交际（CMC）中，技术平台会提供新的交际资源，比如上文讨论的话题标签符号和表情符号，交际者通过使用这些符号，既赋予交际符号新的语用功能，也改变了交际方式，使网络交际呈现出区别于面对面交际的特点；这些符号与不礼貌策略结合使用，可以起到增强或减弱不礼貌力度的作用，实现不同的交际目的。

5.4　不礼貌策略使用受语境多因素影响

"批评/抱怨"这一策略不在 Culpeper（2005）的不礼貌模式中，然而，研究者发现这一策略在中、英两种语料中大量出现，借鉴 Culpeper（2010）提出的不礼貌惯用语（conventional impoliteness formulae）的批评/抱怨语的概念，可将这一策略定义为：说话人故意批评/抱怨目标或听话人。"批评/抱怨"策略标记性的的多次出现与交际话题（Herring 情境模式因素之一）有关。首先，使用批评或抱怨这一策略预设了被攻击的对象有较为明显的过失，该交际活动的目的为"公开表达冲突意见以解决严肃问题"。其次，由于这一策略面子威胁程度较高，说话人应当确保批评或抱怨的行为属实，否则可能会招致更严重的反驳或批评，从而威胁自己的面子。也就是说，这一策略的使用有以上条件的限制。然而，在本研究选定的话题中，由于美联航雇员的行为明显过失，大多用户选择使用批评/抱怨的极端性策略来攻击其积极面子既非偶然。此外，研究者还发现，选择使用何种不礼貌策略与攻击的对象有关。对机构性网络抱怨语的研究（周树江 2016）结果发现，机构性话语对于不礼貌话语的回应总是礼貌的、模式化的。亦即，机构批评与个人批评的后果不一样，说话人承担的面子威胁的风险也非能等同。在本研究语境中，被攻击对象——美联航，不仅有明显过失，且作为机构无法、不宜通过不礼貌的方式来反击这些匿名性、大量的、公开性批评，这使得微博、Twitter 的用户得以回避这一策略可能带来承担的面子风险。最后，"批评/抱怨"的策略在英文语料中使用的频次高于中文语料，并且在积极不礼貌策略中所占比例也更高，且该策略作为一使用模式在英文语料中与其他策略混合使用的比例也更高，应该也与处于当代世界中、多元跨文化背景下的广大的英语人群面对世界性（种族歧视）问题进行不礼貌语言选择（Mills,2009）等的语言文化的变迁有关。

6 结 论

　　采取对比研究的方法，本研究取样研究了中文、英文社交媒体用户在相同话题下使用不礼貌策略的情形，得出以下结论：首先，中文、英文的网络媒体发帖中使用了相似的不礼貌策略：(1)中文、英文语料中使用最多的策略为积极不礼貌策略；(2)在微博、Twitter回复语料中，不礼貌策略的使用均呈现出单个不礼貌策略的重复使用模式和多个策略的混合使用模式；(3)以两种策略混合使用的情况较多；其次，中文、英文语料中不礼貌策略使用有差异性，差异体现在积极不礼貌策略的使用上：(1)英文积极不礼貌数量多于、显性表达强于中文网贴的不礼貌策略；(2)计算机中介交际（CMC）中由技术媒介提供的特殊交际模式、多向度符号的交际资源运用而生语用功能，与不礼貌策略的耦合使用可影响不礼貌策略的力度，易使网络交际者实现交际目的；(3)不礼貌策略的使用与话题、对象等语境因素密切相关，并且受交际活动因素、目的因素、语气因素、交际范式因素的重要影响。最后，语料样本整体的"不礼貌"语义表现及其语用特点的形成源于"美联航打人"这一针对国际品牌劣质服务事件下网络交际的具体语境，对于类似语境中不礼貌现象的研究或有积极意义。本研究借鉴Culpeper的先进理论模式等，并与网络会话交际的社会语用体裁相关联，能够系统解释、洞悉网络语的不礼貌现象，实现对网络语言交际从语言微观走向语用中观、继而走向社会语言学、社会心理认知的宏观的研究。

　　本文对中文微博、英文Twitter社交媒体的中外用户在"美联航暴力事件"发生后的微贴话语使用不礼貌的反馈研究说明，"无论是共享、共鸣还是共情"，网民的话语使用都"在探索中实现价值"，它们突破条条框框去执着探寻、积极参与公共生活，表现出所尚崇的规则和对社会热点的真情关注（《人民日报》2016.12）。两种语言微贴话语的不礼貌使用在形式策略、语用功能和语境机理等方面同异结合、同中有异的现象进行细致的语用分析显示，Culpeper(1996，2005)的不礼貌策略等理论及网络语言多面、动态性语境观和跨文化比较的视角有利于全面深入地对话语活动进行关联的发现和对网络新兴语言精细的描写。研究尤其体现对公共危机事件舆情下的网络争论性语言的对比性发现研究，所以有助于增进人们对网络语用（如，不礼貌现象）、计算机中介交际语言特征的理解，对解决重点时期舆情的监控（引导）问题，开拓跨文化网络传播等交际研究的实践有积极意义。并且，以相关研究了解和掌握中外网络语言使用的现状和预测今后网络话语使用中自然—人工语言混合、私人—公共话语声音共振、言语跨境跨界和互联互通等话语运用的发展趋势,对时代语言变迁等相关语言文化研究的启示意义重大——只有通晓网络社交媒体语言的话语使用,才能胜任新时代语言文化传播的重任。

参考文献

[1] Angouri, J. & T. Theodora. 2010. 'you HAVE NO IDEA WHAT YOU ARE TALKING ABOUT!' from e-disagreement to e-impoliteness in two online fora[J]. *Journal of Politeness Research*, 6(1): 57-82.

[2] Austin, P. 1990. Politeness revisited—the dark side[A]. In A. Bell & J. Holmes (eds.). *New Zealand ways of speaking English*[C]. Philadelphia: Multilingual Matters, 277-293.

[3] Blitvich, P. & M. Sifianou. 2019. Impoliteness and discursive pragmatics[J]. *Journal of Pragmatics*, 145: 91-101.

[4] Bousfield, D. 2008. *Impoliteness in Interaction*[M]. Amsterdam/Philadelphia: John Benjamins.

[5] Brown, P & Levinson, S. C. 1987. *Some Universals in Language Usage: Politeness Phenomena*[M]. Cambridge, Cambridge University Press.

[6] Cashman, H. R. 2006. Impoliteness in children's interactions in a Spanish/English bilingual community of practice[J]. *Journal of Politeness Research*, 2: 217-246.

[7] Chen, X. 2019. "You're a nuisance!": "Patch-up" jocular abuse in Chinese fiction[J]. *Journal of Pragmatics*, 139: 52-63.

[8] Culpeper, J. 1996. Towards an anatomy of impoliteness[J]. *Journal of Pragmatics*, 25: 349-367.

[9] Culpeper, J. 1998. (Im)politeness in dramatic dialogue[J]. In J. Culpeper, M. Short & P. Verdonk (eds.). *Exploring the Language of Drama: From Text to Context*[M]. London: Routledge, 83-95.

[10] Culpeper, J. 2005. Impoliteness and entertainment in the television quiz show: The weakest link[J]. *Journal of Politeness Research*, 1: 35-72.

[11] Culpeper, J. 2015. Impoliteness strategies[A]. In A. Capone and J. L. Mey (eds.). *Interdisciplinary Studies in Pragmatics, Culture and Society*[C]. New York: Springer, 421-445.

[12] Culpeper, J. & O. Holmes. 2013. (Im)politeness and exploitative TV Show in Britain and North America: The X-Factor and American Idol[A]. In N. Lorenzo-Dus & P. Garcés-Conejos Blitvich (eds.). *Real Talk: Reality Television and Discourse Analysis in Action*[C]. New York: Palgrave Macmillan, 169-198.

[13] Dobs, A. M. & P. Garcés-Conejos Blitvich. 2013. Impoliteness in polylogal interaction: Accounting for face-threat witnesses' responses[J]. *Journal of Pragmatics*, 53: 112-130.

[14] Dynel, M. 2015. Impoliteness in the service of verisimilitude in film interaction[A]. In M.

Dynel & J. Chovanec (eds.). *Participation in Public and Social Media Interactions*[C]. Amsterdam & Philadelphia: John Benjamins,157-182.

[15] Eelen, G. 2001. *Critique of Politeness Theories*[M]. Manchester: St Jeromes Press.

[16] Fang, T & Faure, G. O. 2011. Chinese communication characteristics: A Yin Yang perspective [J]. *International Journal of Intercultural Relations*, 35: 320-333.

[17] Harris, S. 2001. Being politically impolite: Extending politeness theory to adversarial political discourse[J]. *Discourse and Society*, 12(4): 451-472.

[18] Harris, S. 2011. The limits of politeness re-visited: courtroom discourse as a case in point[A]. In Linguistic Politeness Research Group (ed.). *Discursive Approaches to Politeness* [C]. BerlinGoogle Scholar: Mouton de Gruyter, 85-108.

[19] Haugh, M. 2010a. Jocular mockery, (dis)affiliation, and face[J]. *Journal of Pragmatics*, 42: 2106-2119.

[20] Haugh, M. 2010b. When is an email really offensive?: Argumentativity and variability in evaluations of impoliteness[J]. *Journal of Politeness Research*, 6 (1): 7-31.

[21] Herring, S. C. 2007. A faceted classification scheme for computer-mediated dis-course[J]. *Language@Internet*. http://www.languageatinternet.de/articles/2007/761.

[22] Holmes, J. 1984. Modifying illocutionary force[J]. *Journal of Pragmatics*, 8 (3): 345-365.

[23] Holmes, J., M. Marra & B. Vine. 2012. Politeness and impoliteness in ethnic varieties of New Zealand English[J]. *Journal of Pragmatics*, 44 (9): 1063-1076.

[24] Kienpointner, M. 1997. Varieties of rudeness: Types and functions of impolite utterances[J]. *Functions of Language*, 4(2): 251-287.

[25] Lachenicht, L. G. 1980. Aggravating language. A study of abusive and insulting language[J]. *Papers in Linguistics: International Journal in Human Communication*, 13(4): 607-687.

[26] Leech, G. 1983. *Principles of Pragmatics*[M]. London: Longman.

[27] Locher, M. A. 2010. Introduction: Politeness and impoliteness in computer-mediated communication[J]. *Journal of Politeness Research*, 6 (1): 1-5.

[28] Lorenzo-Dus, N. 2009. "You're barking mad, I'm out": Impoliteness and broadcast talk[J]. *Journal of Politeness Research*, 5(2): 159-187.

[29] Lorenzo-Dus, N, P. Garcés-Conejos Blitvich, & P. Bou-Franch. 2011. On-line polylogues and impoliteness: The case of postings sent in response to the Obama Reggaeton YouTube video[J]. *Journal of Pragmatics*, 43(10): 2578-2593.

[30] Garcés-Conejos Blitvich, P. 2010. The You Tubification of politics, impoliteness and polarization[A]. In R. Taiwo (ed.). *Handbook of research on discourse behavior and digital communication: Language structures and social interaction* [C]. Hershey, PA: IGI Global, 540-563.

[31] Marquez Reiter, R. &P. Bou-Franch. 2017. (Im)politeness in Service Encounters[A]. In J. Culpeper, J; H, Michael and Kádár, D. Z. (eds). *The Palgrave Handbook of Linguistic (Im)*

politeness[C]. Palgrave Macmillan UK, 661-687.

[32] Mills, S. 2009 Impoliteness in a cultural context[J]. *Journal of Pragmatics*, 41: 1047-1059.

[33] Nishimura, Y. 2008. Japanese BBS websites as online communities: (Im) politeness perspectives[J]. *mLanguage@Internet*, 5: 1-16. www.languageatinternet.de.

[34] Nishimura, Y. 2010. Impoliteness in Japanese BBS interactions: Observations from message exchanges in two online communities[J]. *Journal of Politeness Research*, 6(1): 33-35.

[35] Rudanko, J. 2006. Aggravated impoliteness and two types of speaker intention in an episode in Shakespeare's Timon of Athens[J]. *Journal of Pragmatics*, 38: 829-841.

[36] Scott, K. 2015. The pragmatics of hashtags: Inference and conversational style on Twitter[J]. *Journal of Pragmatics*, 81: 8-20.

[37] Shum, W. & C, Lee. 2013. (Im)politeness and disagreement in two Hong Kong Internet discussion forums[J]. *Journal of Pragmatics*, 50: 52-83.

[38] Taylor, C. 2011. Negative politeness forms and impoliteness functions in institutional discourse: A corpus-assisted approach[A]. In B. L. Davies, M. Haugh & A. J. Merrison (eds.). *Situated Politeness*[C]. London & New York: Continuum, 209-231.

[39] Tracy, K. 2008. Reasonable hostility: Situation-appropriate face-attack[J]. *Journal of Politeness Research*, 4: 169-191.

[40] Tracy K. (2017) Facework and (Im)politeness in Political Exchanges[A]. In J. Culpeper., Haugh M., Kádár D. (eds.). *The Palgrave Handbook of Linguistic (Im)politeness*[C]. Palgrave Macmillan, London, 7-28.

[41] Upadhyay, S. R. 2010. Identity and impoliteness in computer mediated reader responses[J]. *Journal of Politeness Research*, 6(1): 105-127.

[42] 程伟,2013.基于顺应论的网络交际语码转换现象分析[J].山东外语教学,(2):44-49.

[43] 冯薇、王立非,2017.新媒体英文网络语言特征及其教学价值新探[J].西安外国语大学学报,(2):80-85.

[44] 胡凌、刘云、杨传丽,2014.网络语言二十年发展综述[J].湖南大学学报(社会科学版),(5):136-141.

[45] 黄国文,2005.电子语篇的特点[J].外语与外语教学,(12):1-5.

[46] 李国防,2006.网络语言适者生存——以模因的名义[D].硕士论文,广东外语外贸大学.

[47] 毛延生,2014.汉语不礼貌话语的语用研究[J].语言教学与研究,(2):94-102.

[48] 人民日报评论部,2016.怎样对话网络"新世代"——2016舆情观察与思考[P].《人民日报—人民网》2016.12.21(5).引自 http://opinion.people.com.cn/n1/2016/1221/c1003-28964647.html.

[49] 孙亚、赵彬楠,2015.商务话语中的礼貌与不礼貌[J].北京科技大学学报(社会科学版),(6):13-19.

[50] 王彦彦,2010.网络语"杯具"及衍生辞句的认知研究[J].当代修辞学,(1):75-79.

[51] 张挺、武超,2017.自媒体视域下的语言舆情:形成、传播与引导[J].语言文字应用,(1):51-60.

[52] 周树江,2016.机构性网络抱怨语中的不礼貌现象分析[J].西安外国语大学学报,(3):56-60.
[53] 朱晔,2015.论社交媒体在我国外语教学中的应用[J].外语电化教学,(4):47-51.
[54] 左海霞、姚喜明.2006,修辞视角下的网络语言[J].外语电化教学,(1):27-31.

美国 ACTFL 外语能力指导方针研究及启示*

上海对外经贸大学国际商务外语学院　张蔚磊**

摘要：本研究述评了美国现有的外语能力标准，即 ACTFL 外语能力指导方针。首先，梳理了 ACTFL 外语能力指导方针的发展历程，1986 版，1999 版，2001 版和 2012 版。其次，介绍了 2012 版 ACTFL 外语能力指导方针的主要内容，包括五个等级，四个语言技能；分析了该量表的优缺点。再次，对现有的 ACTFL 外语能力指导方针听、说、读、写四大技能的信度效度的研究分别进行了总结和剖析。第四，评论了 2012 版 ACTFL 外语能力指导方针的对美国外语教育的影响和对我国《中国英语能力等级量表》和测评体系的启示。

关键词：外语能力标准；美国；语言熟练度；ACTFL

Title: A review on ACTFL Proficiency Guidelines and their Implications

Abstract: This study reviews the USA current language ability standard, ACTFL Proficiency Guidelines 2012. First, the development history of ACTFL Proficiency Guidelines 2012 is introduced. Second, its main contents of it are analyzed, and its advantages and disadvantages are illustrated. Third, the reliability and credibility of ACTFL Proficiency Guidelines 2012 are discussed. Finally, the effects and implications are analyzed.

Key words: foreign language ability standard; USA; language proficiency; ACTFL

---

* 本研究系教育部人文社会科学研究规划基金项目："基于核心素养的英语测评体系的国别研究"（项目编号：20YJA740060）的阶段性研究成果。

** 作者简介：张蔚磊，女，博士，教授。研究方向为外语教育、语言政策、外语教学理论与实践。联系方式：leisabrina@126.com。

1 引言

"ACTFL 外语能力指导方针"一直是一项全球性语言综合能力测评标准。美国的外语能力指导方针(ACTFL Proficiency Guidelines)区分了不同外语能力水平(Fagan,2018),它适用于教学中的不同阶段,同时为教学测评和学生成绩测评提供参考(Kissling and O'Donnell, 2015)。它可以测评四种不同能力,有助于教师和研究者更好地了解英语教学的特点和不足之处。经梳理,笔者发现对美国"ACTFL 外语能力指导方针"的研究,除史成周(2014)的内容描述外,系统地从发展历程,影响力的角度进行研究的文章较少,对其信度与效度进行研究对文章更是寥寥无几,因此笔者拟从这几个角度进行探究。详细了解 ACTFL 量表对于发展和完善我国现有的能力量表大有裨益。

2 ACTFL 外语能力指导方针的发展历程述评

目前,ACTFL 外语能力指导方针的发展包括四个阶段:1986 年的 ACTFL 语言能力指导方针(听,说,读,写)(ACTFL Proficiency Guidelines);1999 年的 ACTFL 语言能力指导方针(ACTFL Proficiency Guidelines—Speaking);2001 年的 ACTFL 语言能力指导方针(Preliminary Proficiency Guidelines—Writing Revised, 2001);2012 年的 ACTFL 语言能力指导方针(ACTFL Proficiency Guidelines)。

1986 年版的语言能力量表,在口语、听力、阅读和写作四个方面的外语综合能力进行了分级。每一等级也都对较低等级的语言能力进行了测评,使语言学习成为了一种从简单到复杂的过程。这在当时是一种进步。但 86 版量表的不同等级代表的是对特定语言能力进行测评,并不代表全部语言能力。

10 年后 ACTFL 量表逐渐适用于学术领域。1999 年,ACTFL 颁布了口语量表的修订版(ACTFL Proficiency Guidelines—Speaking),对"高能力等级"(ILR 3-5)进行合并,又对"低能力级"进行了细分(ILR 0-1),对"优秀能力等级"(Superior level)进行了明确的界定,最终确定了语言能力的各等级划分细则。这满足了学术界和商业界日益增长的对高能力等级的学生进行细分的需求。1999 年修订口语能力量表,使口语能力得到了更充分的描述,明确了测试员和教师之间的区别,纠正了委员会对量表早期版本的等级方面的误解。1999 量表采用了不同的阐述方法:将重点摘要图(Chart of Summary Highlights)附于量表后,来提醒学生注意各等级的主要特征,并提供快速索引功能。这为后来量表索引的进一步完善奠定了基础。(参见：ACTFL Proficiency Guideline—Speaking，1999：13)

  2000年研发人员已经对ACTFL口语量表进行了大量测评和阐释,并将其作为口语能力面试(Oral Proficiency Interview,简称OPI)的核心和研究课题。2001年又单独修改了写作方面的内容。修改后的量表进一步对"高能力等级"(Advanced level)进行了细分。最初,高能力等级仅包括两个子等级:高级(Advanced)和高级高等[①](Advanced high)。修订的写作量表(2001)和修订过的口语量表(ACTFL 1999)相同,呈现了自上而下的顺序(从高能力等级到低能力等级),这使每个等级及次级等级具有了更具体的解释,同时强调了学生需掌握的语言核心能力,弱化了对次要能力的要求。这种自上而下的排序通过强调能力之间的细微差别,更清晰地展现相邻等级之间的紧密联系,而不仅仅是关注测评之间存在的差异性和取得更高能力等级。2001年的量表的写作是指自发性写作和反思性写作。作为两种输出型技能(口语和写作),商业界和学术界要求对量表中高能力等级进行细分(ILR2级为:有限工作能力)。这与对写作量表中低能力等级进行细分,或与修改后的口语量表一样,将高能力等级的划分为高级高、高级中和高级低是为了满足社会需求。2001年修改的写作量表只是整个修订过程的第一步。委员会邀请专业测试员使用量表来进行写作能力的测评,并研究这些修改对教学和大纲设计产生的影响。为了更精确地评判写作能力,委员会还请了专业人士继续研究、讨论和审查写作量表,以便进一步细化。

  2012年,ACTFL发布了新的ACTFL外语能力指导方针。这是自1986年来,首次对阅读和听力量表进行大幅修改。口语和写作量表主要修改了比"优秀能力等级"(Superior)更高一级的名称:"杰出能力等级"(Distinguished),该能力等级满足了专业交流的需求。"杰出能力等级"从最初到2012年修订版,一直是阅读和听力量表的最高级别。新的2012版能力量表将听力和阅读量表的高能力等级划分成:高级高、高级中和高级低,并为其他四个语言能力的高级、中级和初级都增添了简单的等级描述。2012版的语言能力量表也发布了网络版本,其中包含有大量术语和多媒体示例,并与不同能力测评和不同能力等级相关联。2012版的ACTFL语言能力量表直接应用于语言能力的测评当中,并准备运用到学术界和工作环境中去。ACTFL研发了与2012版量表配套的新教材和测试系统,并且已经开始重新评估现有的被试者和测试员。

  透过ACTFL的发展历程,我们可以发现任何一个语言能力量表都不是一蹴而就的,需要随着实践而不断地修订和完善。

---

  ① 具体的分级名称可以参照:邹鹏《基于口语能力测试(OPI)评价体系的汉语口语教学模式探究》,四川师范大学国际教育学院,2016.02.13。

3 ACTFL 外语能力指导方针(2012)的主要内容

ACTFL 外语能力指导方针(2012)是目前美国主要应用的一款语言能力量表。它包括五大等级,四个能力。

3.1 五大等级

2012 ACTFL 外语能力指导方针对不同语言能力都划分了五个关键等级:杰出级(distinguished),优秀级(superior),高级(advanced),中级(intermediate)和初级(novice)。参见下图1:

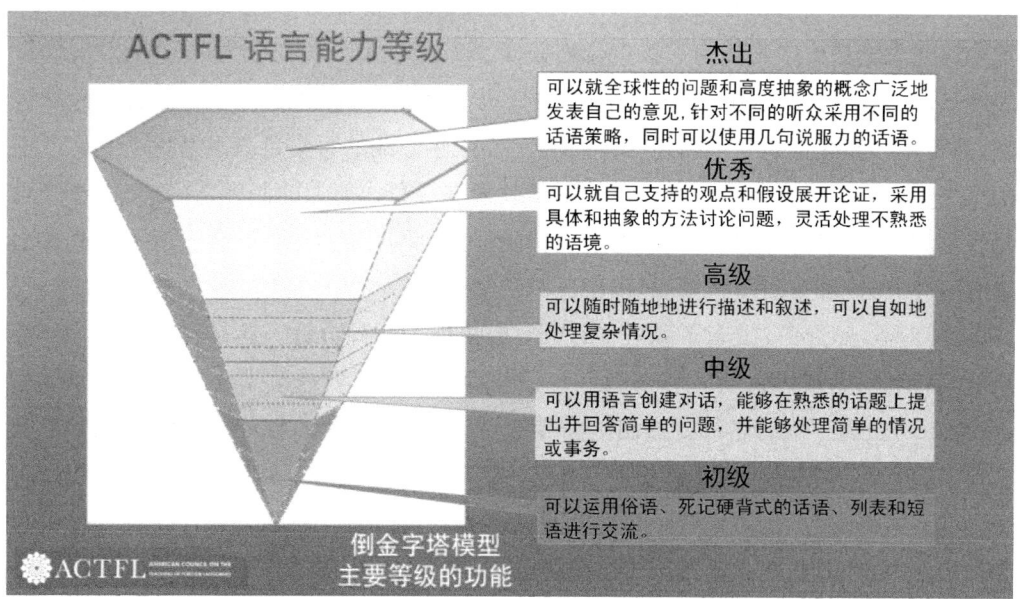

图1 《美国 ACTFL 语言能力指导方针》(2012)

其中高级,中级和初级又各自分出:高、中、低三个次级等级(例如:高级高、高级中、高级低),参见图2:

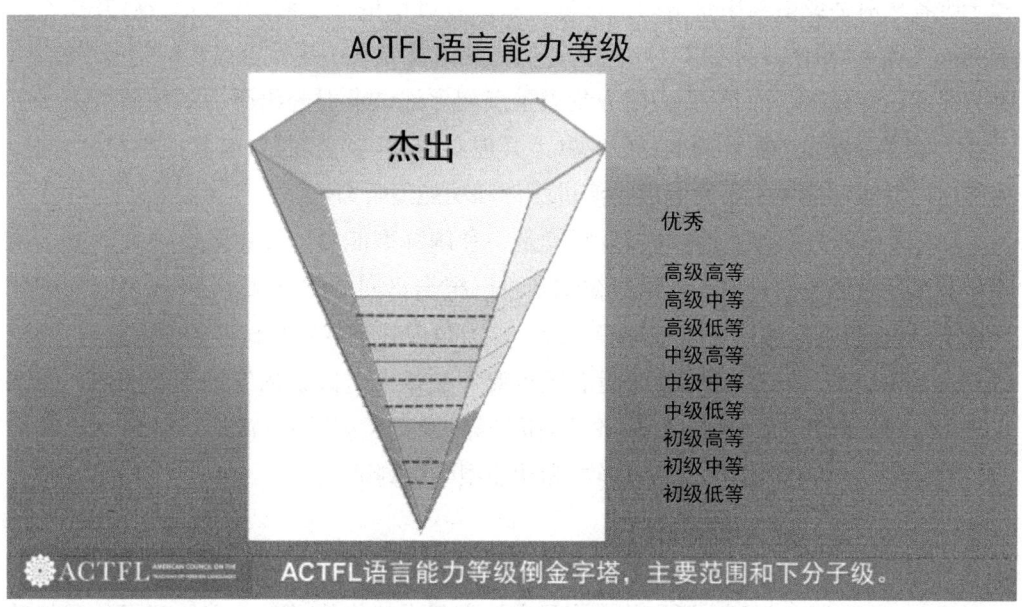

图 2 《美国 ACTFL 语言能力指导方针》(2012)

2012 版 ACTFL 语言能力指导方针主要测评学生在自发性的真实情景中对口语、写作、听力和阅读这四个语言能力的应用情况。

3.2 四大语言能力

2012 版 ACTFL 能力指导方针的每一个语言能力都包括上述五个关键能力等级。关键能力等级都代表了不同特定范围的语言能力水平。进行测评时，被试者可以测评不同等级、内容、语境、准确度和文本类型，并且不同的测评模式也会使被试者了解自身的局限性。纸质版和电子版能力量表为每一种能力都提供了样本。

（1）口语能力指导方针（2012），语能力量表可以用来测评交互型（Interpersonal）和单向无交互型（Presentational）口语能力。纸质版和电子版口语能力量表都包含了不同等级的口语样本。

（2）写作能力指导方针（2012），写作能力量表可以用来测评例如：展示型（论文，报告，信件）或交际型（短信，电子邮件）写作能力。另外，量表强调写作成果的产出，因此学生需要进行自发型（即时，无编辑）或反思型（修改，编辑）写作。纸质版和电子版写作能力量表都提供了不同等级的写作样本。

写作能力指导方针的参数和描述语描述了不同级别的作者能完成的任务、内容、语境、准确性和话语类型以及完成更高级别的任务时在能力上的局限性，涉及很多具体的能力描写参数。

（3）听力能力指导方针（2012），听力是一种阐释型能力。听力理解很大程度上依赖于听者从对话或语篇中获得的信息量。被试者可以根据不同的听力文本,并在不同的测评环境下,测评自身对文本的理解。听力能力量表并不规定被试者的学习进程,听力方式及认知过程。而且,听力能力量表重点测评被试者对外语听力的理解能力。听力能力量表可以用来测评例如:展示型(无其他参与者)或交互型(有其他参与者)的听力能力。量表都提供了不同等级的演讲示例和功能型听力测试。

(4)阅读能力指导方针(2012),阅读是一种阐释型能力。阅读理解很大程度上依赖于被试者对文本信息的获取量。被试者可以根据不同的阅读文本,并在不同的测评环境下,测评自身对阅读文本的理解。阅读能力量表并不规定被试者的学习进程,阅读方式及认知过程。而且,阅读能力量表重点测评被试者对阅读内容的理解能力。阅读量表用来测评例如:展示型(书籍,论文,报告等)或交互型(即时消息,短信,电子邮件等)阅读能力。量表都提供了阅读样本和功能型阅读测试。

3.3 优势与不足

综上,2012版ACTFL语言能力指导方针有很大的优势:第一,它体现了从零基础或低能力等级到完全掌握语言能力的连续统一。语言能力量表包括不同语言能力等级,并规定了每个等级中学生需达到的特定能力水平。各个能力量表共同组成了一个分级系统,其中每个等级都融入了较低等级的语言能力。第二,与学习成绩不同,该语言能力量表强调了外语能力的习得,测评并不试图去衡量学生在课堂教学中的各方面表现,而是测评在不同时间地点,不管以何种方式,学生在实际生活中的语言应用情况;因此,"学习语言"和"获得能力"具有了更深远的意义。第三,该语言能力量表是基于能力水平的一项全球性语言评估。

但同时我们也发现语言能力量表并不基于任何特定的语言理论、教学方法或教育大纲。能力量表也不会指导学生学习语言,也不规定学生的学习方法,因此只能作为一种语言能力等级测评工具。其次,该指导方针也存在一定的不足:例如有些描述语意义模糊,不利于应用;有些描述语只出现在某一个能力的某一个等级,不符合实际情况;有些描述语使用比较级进行表述,使等级不能独立使用,须参照其他等级,降低了标准的可操作性(史成周,2014);否定形式的描述语降低了量表的可操作性。再次,ACTFL语言能力指导方针还需要更进一步的理论事实研究,以验证指导方针的效度。尤其是,对每个等级的划分说明还需要程序研究。而且,为了更加有效地解决每个等级上阅读能力的问题,需要不断地进行修正。

4 ACTFL 语言能力指导方针的信度效度探究

4.1 ACTFL 语言能力指导方针四大能力的信度效度

美国 ACTFL 语言能力大纲出台之后,就有相关组织对其信度效度进行专项研究,这些信度和效度研究包括写作、阅读和听说。

(1) 写作量表的信度效度研究

《美国外语教育委员会写作能力测试信度效度分析报告》(Dierdorff,2004)呈现了该量表的初步信度和效度信息。

为了更加准确地评估评估间一致性的程度,他们使用了多重方法。他们从评估间效度,评估间联系性等角度解释评估间一致性。多重方法可以让评估间一致性的程度进行更为完整的说明呈现。整体的原理就是扩大评估间一致性(interrater consistency)的广度。评估间一致性的测试面向写作能力测试的全部样本,以促进评估者一致性之间的相对比较。他们采用了皮尔逊相关系数、斯皮尔曼秩次相关系数、肯德尔 τ、古德曼和克鲁斯卡尔 γ、科恩 κ、一致性的原比例等方法进行了测试。他们测算了写作能力测试评估间一致性,全部样本的写作能力测试能力类别的评估间一致性,西班牙语样本的写作能力测试能力类别的评估间一致性,西班牙语样本的写作能力测试能力等级的评估间一致性、未修正的评估间信度、修正的评估间信度等。还研究了写作与口语之间的关系。

研究结果表明:评估者间的皮尔逊和斯皮尔曼信度水平都高于 0.90,评估间效度为有效。信度结果在一致性分析的比例中有所显现,其中绝大部分呈现出绝对的一致性。换句话说,大部分的评估人员配对组合在给写作能力测试打分时,都给出了一致的能力等级。

(2) 阅读量表的信度效度研究

ACTFL 外语能力指导方针(阅读)出台不久就有几份针对其效度的研究报告,例如 Lee 和 Musumeci(1988)、Dandonoli 和 Henning(1990)等。其中最具代表的是《美国外语教育委员会阅读测试文本和能力等级方针的效度报告》(Park, Siwon. 2004)。该报告提出了 2 个研究问题:研究问题 1:运用美国外语教育委员会(ACTFL)阅读指导方针能够促进可靠可信的测试的研发吗? 研究问题 2:ACTFL 阅读指导方针中对等级的说明能够体现从初级中等到优异等级的提升吗? 这两个问题用以探究该量表等级划分的效度。

首先,研究人员采取了经典等项目分析法来检验题目的质量,利用 Cronbach alpha

算出信度系数为 0.81；之后，研究人员估算了点双列相关系数 r（point-biserial correlation），最终确定初测的文本。然后，他们采用古特曼量表法和方差分析（Guttman scaling and ANOVAs）检测了美国外语教育委员会阅读方针的效度。由于指导方针的出台是建立在阅读文本和能力要求的两个连续等级之上的，所以在设置测试题目时，他们仔细考虑了每个文本的复杂性和能力要求。通过运用古特曼量表法来研究文本和能力要求之间的联系性。随后再运用方差分析法去对初级、中级、高级、优异的等级（Novice, Intermediate, Advanced, and Superior levels）进行进一步划分。

研究发现，古特曼量表法分析结果呈现出由初级到高级的能力等级水平。同时，经方差分析，连续等级的样本之间存在数据上的显著性差异。但是，有些样本还不够有代表性，无法体现上述的等级要求。这些样本在 2012 年的 ACTFL 语言能力指导方针中有所改进。从信度效度研究分析中，我们可以发现 ACTFL 语言能力指导方针中的阅读等级划分，高级和优异之间的界限不明确，但是其他等级的划分还是比较清晰的。总之，目前该量表可以为阅读能力测试提供一个很好的标准。

（3）听说量表的信度效度研究

ACTFL 口语能力标准的效度主要通过 ACTFL 口语能力测试（OPI）来体现。ACTFL 口语能力测试（OPI）是有效可信的互动式直接口语等级评估，它通过有资历的测试员跟测试者进行面对面或者通过电话的方式进行考试。测试员遵循标准化的程序，有目的性地挑选出语音样本，根据语音样本的功能和任务的完成情况、样本的数量和质量、文本类型、语境和内容，对被测试者进行评级。

OPI 本身的信度和效度至关重要。纵观文献，对 ACTFL 的 OPI 信度和效度的研究有不少，其中 2012 年的 Olaf Barenfanger 和 Erwin Tschirner 参照欧洲语言能力标准框架（CEFR）对 ACTFL 的 OPI 的信度和效度做的实证研究较有代表性。研究该过程包括三个阶段：(1) 熟悉阶段：测评员首先要熟悉 CEFR 能力量表体系，这基于刻度化的 CEFR 等级的语音样本；(2) 校准阶段：每个测评员能否按照 CEFR 等级的精准刻度来对语音样本进行精准评级，决定了测评员评级的可靠性（信度）；(3) 狭义的标杆/基准设定是指测评员在未知 CEFR 等级的情况下对语言样本进行评级，之后再把这些评级结果和官方的 ACTFL 标准的评价结果相比照。这样刻度数据和标杆数据的可信度都可以被计算出来。该研究采用了拟合优度检验、斯皮尔曼系数、肯德尔 τ、古德曼和克鲁斯卡尔 γ、Kendall's W 系数等验证了评级者的可靠性和数据校正的一致性；CEFR 和 ACTFL 评级的一致性（这包括 ACTFL 和 CEFR 的等级比较、CEFR 和 ACTFL 等级的相关性和一致性测量、根据 ACTFL 口语能力等级观察出 CEFR 的每个等级的可能性）（该研究得出的对应关系是：NH＝A1, IL＝A2, IM 和 IH＝B1, AL 和 AM＝B2, AH＝C1, S＝C2。）；测评员对评级过程的认知的一致性（研究了评级简易度、可理解度、自信程度）。该研究说明现有的 ACTFL 口语能力是有效可信的。

4.2 ACTFL 语言能力指导方针信度效度研究的启示

美国的 ACTFL 语言能力指导方针信度效度研究具有一定的局限性。第一,在数据收集阶段,由于研究的时间有限,研究人员不能给测试者充足的时间,去完成所有的题目,这就会导致数据之间存在不一致性。由于许多数据分析都是依赖于相关系数分析的,这种不一致性就会有些问题,因此需要对数据的获取进行更加繁琐的调查研究。第二,参与人员的水平跨度问题。因为试行研究阶段没有足够的高水平人员的参与,许多难题就没有人是答对的,而是完全猜对的。这就会导致数据分析和结果存在问题,如:点双列相关系数值较低,项目反应理论的卡方拟合统计值较低。这也就导致研究人员必须要把杰出水平排除在效度研究之外。要找到一些高水平的参与人员并不现实,因为这些人本来就不多。第三,题目的数量问题。从逻辑上来说,题目越多,研究人员实现研究目的的效度就越多。但是考虑到参与人员和研究人员所需要投入的时间和精力,研究人员必须要在现实考虑和研究理想状况之间实现平衡。尤其是,因为研究人员非常清楚,没有众多学术机构的合作,这种研究是根本不可能完成的。

因此我国在进行现有能力标准的信度效度测量是需要注意以上几点。

5 ACTFL 外语能力指导方针的对测评系统的影响

ACTFL 语言指导方针在语言教育的许多方面都发挥了重要作用。指导方针成为各语言机构共同的行动纲领,推动语言项目的发展(Brown,1996)。ACTFL 外语能力指导方针确实具有指导性功能,ACTFL 能力量表是中小学能力量表的基础,与 2006 年版的国家外语学习标准(National Standards for Foreign Language Learning)相配合来进行学生的语言能力测评。从 1987 年至今,ACTFL 能力量表在美国的语言教学中的影响力不断加深。

第一,经过多项相关测试后,ACTFL 外语能力指导方针显然已经对美国的外语能力考核产生了影响。指导方针给测试研发人员提供评估标准,他们在设计题目的时候,可以预测自己的难度是否符合指导方针的要求。他们可以根据指导方针,对测试结果进行解读,并做出下一步计划。ACTFL 外语能力指导方针的颁布不仅为外语能力测评提供了依据,同时培养了一批受过训练的专业外语教师,他们会根据程序来进行不同语言的能力测评,这种综合性方法推动了 ACTFL 外语能力指导方针的传播,同时也引进了新的量表模型,包括:总体框架,测试结构,以及配套的教材和认证体系。

第二,ACTFL 测评系统是建立在基于标准的官方测评框架之上。所有测评都强调量表中几个关键等级所各自规定的语言功能。这些功能都以相关等级的额外标准进行测评(例如:语境/内容(context/content),文本类型或语篇(text type or discourse),及对正确值的期望(accuracy expectations)等)。从量表衍生出来的独立的 ACTFL 外语能力指导方针模型规定:特定语言能力需与相应等级标准保持一致,该等级的测评才可进行。ACTFL 根据能力指导方针研发了与之匹配的口语测评系统(Oral Proficiency Interview,简称 OPI)、写作测评系统(ACTFL Writing Proficiency Test,简称 WPT)、听力测评系统和阅读测评系统。

第三,基于 ACTFL 指导方针的 ACTFL 能力测评具有教育功能,例如:入学,实习和毕业等;经济功能,例如:项目研究,项目估值,人员的雇佣和提拔等;政治功能,例如:教师和语言专家的证书颁发等;以及其他需要私人语言能力评级的情况。目前,由 ACTFL 测试中心,即 LTI(Language Testing International)进行安排,管理和发布每年二十万份能力评级报告。ACTFL 测评已经由美国教育委员会(American Council on Education,简称 ACE)授权,并引入大学校园。ACTFL 测评也出现在了政府总务管理局的日程安排上。美国教育局、外语辅助程序机构、星语、国防语言学院、国家语言服务团、北大西洋公约组织、国土安全部也分别和 ACTFL 签署了协议,并给予赞助,ACTFL 也会给他们提供能力测试,并在测试的开发和研究方面给他们提供专业指导。

第四,ACTFL 外语能力指导方针对基础教育考核系统也产生了影响。由于高能力等级(高级和高级高)还未在中小学教育中普及,尤其是在输出技能方面,因此 ACTFL 早在 1998 年为中小学生开发了能力量表。中小学生 ACTFL 外语能力量表(K-12)以 ACTFL 外语能力指导方针为基础,并且规定了中小学生语言能力的不同准入点和准出点。他们还确定了不同准入点的,三个不同交流模式的学生所可能获得的语言成绩。这三个交流模式分别是:交互式(对话者进行动态交流的方式),解释式(将深层含义从书面或口头交流中提炼出来的方式)和表述式(可以通过口头或书信进行交流的方式)。

第五,ACTFL 外语能力指导方针对国家外语考核体系也有很大的影响。2006 年,ACTFL 接受多个赞助,用以研发国家级外语考核体系,并称为 ACTFL 语言能力测试(ACTFL Assessment of Performance Toward Proficiency in Language,简称 AAPPL)。AAPPL 测试利用网络,进行交互式听/说,创意写作,阅读理解,和听力理解等考核。另外,美国一些学校开始使用 ACTFL 外语能力指导方针做一些随堂考核。例如,弗吉尼亚州(Virginia),费尔法克斯县(Fairfax County)根据 ACTFL 外语能力指导方针创建了当地的口语能力评级标准,专门为了随堂考核使用。

第六,ACTFL 外语能力指导方针的积极影响已经在教学和研究中慢慢显现。ACTFL OPI 量表已经成为一些调查研究的工具,例如:对 OPI 的评分者信度的研究;对不同形式 OPI 考核的研究(Brooks,2009;Kasper and Ross,2007;Thompson 等,2016);对 OPI 效性和测试的研究(Carey 等,2011;Ross,2007;Kissau,2014);对 OPI

和相关考核中语篇的研究(Tominaga,2013)。另外,许多研究已经开始将 OPI 和其相关测试视为能力考核方法(Malone and Montee,2010；Sullivan,2011)。此外,基于地方性外语教学和大学课程的美国国家级调查表明：ACTFL 外语能力指导方针已经为考核当地学生的语言能力提供了参考。

6　ACTFL 外语能力指导方针对我国的启示

虽然 ACTFL 外语能力指导方针存在一些不足,有值得商榷的地方,但是它仍然对我国语言能力标准的完善具有一定的指导参考意义。

第一,我们需要在标准制定之后,进行大范围的试验、测试和评估,提升我国标准的信度效度。在评估过程中,尽可能地让更多来自不同地区,不同水平的英语学习者参与进来,为他们设置数量适中,难度适中而又很有区分度的题目。确保数据搜集时间充足,同时尽可能地解决参与人员的水平跨度问题,保障测试的信度。

第二,完善现有标准过程中要注意,充分考虑各方面的相关因素,细化能力等级,明确等级的说明和要求；对标准中的描述语进行优化,确保其意思清晰,没有歧义,减少人为因素对评估结果的影响,增强标准的可操作性。

第三,我们还需要争取与更多的学校、教育机构、教育主管部门以及学术机构的合作,扩大标准的使用范围,希望他们在标准的完善和评估过程中,能够提供更多更有建设性的建议。尽快研制出与之配套的不同学段的测评体系,在大、中、小学中投入使用,以便为标准评估提供反馈。不断完善现有标准,最终为我国的外语教学保驾护航。

参考文献

[1] ACTFL. 2012. ACTFL Proficiency Guidelines[OL]. Retrieved. Aug. 15, 2015, from http://www.actfl.org/publications/guidelines-and-manuals/actfl-proficiency-guidelines-2012.

[2] Brown, J. D. 1996. *Testing in Language Programs*[M]. Englewood Cliffs, NJ: Prentice Hall Regents.

[3] Dandonoli, P., & Henning, G. 1990. An investigation of the construct validity of the ACTFL proficiency guidelines and oral interview procedure[J]. *Foreign Language Annals*, 23(1): 11-22.

[4] Dierdorff, E. C. 2004. Preliminary reliability and validity: findings for the ACTFL writing proficiency test[O]. *SWA Technical Report* C04-R01.

[5] Fagan, D. S. 2018. Using the ACTFL proficiency guidelines in the classroom: Perspectives from practicing L2 Instructors[J]. *Working Papers in Applied Linguistics and TESOL*, 7.

[6] Kissling, E. M., M. E. O'Donnell. 2015. Increasing language awareness and self-efficacy of FL students using self-assessment and the ACTFL proficiency guidelines[J]. *Language Awareness*, 24 (4): 283 – 302.

[7] Kasper, G., S. J. Ross. 2007. Multiple questions in oral proficiencyinterviews[J]. *Journal of Pragmatics*, 39 (11): 2045 – 2070.

[8] Thompson, G. L., T. L. Cox. 2016. Nieves Knapp, Comparing the OPI and theOPIc: The effect of test method on oral proficiency scores and student preference[J]. *Foreign Language Annals*, 49 (1):75 – 92.

[9] Hastings-on-Hudson, NY: ACTFL. 2001. American Council on the Teaching of Foreignlanguages[O]. *ACTFL Proficiency Guidelines*.

[10] Hastings-on-Hudson, NY: Author. ACTFL. 1999. *ACTFL Proficiency Guidelines*[O].

[11] Sullivan, J. H. 2011. Taking charge: Teacher candidates' preparation for the oral proficiencyinterview[J]. *Foreign Language Annals*, 44(2), 241 – 257.

[12] Lee, J. F, &. D. Musumeci. 1988. On hierarchies of reading skills and text types[J]. *The Modern Language Journal*, 72: 173 – 187.

[13] Brooks, L. 2009. Interacting in pairs in a test of oral proficiency: Co-constructing a betterperformance[J]. *Language testing*, 26(3): 341 – 366.

[14] Margaret, E, M., M. J. Montee. 2010. Oral proficiency assessment: Current approaches and applications for post-secondary foreign language programs [J]. *Language and Linguistics Compass*, 4(10): 972 – 986.

[15] Mecartty, F. H. 1998. The effects of proficiency level and passage content on reading skills assessment[J]. *Foreign language Annals*, 31(4): 517 – 534.

[16] Park, S. 2004. Validation of the text and skill hierarchy of the ACTFL Reading Guidelines[J]. *English Teaching*, 59(3): 145 – 166.

[17] Scott, K. 2014. The impact of the Oral Proficiency Interview on one foreign language teacher educationprogram[J]. *Foreign Language Annals* 47(3): 527 – 545.

[18] Steven, J. R. 2007. A comparative task-in-interaction analysis of OPI backsliding[J]. *Journal of Pragmatics*, 39(11): 2017 – 2044.

[19] Tschirner, E, E. Swender., O. Bärenfänger. 2012. *Comparing ACTFL/ILR and CEFR Based Reading Test*. Aligning frameworks of reference in language testing: The ACTFL Proficiency Guidelines and the Common European Framework of Reference[O].

[20] Tominaga, W. 2013. The development of extended turns and storytelling in the Japanese oral proficiency interview[J]. *Assessing second language pragmatics*, 220 – 257.

[21] Yonkers, N. Y. 1986. American Council on the Teaching of Foreign Language[O]. *ACTFL proficiency guidelines*.

[22] 史成周,2014. 美国 ACTFL 阅读能力标准及评论[J].《海外英语》,(5):100 – 101.

外国文学研究

"灰姑娘反串版"的四种现代叙事变体*

江南大学　张俊萍**

摘要：传统的"灰姑娘反串版"往往叙述男主角通过婚姻"逆袭"成功的故事。而在近现代叙事中，"灰姑娘反串版"故事出现新的表达。文本以司汤达的《红与黑》、菲兹杰拉德的《夜色温柔》、劳伦斯的《查泰莱夫人的情人》和金斯利的《幸运的吉姆》为例，具体研究了男性"灰姑娘"功败垂成、喜尽悲来、被工具化和变成滑稽模仿的四种变体。研究发现，这些变体不仅在故事模式上发生了一些调整，更重要的是，作品的主题立意发生了深刻变化，特别是重构了传统版灰姑娘故事中的"性别政治"形态，体现了男权的衰落、男性英雄形象的瓦解和女权的兴起。

关键词：男性灰姑娘；变体；男性权威；女权

Title: Four Narrative Variants of "Male Cinderella Story"

Abstract: The traditional "male Cinderella story" narrates heroes' successful "class promotion" by way of marriage upward, while in modern narration "male Cinderella story" finds new expressions. This paper takes Stendhal's *The Red and the Black*, Fitzgerald's *Tender Is the Night*, Lawrence's *Lady Chatterley's Lover* and Amis's *Lucky Jim* as examples to present the four typical modern variants, in which male Cinderella either fails on the verge of success or experiences grief after a bout of

---

* 本研究是江南大学基本科研计划—重大项目培育课题"新经济批评视野下的20世纪初美国城市小说研究"（编号：JUSRP1910ZD)、江南大学基本科研计划重点项目"语言认知与跨文化研究"（编号：2020JDZD02)的部分成果。

** 作者简介：张俊萍，文学博士，江南大学外国语学院语言认知与文化传播研究中心副教授、硕导，主要研究方向为比较文学与世界文学、小说理论。电子邮箱：jndxzjp@163.com。

pleasure, either becomes an instrument or a travesty. These variants not just show some adjustments in the story pattern. More importantly, they reconstruct traditional "male Cinderella story's" "gender politics", presenting totally new themes, reflecting the decline of masculine authority, the smash of "hero" image, and the rise of feminine power.

Key words: Male Cinderella; variants; masculine authority; feminine power

1 "灰姑娘反串版"故事模型

童话《灰姑娘》故事模型流播久远,深受作家和读者喜爱。文学史上与灰姑娘故事模型相对应的,还存在着一种"反串版",即故事主角由女性变为男性。其故事模式如下:穷小子出门谋生,最终凭借其勇敢、智慧、善良或才干,赢得了高贵家庭的年轻貌美女士(一般是公主)的芳心,自然,也获得了来自女方的高贵地位和丰厚财产。民间故事研究专家普洛普在《民间故事形态学》一书中,把"灰姑娘反串版"这种千篇一律的结尾当作是民间故事31种故事功能中的第31种——男主角受到命运的奖励,娶公主、登王位、得王国(Propp, 1968:43)。与"灰姑娘故事"相似,在"灰姑娘反串版"故事里,男女主角在阶级地位、社会财富等方面也存在巨大差异,但通过婚姻,男方彻底改变了原先卑微的身份,实现社会地位阶梯上的"晋升"梦想。与灰姑娘主要凭借过人的美丽和善良不同的是,穷小子作为故事中的"英雄",依仗的是其勤奋、才干或者其他特殊品质。在古老的"灰姑娘反串版"故事中,表面上,男方在出身地位上处于劣势,在"婚姻市场"上价值不高,而女方处于优势;但随着情节发展,女方被动、弱小、需要保护的特征逐渐显露出来,而男性则无论是智力上还是体力上都成为强者,并且总是积极主动地去拯救女方或去解决其王国面临的困难。由此可见,"灰姑娘反串版"故事创造出来的其实是一种"男权的胜利"神话:男主角虽然卑贱低微,但天赋异秉,最终成为高贵家族的"乘龙快婿",并成为一家之主,统领女方原来的"王国"。

以上这种传统的"灰姑娘反串版"故事模型,在近现代小说创作演进中,发展出四种新的变体。在这四种故事变体中,男性"灰姑娘"或是功败垂成,或是喜尽悲来,或是被工具化,或是变成滑稽模仿。这些变体不光光是故事模式上发生了一些调整,更重要的是,作品的主题立意发生了深刻变化,特别是重构了传统版灰姑娘故事中的"性别政治"形态,表现出男性权威的衰落和男性英雄形象的瓦解,并朝着女权和女性主义方向掘进。本文将以司汤达的《红与黑》(1830年)、菲兹杰拉德的《夜色温柔》(1934年)、劳伦斯的《查泰莱夫人的情人》(1928年)和金斯利·艾米斯的《幸运的吉姆》(1954)为例对四种故事变体予以具体阐述和探讨。

2 于连：功败垂成的"灰姑娘"

"灰姑娘反串版"的第一种变体是，男性"灰姑娘"无限接近梦想，但最终倒在成功的门槛之外。最为典型的是《红与黑》中于连的故事。

于连出生低微，却富有才智和勇气，从小渴望像拿破仑一样赢得美妇芳心，跻身上流社会、成为世界的主人："他自幼经常心潮澎湃，美滋滋地幻想有朝一日自己会被引见给巴黎的美貌女人，会以惊人的事迹引起她们的注意。当拿破仑还是穷小子的时候便已经使光彩照人的德·博阿尔内夫人对他一见钟情，他又为什么不能赢得其中一位佳丽的芳心呢？这个想法给认为自己非常不幸的他带来安慰，在他快乐的时候更增添了他的快乐"(Stendhal，1958：37)。他明白，像他这样出生于平民家庭、无钱无势之人，"不用手段而飞黄腾达，绝对不可能"(范学亮，2010：11)。当皮拉尔神父把于连介绍给德·拉莫尔侯爵做秘书时，于连欣喜地进入这个"巴黎权力漩涡的中心"、"阴谋与虚伪的大本营"(Stendhal，1958：244)，而且他很快想出一条捷径，那就是捕获侯爵女儿玛蒂尔德的芳心。虽然并不喜欢玛蒂尔德奇特而高傲的性格，但当他想到与她结婚可以爬上高位、获取贵族阶级的荣誉、青云直上时，于连就开始热烈地追求起玛蒂尔德小姐。因此，在收到玛蒂尔德的爱情告白信的时候，于连首先想到的是他终于战胜了情敌，可以平等地与贵族情敌站在同一起跑线上了。由于玛蒂尔德怀孕，他获得侯爵赠送的一个骑士称号、一份田产和一个骠骑兵中尉的军衔时，他又做起了"30岁当司令"的美梦。当于连几乎美梦成真时，司汤达却让事态一直往相反的方向发展。最后，在权贵与教会合谋下，于连的前一任情人德·雷纳尔夫人出手写了一封揭发于连的告密信。信中说："此人既穷且贫，企图以极虚伪的手段，通过勾引一个不幸的弱女子来达到向上爬的目的"(Stendhal，1958：450)。于是，侯爵取消了于连与侯爵小姐的婚约；于连在盛怒之下射伤德·雷纳尔夫人并被判处死刑。至此，于连的美梦最终成为一枕黄粱。

在《红与黑》中，虽然男主角最终功败垂成，但并不影响其实际上仍然是一个"灰姑娘反串版"故事。从"性别政治"的角度看，《红与黑》仍然精彩地表达了一个男权神话，即便这个神话典型性较弱。可以说，虽然于连在婚恋策略上如此卑下，故事结局也远离古老的"灰姑娘反串版"的套路，但作家还是让男主角成了爱情上的大赢家——德·雷纳尔夫人饱受情感折磨并遭到枪击，但自始至终深爱于连；侯爵小姐在于连入狱后，也为营救他四处奔走，甚至愿意为之殉情，"用她无比的爱和崇高的行动作出惊世之举"(Stendhal，1958：470)，而且在于连被处死之后，她坐上马车，手捧于连的头颅，来到于连生前选定的墓地,亲手埋葬了他,表现出莫大的勇气和忠贞。男主角虽然没有像民间故事中那样赢得女方的地位、金钱和王国,却赢得了"公主"的刻骨铭心之爱。

3 迪克:喜尽悲来的"灰姑娘"

20世纪初美国作家菲茨杰拉德所著的小说《夜色温柔》提供了"灰姑娘反串版"的第二种变体:异性"灰姑娘"实现"晋升"梦想后喜尽悲来。小说中的男主角与"公主"结了婚并继承了"公主"的王国,但从此男性"灰姑娘"并未过上幸福的生活,而故事从一个喜剧走向了一个悲剧。

《夜色温柔》小说一开头,中下阶级出身的年轻精神病理医生迪克与上流社会的患者、百万富翁的女儿尼科尔·沃伦结婚,穷小子已经娶得"公主",并继承了"公主"的"王国";然而随着故事的进展,这个立志"做一个出色的心理学家,也许是有史以来最伟大的心理学家"(Fitzgerald,1933:132)的有为青年,在精心照顾妻子的过程中荒废了自己的事业,并失去了其"自我控制、自我约束"的优点。而其妻子病愈后,从一个依附于丈夫的病人成长为独立的女性,甚至具备了足够的勇气,觉得自己"无需听从其中任何一个男子的摆布,甚至无需爱他们"(Fitzgerald,1933:294)。彻底让迪克幻梦破灭的是,尼科尔有了婚外情,并提出与迪克离婚。和传统"灰姑娘反串版"故事喜剧结局不同的是,这部小说以婚姻破灭、男主角自我放逐的"悲剧"结束。女性人物也一改传统"灰姑娘反串版"故事中的女性形象,不再是被动、弱小、需保护的对象。

正如一些学者所说,《夜色温柔》表现的是"一个典型的现代父权文化崩溃、女权主义崛起的隐喻"(张勤,2001:71)。一般而言,"在男权制社会中,妇女的地位始终与她们的经济依赖性紧密相关。正如其社会地位是间接地,是通过男性获得的,妇女与经济的关系也具有典型的间接性和附带性"(米利特,2000:48)。而在《夜色温柔》中,尼科尔作为巨额财富的继承者,在经济方面无需依赖男性、依赖婚姻。小说中,虽然尼科尔也属于那类"性感迷人"的柔情女郎,但"对与她有关系的男人却有着一种毁灭性的影响"(库普曼,1996:117)。

小说背后表达的是男权的焦虑。从故事开头看,男主人公也许有可能控制掌握了一切:治疗女主人公、娶了女主人公、逆袭进入女主人公的社会阶层,但最终女主人公"反制"成功,给男主人公留下一个悲剧的结尾。菲兹杰拉德实际上讲述了一个男权控制失败的故事:男性"灰姑娘"在不同层面上受到阻挠,而女主角在两性关系中获得了越来越大的权力。如果说传统"灰姑娘反串版"故事表现的是男权的胜利,而《夜色温柔》表达的则是男权的失败。

4 梅乐士：被"工具化"的"灰姑娘"

英国文学巨匠劳伦斯的《查泰莱夫人的情人》则讲述了另一则底层男子试图与上层妇女联姻的"灰姑娘反串版"故事。然而在这一故事变体中，男性"灰姑娘"与"公主"的结合是灵肉分离的结合，前者虽然得到了"公主"，但某种程度上只是充任了"公主"的肉体和情感的工具，既不可能继承财产，也无法获得"王国"，当然也谈不上地位的晋升。梅乐士在整个故事中都处于一种被动、虚弱和焦虑的状态之中。

男主人公梅乐士——男爵家的狩猎人——与其他几个男性角色相比，是唯一一个可以在性爱中满足男爵夫人康妮（女主人公查泰莱夫人）、并显示出男性力量的人物。然而，可悲的是，"梅乐士的作用似乎与他的男性同胞无二，只是康妮享受性爱的工具"（杨新宇，2011：144）。更有甚者，这个在性爱方面最强有力的男人在情感上却十分无能。这种无能无异于康妮其他性伴侣在性爱上的无能。反而是康妮在被梅乐士的性爱唤醒的同时，也帮助梅乐士摆脱了孤独，实现了回归，成为他的守护神、精神的安慰者、引导者（Spilka，1955）。当梅乐士担心两人的关系被人发现时，康妮斩钉截铁地说："那么，我可以走。"、"无论哪儿！我有我自己的钱……"（劳伦斯，1992：177）。当梅乐士担心康妮割舍不掉她的地位时，康妮表示："我不，我的男爵夫人又怎么样！我实在恨这个名称，人们每次这样叫我的时候，我总觉得他们在嘲弄我"（劳伦斯，1992：177）。准确地说，这部小说中的两性关系是这样的："他们[男性]是新生的，只有通过女性才得见精神世界永恒的光"（Pinion，1978：72）。女性在精神世界中的强大衬托了以梅乐士为代表的男性的虚弱。劳伦斯本人曾说："在男女关系中，表面看来似乎是男性处于支配地位，这种表面现象给人以错觉。从两性关系的深层看，男性在女性面前具有一种（因）自身虚弱而产生的恐惧，因为一旦女人离开了他，他就会像灰尘那样空寂"（侯朝峰，2009：23）。小说以男主角俯首帖耳，宣告女主角是他生命的结尾："那么我相信我们间的小火把，现在在我看来，这是世界上唯一的东西了。我没有朋友，没有知己的朋友。只有你。现在，那小火把是我生命中唯一在怀的东西了"（劳伦斯，1992：438）。

与《夜色温柔》一样，《查泰来夫人的情人》的结局对男主角来说也并不理想，从小说结尾我们可以得知，梅乐士辞去了在康妮家做狩猎人的职位，在一家农场找到了新的工作，"他要在农场做六个月的工，以后他和康妮或可有个自己的小农场……他得工作，甚至是劳苦的工作。他得谋自己的工作，即便康妮有钱帮助他开始"（劳伦斯，1992：433）。看来，梅乐士即使与上层女子顺利结婚，似乎也得不到民间传说中男子的"高攀"式婚姻所附带的财富地位等其他好处。细读小说结尾处梅乐士写给查泰来夫人的信，如若撇开信中那些激情洋溢的情话，读者看到的是梅乐士对金钱的关注和对未来与康妮一起生活的担忧。信中有五次提到金钱:在介绍自己当前的工作和生活时梅乐士似乎是无意识地提到自己的"工资是每星期30先令"(劳伦斯,1992:434),但在此信的另一处他发出无奈的叹息,"25到30先令的工钱,怎么养活一家人呢?"(劳伦斯,1992:436)。他在抨击他人奢侈消费的现象和导致这种现象的社会教育、评价金钱的作用时说"叫群众为花钱而生活,然后金钱便流出来了……你有了的时候,它便毒害你;你没有的时候,它便饿死你"(劳伦斯,1992:437),以及最后他明明白白地向康妮袒露忧思时提到"觉得恶魔在空中,它将试图把我们捉住。或者这不是恶魔,而是贪财鬼"(劳伦斯,1992:437)。因此,读者可以发现这个处于社会低位的男子对与上层女子共同生活的全部忧虑。这也表明像劳伦斯这样一位极其关注"金钱与阶级、性欲与性别"(money and class, sexuality and gender)(Richetti,2005:715)主题的男性作家并不看好跨越阶层的爱情和婚姻。

5 吉姆:滑稽模仿的"灰姑娘"

英国现当代作家金斯利·艾米斯的《幸运的吉姆》,无论从立意和结构上看,都是一个"灰姑娘反串版"典型故事,它的情节与古老的"灰姑娘反串版"故事模式最为接近。但必须指出,在这个故事变体中,男主角不再具备古老民间故事中男主角身上的"英雄"特质,而是呈现出一些"反英雄"的特征。类似于堂·吉诃德是对古典主义英雄骑士的滑稽模仿,吉姆的男性的英雄形象和成功之道也是对传统"灰姑娘"故事的一种滑稽模仿。

出身中下层的"灰姑娘"——吉姆·迪克逊(男主角)在一所大学的历史系担任临时教职,因出身低微,不熟悉中上阶级的社会交往与文化生活,他在社交场合出了很多洋相;为了保住这份能够维生的工作,他不得不在学院里那些出身高贵、趾高气扬、装腔作势的资深人士面前,尤其是在几乎以恩主自居的威尔奇教授面前低三下四、忍气吞声。吉姆在感情上也颇为不顺,他爱上了美丽大方、出生上流社会的女孩克里斯汀,但她是威尔奇教授儿子贝尔特朗的女友。在一场名为《可爱的英格兰》的大学演讲会上,吉姆由于怯场与酒醉而胡言乱语,搞砸了演讲,自然也丢了工作。出人意料的是,克里斯汀的富商舅舅很欣赏吉姆演讲时的直率,他给吉姆打来电话,提供给他一份人人觊觎的商务职位——贝尔特朗梦寐以求的美差;而且吉姆的幸运不仅仅如此,克里斯汀得知贝尔特朗对自己不忠后,毅然放弃贝尔特朗走向吉姆。一直遭受精神迫害的"灰姑娘"吉姆最终可谓事业、爱情双丰收,他跟威尔奇父子的"战争"以胜利告终。

但是,吉姆并非传统"灰姑娘反串版"故事中伟岸的"英雄",而是"反英雄":他是一个小丑式的主人公,相貌平平,没有才能,言行举止常常无比夸张,丑态百出;他身处社会边缘,承受生活的重负,他的法宝只是扮"小丑"、做"鬼脸"、发出"笑"声,丝毫算不上英雄壮举。小说中充满了对吉姆这些琐碎无聊的"反英雄"姿态描写,如他会"把舌头咬在两排牙齿中间,使两颊隆起,变成两个半圆形的小气球;然后,他使劲让上唇往下压,压出一个白痴般的噘嘴;接着,他又把下巴朝外翘起,翘得像把铁铲一样。从头至尾,他还时而鼓起眼睛,时而像长着斗鸡眼一样地转动眼珠"(Amis,1968:224)。整部小说中对吉姆各类并不雅驯的笑声的描写出现了120处之多(阮炜,1996:48)。至于他在演讲会上的"勇敢"至多只能算是他的怯场和醉酒导致的直言不讳。然而,富有反讽意义的是,正是这样一个"反文化"的、"非英雄"的、"勇敢"和"率直"的吉姆赢得了"公主"克里斯汀的心,获得了她那做商业大亨的舅舅的欣赏和奖赏。

6 "灰姑娘反串版"和性别政治重构

"灰姑娘反串版"的变体无论是功败垂成、喜尽悲来的男性"灰姑娘",还是被工具化、变成滑稽模仿的"灰姑娘",改变的不仅仅是故事模式,还有传统"灰姑娘反串版"所极力张扬的性别政治形态:男性主导控制命运、女人、财富和权力等一切。

传统"灰姑娘反串版"故事往往塑造男权"英雄"形象,表现男权的彻底胜利:男方即便出身低贱,最终总能凭借其英勇和智慧娶到公主,统领公主的"王国";而女性,即便是妇女中那些拥有地位、财富或者王国的幸运女性,也是软弱无力、掌握不了自己的世界的,她们本人和她们所拥有的一切最终都须归男人掌握。正如波伏娃(Beauvoir,1952:142)所说,"定义和区分女人的参照物是男人,而定义和区分男人的参照物却不是女人。她是附属的人,是同主要者相对立的次要者。他是主体,是绝对,而她是他者。"女性,即便是富有的上层阶级的女性也只有通过这种方式才能"定义"自身,而且"定义"她们、掌握她们世界的是男性中经济地位低下的"穷小子"。

相反,在"灰姑娘反串版故事"的四种近现代叙事变体中,上述的性别政治形态获得重构。女性人物,不管是玛蒂尔德、尼科尔,还是康妮、克里斯汀,均不像民间传说中被动、弱小、需保护的对象,而是一改"第二性""他者"形象,表现出很大的主动性、独立性,在两性关系中获得越来越大的权力。而男性原本在"婚姻市场"上的"劣势"却并未随着故事的进展逐步转为优势,其男性"权力"和男性权威没有进一步扩大,其英雄形象也逐步解构。男主角们,无论是于连,还是梅乐士、迪克,也许一开始承担或企图承担拯救女方或解决女方王国困境的角色,但他们很快就无能为力,再也无法充当强者,甚至自身也成为需救赎或施舍的对象,于连的失败、梅乐士的焦虑、迪克和吉姆的挣扎都是明证。因此,他们的"晋升"美梦或极难实现,或即便勉强实现也是忧虑重重,甚至很快幻灭。唯独吉姆十分幸运,被称为"幸运的吉姆"。但称其为"幸运的吉姆"正表示他的成功只是一种偶然,甚至是一种荒诞叙事。而且正是这个小丑般的吉姆,在最大程度上瓦解了男性"英雄"形象。

参考文献

[1] Amis, K. 1968. *Lucky Jim*[M]. London: The Camelot Press.

[2] Beauvoir, D. S. 1952. *The Second Sex*[M]. New York: Alfred A. Knopf, Inc.

[3] Fitzgerald, S. 1933. *Tender is The Night*[M]. New York: Charles Scribner's Sons.

[4] Pinion, F. B. 1978. A *D. H. Lawrence Companion: Life, Thoughts and Works*[M]. London: The MacMillan Press Ltd.

[5] Propp, V. 1968. *Morphology of the Folk Tale*[M]. Bloomington IN: The American Folklore Society and Indiana University.

[6] Richetti, J. 2005. *The Columbia History of the British Novel*[M]. Beijing: Foreign Language Teaching and Research Press, New York: Columbia University Press.

[7] Spilka, M. 1955. *The Love Ethic of D. H. Lawrence*[M]. Bloomington IN: Indiana UP.

[8] Stendhal. 1958. *The Red and the Black* (L. Bair, trans.)[M]. New York: Bantam Books, Inc.

[9] 范学亮,2010.于连的悲剧根源与小说主题探微——重读小说《红与黑》[J].西安文理学院学报(社会科学版),(6):11-13.

[10] 菲茨杰拉德,1999.《夜色温柔》(贾文渊译)[M].北京:中国和平出版社.

[11] 侯朝峰,2009.劳伦斯文学创作的女性主义思想——《查泰莱夫人的情人》重读[J].文教资料,(8):22-23.

[12] 劳伦斯,1992.《查泰莱夫人的情人》(饶述一译)[M].长沙:湖南人民出版社.

[13] 米利特,2000.《性政治》(宋文伟译)[M].南京:江苏人民出版社.

[14] 库普曼、弗·斯科特,1996.《菲茨杰拉德的〈了不起的盖茨比〉:英汉对照》(王小梅译)[M].北京:外语教学与研究出版社.

[15] 阮炜,1996.吉姆的笑[J].外国文学评论,(3):46-52.

[16] 司汤达,1999.《红与黑》(张冠尧译)[M].北京:人民文学出版社.

[17] 杨新宇,2011.男性的衰落——再评《查泰莱夫人的情人》[J].时代文学,(12):144-145.

[18] 张勤,2001.一曲现代父权文化衰落的哀乐——《夜色温柔》的女性解读[J].国外文学,(1):71-75.

无法逃离的精神藩篱
——艾丽丝·门罗《逃离》的文体学分析

清华大学　中华女子学院　张淑玲[*]

摘要: 本文运用系统功能文体学选择与功能的关系、话语文体学的会话分析理论,以及认知文体学的概念整合理论对艾丽丝·门罗的短篇小说《逃离》进行文体研究,主要考查了男主人公 Clark 分别与妻子 Carla 及 Sylvia 的对话以及 Clark 对待 Carla 和山羊 Flora 相似的方式。通过对会话细节及男主人公 Clark 思维风格等的分析,揭示了 Clark 霸道强势的大男子主义形象及对妻子 Carla 的绝对控制地位,阐释了女主人公 Carla 选择逃离的必然性。同时,Carla 的软弱又预示其逃离的失败,她最终无法逃脱精神藩篱的束缚,这注定了其日后生活的悲剧性。

关键词:《逃离》;文体学;功能语言学;话语分析;概念整合

Title: Inescapable Mental Fence: A Stylistic Analysis of *Runaway* by Alice Munro

Abstract: Drawing on the relationship between choice and function in systemic functional stylistics, conversation analysis theory in discourse stylistics, and the conceptual integration theory in cognitive stylistics, this paper provides an analysis on the short story *Runaway* by Alice Munro, including the analysis of the conversation between Clark and Carla, between Clark and his neighbor Sylvia, and a conceptual integration analysis of Clark's attitudes toward Carla and the goat Flora. Through the analysis, the paper demonstrates the power of the hero Clark and his absolute mental control over Carla, explains the inevitability of Carla's runaway and return, indicates

---

[*] 作者:张淑玲,清华大学外文系在读博士研究生,中华女子学院外语系讲师。主要研究方向:功能语言学、文体学、会话分析。邮箱:alinger2008@163.com。

the inescapable mental fence set up by Clark. At the same time, Carla's sluggishness and dependency on Clark leads to her return, and predicts Carla's tragic life in the future.

Key words: *Runaway*; stylistics; functional grammar; conversation analysis; cognitive integrity

1 引言

有着"当代契科夫""当代最伟大小说家"美誉的艾丽丝·门罗(Alice Munro),2013年荣获诺贝尔文学奖,成为诺贝尔文学奖历史上第13位女性获奖者,并被瑞典学院誉为"当代短篇文学小说大师"。在此之前,她还曾多次获得加拿大总督文学奖、英联邦作家奖、加拿大吉勒文学奖、爱尔兰时报国际小说奖等多个文学奖项。门罗的作品包括1部长篇小说,13部短篇小说集,如短篇小说集《快乐影子之舞》(Dance of the Happy Shades)、《石城远望》(The View from Castle Rock)、《逃离》(Runaway)、《亲爱的生活》(Dear Life)等。其作品多以女性为中心,描写加拿大郊区小镇中平民的爱情、家庭日常生活,探索普通女性复杂的心理与情感世界。

《逃离》是其短篇小说集代表作之一,出版于2004年,曾荣获加拿大吉勒文学奖和英联邦作家奖。全书由八个短篇小说组成:《逃离》、《机缘》、《匆匆》、《沉寂》、《激情》、《侵犯》、《播弄》和《法力》,从不同角度讲述了不同普通女性的"逃离"经历。其中,同名短篇小说《逃离》是这部小说集的开篇,也是最能代表其风格的一部作品。它讲述了女主人公Carla两次出逃的经历:第一次是为了爱情,她成功地"逃离"了自己的原生家庭和父母;第二次是为了"逃离"令她倍感压抑的丈夫和婚姻生活去寻找自我,却以失败告终。

2 对小说《逃离》的前期研究概述

国内学者近几年热衷对《逃离》这部小说集进行研究,其开篇同名小说《逃离》更是引起很多学者的兴趣。其中,大部分学者从女性主义文学批评的角度进行研究,主要涉及女主人公Carla女性意识的觉醒及女性成长的历程(于艳平,2011;王雪玲,2014;章芸,2017;周雪,2019),女性主义的解读(陈思,2014;刘金萍,2015),山羊Flora的意象及其与女主人公Carla的象征关系(李亚莉,2015;杨娜,2015;张亚娟,2019),小说的

"逃离"主题(梁艳,2012;周庭华,2014)。还有一些学者研究小说的叙事策略,包括空间叙事(傅琼,2011;高迪、李奇志,2020;王云侠,2015)等。

前期研究表明,很多学者都从女性主义的角度研究主人公Carla女性意识的觉醒,以及最后回归的必然性。而令Carla选择逃离的根本原因,即丈夫Clark对她的霸道无礼和精神控制,并没有得到足够关注。Clark对待Carla的精神控制体现在小说篇幅不多的对话中,以及他对待Carla和山羊Flora的相似态度上,这些能突出Carla逃离的必然性及日后生活悲剧性的主题。对于该主题的阐释,先行研究主要从女性解放的环境限制和阻力(杨司桂,2016)、女性被动性"自我选择"(胡恩璇,2018)、态度系统(刘娜,2019)等角度展开的,从文体学方向研究该主题的较少。本文将从系统功能与话语文体学和认知文体学的角度,通过细致分析人物间会话以及男主人公Clark的心理风格,从一个新的侧面来阐释Carla逃离的必然性及回归后生活的悲剧性。本文主要回答以下两个问题:

(1) Clark与Carla的权势及地位关系是如何通过人物对话体现出来的?
(2) Clark对山羊Flora的态度如何进一步突出主题?

3 理论基础:功能文体学与认知文体学

3.1 系统功能文体学与话语文体学

系统功能文体学正式诞生的标志,可以说是韩礼德发表的著名论文"语言功能和文学文体:威廉·戈尔丁的《继承者》的语言分析"。它的文体观是:文体即意义潜势。根据韩礼德的观点,语言有三大元功能,即:概念功能、人际功能和语篇功能,这三大功能是"意义潜势"(刘世生,2016:87)。

随着功能文体学的发展,其研究已不限于仅仅从某个元功能对语篇进行描述,而是把不同方面结合起来进行分析,从而更好地对作品的主题进行阐释,比如对文学作品中及物性系统、名词化、人称代词等方面的分析。而且,这些研究开始朝着语言使用所揭示的权力和意识形态关系的方向发展,拓展了功能文体学的研究视野(刘世生,2016:89)。

从一定意义上来说,话语文体学也是功能主义的。话语文体学是在20世纪80年代发展起来的,是当今文体学研究的主流派别之一,它的理论基础是"话语分析理论"(刘世生,2016:99)。早期的话语分析研究以实际交际中的会话分析为主,如话轮转换,衔接,语义关系等。后来,不同的话语文体学家开始通过分析对话中的话步、沉默、行为等探讨语言背后所掩盖的阶级压迫、种族歧视和性别不平等等权力关系。在语篇阐释过程中,话语文体学家需要探讨系统的语言描写如何与性别、阶级和意识形态立场等兼容(刘世生,2016:102)。

3.2 认知文体学

认知文体学,也被简称为认知诗学,是建立在认知科学,尤其是认知语言学发展的基础之上的,利用认知语言学的理论来研究文本的特征。刘世生(2016:160)在他的《什么是文体学》中指出,认知文体学的主要理论包括:斯珀波(Sperber)与威尔逊(Wilson)的相关性理论,莱考夫(Lakoff)的概念隐喻理论,兰格科(Langacker)的认知语法,福柯尼艾尔(Fauconnier)的心理空间理论,福柯尼艾尔(Fauconnier)与特纳(Turner)的概念整合/融合理论等等。申丹(2009)总结的认知文体学的特点中很重要的一点就是,着眼点从分析语言结构与各种意义的关联转向分析作者创作和读者阐释的认知机制。

基于以上两种理论,本研究拟从两个方面对短篇小说《逃离》进行文体分析。一是运用功能文体学中对人称指示语等语言选择的分析,主要涉及失衡理论,以及话语分析理论对小说主要人物之间对话的分析,试图揭示语言现象背后的性别特征与性别不平等的权势关系。此外,本文利用福科尼尔和特纳(Fauconnier & Turner,2002)的概念整合理论,通过对主要人物行为态度的分析,阐释其思维风格或意识形态。通过分析探索小说女主人公悲剧的根源,进一步突出主题。

4 《逃离》的文体学分析

前期的研究表明,小说《逃离》反映了在男权社会中,丈夫和妻子之间的权势关系。这种权势关系,即丈夫对妻子的控制,反映在小说篇幅不多的对话中,不仅包括 Clark 与妻子 Carla 的对话,还在他与邻居 Sylvia 的对话中有所体现。

4.1 Clark 与 Carla 的对话

4.1.1 Clark 的霸道无礼

Clark 经常与人发生口角而气急败坏,有一次他和一个患肺气肿的老妇人因排队发生口角并愤然离去,对此 Carla 与其有一个简短的对话:

节选(1):
…
"You flare up," said Carla. ("你发怒了,"Carla 说。)
"That's what men do."("男人就是这样。")

(Munro,2004:6)

对于 Clark 的粗鲁无礼，Carla 没有大加指责，只客观地说"你发怒了"，而 Clark 对此却嗤之以鼻，认为粗鲁无礼、发脾气是男人的本性。从及物性、名词化、人称代词的运用进行批评语言学角度的分析，这是对功能文体学的发展(刘世生，2016：89)。在这段简短的对话中，Carla 用 you 来指 Clark 本人，但 Clark 在回答中不是用 I 而是选择用 men 回答。Men 是 I 的上义词，Clark 是 men 中的一个个体(Halliday & Hasan，1976)，Clark 选择用指代所有男性的 men 而非指代个体的 I，表明了他把自己的霸道行为解释为男人这一类人的行为，暴露了他对男人本性的认知。

4.1.2　Clark 的强势地位

Clark 不仅对周围人粗暴无礼，对 Carla 更是甚之。可以说，他对 Carla 有绝对的控制权，这充分体现在 Clark 对交谈话题的主导和控制上。以下这段对话是 Clark 告诉 Carla，Sylvia 打过电话，并让其尽快回复她。

节选(2)：

…

Carla：Do you want tea?（你喝茶吗？）

Clark：So, So, Carla.（那个，那个，Carla。）

Carla：What?（怎么了？）

Clark：So she phoned.（她打电话了。）

Carla：Who?（谁？）

Clark：Her Majesty. Queen Sylvia. She just got back.（尊贵的王后 Sylvia。她刚回来。）

Carla：I didn't hear the car.（我没听到车的声音。）

Clark：I didn't ask you if you did.（我也没问你这个啊。）

Carla：So what did she phone for?（那她打电话什么事？）

Clark：She wants you to go and help her straighten up the house. That's what she said. Tomorrow.（她想让你去帮她整理房间。她是这么说的。明天去。）

Carla：What did you tell her?（你和她怎么说的？）

Clark：I told her sure, but you'd better phone up and confirm.（我说当然可以，但你最好和她电话确认一下。）

Carla：I don't see why I have to, if you told her, I cleaned up her house before she left. I don't see what there could be to do so soon.（我不明白我为什么去，如果你告诉她，我在她离开之前就打扫过房间了。我不知道这么快又有什么活需要干。）

Clark: Maybe some coons got in and made a mess of it while she was gone. You never know. (可能她不在的时候几个浣熊闯进去给弄乱房间了。谁知道呢。)

Carla: I don't have to phone her right this minute, I want to drink my tea and I want to have a shower. (没必要现在就打吧,我想喝点茶再洗个澡。)

Clark: The sooner the better. (越快越好。)

Carla: We have to go to the laundromat. Even when the towels dry out they smell moldy. (我们得去一趟洗衣店,毛巾干的时候闻起来都有一股发霉的味道。)

Clark: We're not changing the subject, Carla. I am not going to let you off the hook, Carla. (别转移话题,Carla。我不会让你脱身的,Carla。)

(Munro, 2004: 10 – 11)

对话一开始,Carla 问 Clark 是否想喝茶,Clark 没回答她的问题,而是直接引出新的话题"Sylvia 打电话了"。一般来说,交际双方遵守着话轮的规则,一方说完,对方要给予回应。一方提出问题后,需要另一方通过回答做出回应(谢格罗夫,2013:4)。该对话由 Carla 引起,询问 Clark "是否想喝茶",Clark 理应先回答这个问题,再谈论其他才符合谈话的基本规则。但 Clark 强势打破了该规则,直接忽略 Carla 的问题,把话题转到 Sylvia 身上,仅仅两句话就可以看出两人权势关系的强弱。

在接下来的对话中,Clark 让 Carla 打电话给 Sylvia 确认明天去帮忙整理房屋,Carla 不想去,而且认为没必要马上就打电话,因此 Carla 在一个新的话轮中意欲改变话题"we have to go to ..."。但 Clark 却紧咬着话题不放,直接说"we're not changing the subject",并宣称"I am not going to let you off the hook"。off the hook 意思是"脱身",是从钓鱼衍变而来的,最早的时候是指一条本来已经咬钩的鱼又脱了钩,重获自由。Clark 这句话用在自己妻子身上,妻子如小鱼一般无法挣脱他的鱼钩,让人毛骨悚然。沃德霍(Wardhaugh,1986:292)指出如果一个话题没有谈论穷尽的话,一方试图改变话题很可能会遇到阻挠,除非试图改变话题的人有着特殊的权势。同样,封宗信(2002)也提到在交际者的对话往来中,占主导地位的说话者有权来定义话题是否有关,并决定什么是与当前语境不相关的。从对话可看出,话题毫无疑问是由 Clark 决定的,他直接引出 Sylvia 的话题又强势锁定话题,不允许 Carla "脱身"。Clark 对整个对话的控制彰显了其对妻子 Carla 语言和行为的绝对掌控权。

后来的一段对话也同样反映了 Clark 的霸道与强势地位。Clark 极力说服 Carla 敲诈 Sylvia,Carla 强烈反对:

节选(3)：

……

Carla said, "No. No."(Carla 说道,"别这样,别这样。")

<u>Clark went on as if she had not spoken.</u>(Clark 继续说,就像她什么都没说过一样。)

Clark：We could say we're going to sue. People get money for stuff like that all the time.

（咱们可以威胁她要告他。人们一直都能因为这种事得到钱的。）

Carla：How could you do that? You can't sue a dead person.（你怎么能这么做？你不能告一个死人。）

Clark：Threaten to go to the papers. Big-time poet.（威胁她给他上报纸,给那个大诗人上报。）

……

Carla：You're just fantasizing. You're joking.（你在异想天开。你在开玩笑。）

Clark：No, actually, I'm not.（不,我并没开玩笑。）

Carla said she did not want to talk about it anymore and he said okey.（Carla 说她不想再谈论这个了,他说好。）

<u>But they talked about it the next day, and the next and the next.</u>（但他们第二天还是谈论这个,第三天、第四天也一样。）

(Munro, 2004：13)

这段节选表现出 Clark 想敲诈 Sylvia 的急切心理,更表达了 Carla 在这件事情上丝毫没有发言权。如上所述,交谈双方只有权势高的一方能决定某一语境中话题的相关性。划线句子:Clark went on as if she had not spoken；They talked about it the next day, and the next and the next, as if 引出的虚拟语气在此处表达的是对已经发生的事情的假设,假设其没有发生,Carla 的反对就如没有发生过一样被忽视。三个 next 的使用是一种反复,简短的一句话中出现了三个 next,造成了数量的"失衡"。根据韩礼德的功能文体学理论,失衡属于前景化的一种,可以加强小说的文体效果（刘世生、宋成方,2014）。as if 和三个 next 都表达了 Clark 不顾妻子反对,对该话题无休止地纠缠,进一步证明 Clark 拥有对话题的绝对掌控权,强化了小说的主题。

在下面节选(4)中,Carla 试图缓和他们的关系：

节选(4)：

Carla：Just don't be mad at me.（别生我的气。）

Clark: I am not mad. I hate when you're like this, that's all. (我没生气,只是你这样的时候令我很讨厌,仅此而已。)

Carla: I'm like this because you're mad. (我这样是因为你的想法太疯狂。)

Clark: Don't tell me what I am. You are choking me. Start supper. (用不着你来告诉我我怎么样,你真让我窒息。准备晚饭去。)

(Munro,2004:11)

  Carla 几乎用讨好的语气让 Clark 不要生她的气,而 Clark 却说出了 hate(讨厌)这样的词。当 Carla 指出 Clark 这种想法很不可思议时,他却说,Don't tell me what I am. You are choking me. (用不着你告诉我我怎么样,你真让我窒息)和 Start supper. (准备晚饭去!)。两句都是祈使句。根据韩礼德(Halliday,2008:139)对人际功能中语气的分析,祈使语气的言语功能一般是用来表达命令或提供。但如何判断其言语功能需要借助于语境(context)。此处结合上下文语境可以确定,在一系列的指责之后,Clark 毫无疑问在命令 Carla 不要评判他,并命令她去做饭,言语之中充满强势与呵斥。

  话语分析不仅仅停留在语言表面,而是揭示语言背后的权力关系或意识形态(刘世生,2016:89)。Clark 对话题的纠缠不休,不顾妻子反对执意要骗人钱财,塑造了他霸道贪婪的形象。而 Carla 无力的反对反映了她拥有与丈夫完全不同的道德标准,但却没有任何家庭地位和发言权,逆来顺受。该部分通过篇幅不长的几段对话,彰显了 Clark 意欲控制周围环境和其他人的欲望,揭示了 Carla 在婚姻生活中的压抑,预示她日后逃离的必然性。

4.2　Clark 与 Sylvia 的对话

  Clark 与 Sylvia 的对话也从另一个侧面反映 Clark 对 Carla 的控制地位。在 Carla 逃离又回归后,Clark 去 Sylvia 家归还衣服,两人有一段不算短的对话:

节选(5)

……

Sylvia: Where's Carla? (Carla 在哪儿?)

Clark: You mean <u>my wife Carla</u>? <u>My wife Carla</u> is home in bed. Asleep in bed. Where she belongs. (你指的我妻子 Carla? 我妻子 Carla 在家里的床上。床上睡着呢,那才是她的归宿。)

……

Clark：I came here to tell you I don't appreciate you interfering in my life with <u>my wife</u>.（我来这儿为了告诉你，我不喜欢你介入我和我妻子的生活。）

Sylvia：She is a human being, besides being <u>your wife</u>.（除了是你妻子外，她还是个人。）

Clark：My goodness, is that so? <u>My wife is a human being</u>? Really? Thank you for the information. But don't try getting smart with me. Sylvia.（天啊，是吗？我妻子还是个人？真的吗？谢谢你的提醒，但别想和我耍小聪明，Sylvia。）

Sylvia：I wasn't trying to get smart.（我没有想和你耍小聪明。）

Clark：Good, I'm glad you weren't. I don't want to be mad. I just have a couple of important things to say to you. One thing, that I don't want you sticking your nose in anywhere, anything, in my and <u>my wife</u>'s life. Another, that I'm not going to want her coming around here anymore. Not that she is going to particularly want to come, I'm pretty sure of that, she doesn't have too good an opinion of you at the moment. And it's time you learned how to clean your own house.（那就好，很高兴你没有。我不想发火，只是想和你说清几件事。第一，我不希望你介入我和我妻子生活中的任何事情；另外，我不会让她再靠近这儿半步。她并不想来这儿，我很确定这点，只是当时她对你缺乏正确的认识。而且，你也应该学会如何打扫自己的房屋了。）

(Munro, 2004: 37 - 38)

在这段关于 Carla 的对话中，两个人对 Carla 不同称呼的频率如下表 1 所示：

表 1　对 Carla 的称呼指示语

人物＼称呼	Carla	My (your) wife/My wife Carla	She/her
Clark	0	5	19
Sylvia	1	1	6

该对话是 Clark 与 Sylvia 谈论 Carla 逃离的事。在两人的对话中，Clark 对 Sylvia 冷嘲热讽，态度强势恶劣，这似乎也在情理之中，因为毕竟是在 Sylvia 的鼓励下他妻子才离家出走。值得一提的是，在谈及 Carla 时，两个人对 Carla 称呼的选择有着明显的不同，Clark 用了 5 次"我妻子"（My wife，3 次）或"我妻子 Carla"（My wife Carla，2 次），分别如下：

1) You mean <u>my wife Carla</u>?
2) <u>My wife Carla</u> is home in bed.
3) I came here to tell you I don't appreciate you interfering in my life with <u>my wife</u>.
4) <u>My wife</u> is a human being?
5) I don't want you sticking your nose in anywhere, anything, in my and <u>my wife's life</u>.

系统功能语言学认为我们在语言使用中做的每一个选择,都是为了实现一定的功能,实现其意义潜势(刘世生、宋成方,2014)。萨克斯和谢格洛夫(Sacks & Schegloff, 1979)首次指出我们怎样指称他人,是由我们认为听话人对此人了解多少决定的(recipient design)。我们都遵循一个社会规范,那就是不告诉别人已经知晓的信息(Sacks & Schegloff, 1979)。My wife, my husband 这样的称呼一般是当听话人不认识被提及的人时,说话人用来加以解释说明的。但在该小说中 Clark 在明知对方熟识 Carla 的基础上多次使用 my wife,有时甚至和 Carla 名字连用。这暗示他在特意强调 Carla 是他妻子的身份。

韩礼德吸收了英国语言学家利奇(Leech)的观点,肯定突出的存在,并把突出分为失协和失衡。失衡强调数量上的偏离,并且韩礼德认为失衡现象在文体分析中更有意义(刘世生、宋成方,2014)。在 Sylvia 问 Carla 在哪儿时,她直呼 Carla 的名字。但 Clark 回答时,先明知故问地用 My wife Carla,即 1),又通过重复 my wife Carla 继续强调,即 2)。虽然在该话轮中 My wife Carla 只出现了两次,但在相邻的两句话中重复出现这样较复杂的指示语来指称对话双方都熟悉的人,这是不符合常规的说话习惯的,他完全可以用 Carla 或 She 来回答。两次重复使用 My wife Carla 是一种失衡,暗示他想通过这种方式向 Sylvia 宣布 Carla 的身份,即他的妻子。3)和5)则验证了他用 my wife 而非其他指称的目的,他不喜欢 Sylvia 干涉他与他妻子的生活,此处的 my wife 进一步强调 Carla 的身份,即"我妻子",而不是一个独立的人 Carla。对此,Sylvia 反驳"Carla 除了是你妻子还是个人"时,Clark 极其挑衅地反问"我妻子是人吗?",即句4),来嘲讽奚落 Sylvia。

从表1可以看出,Clark 对 Carla 的指称除了用"我妻子"(My wife)或"我妻子 Carla"(My wife Carla)外,用了很多代词"她"(she 或 her),但他从没单独使用 Carla 这个称呼,其目的不言而喻,Clark 想通过这种方式宣布 Carla 只有一个身份,即他的妻子,以宣布他对 Carla 的所有权。相反,Sylvia 则首先把 Carla 当做一个独立的个体,只用其名字 Carla,唯一用到 your wife,是为了向 Clark 说明,Carla 不仅是"你的妻子"还是一个独立的人。即6):

6) She is a human being, besides being your wife.

Sylvia 尊重女性、尊重人性的光辉形象与 Clark 的大男子主义霸道形象形成了鲜明的对比。Sylvia 是女性主义先进思想的代表,认为女性具有独立的人格;而 Clark 则可以被看做男权主义的代表,他强调女性在社会和家庭中的从属和服从地位,认为女人首先应该是"妻子"。

Clark 在与 Sylvia 的对话中几次选择用 My wife(Carla)而不用 Carla 或 she,他做出的语言选择透露了他欲达到的目的,即向 Sylvia 宣布:不要再介入我和我妻子的生活了,你没有权利,强调他对 Carla 的绝对拥有和控制权。重复使用 My wife(Carla)达到了一种失衡的效果(刘世生、宋成方,2014),同时违反了社会规范,即反复告诉交际另一方已知的信息(Sacks & Schegloff, 1979),使 Clark 霸道强势的形象得到了凸显。这段对话揭示了加拿大郊区小镇男性的霸权和大男子主义思想,预示 Carla 日后婚姻生活的悲剧性。

4.3 Clark 对待 Carla 和山羊 Flora 的态度

Clark 的霸道权势地位也体现在他对待山羊 Flora 的态度上,而 Clark 对 Carla 的态度和方式也可以从他对山羊 Flora 上反映出来。因为小说诸多细节会让读者把 Carla 与温顺的山羊 Flora 联系起来。小说一直在强调 Carla 和 Flora 关系亲密,犹如闺蜜,在 Flora 消失的那段时间,Carla 心情很糟,犹如失了魂(Munro, 2004:7)。这就为两者的隐喻关系奠定了基础,也为两个空间的映射提供了可能,这是概念整合的重要原则之一(Fauconnier, 2010)。

概念整合理论是以心理空间为基本单位,根据建立在一系列心理活动基础上的认知操作过程,建立四个抽象空间,包括两个输入空间(input spaces)(从隐喻上讲,与概念隐喻理论中的源域和目标域相关)、类属空间(generic space)(表示两个输入空间共享的抽象的概念结构)、整合空间(blending space)(在此空间内,两个输入空间结合并相互作用)(Ungerer & Schmid, 2008:258-259)。以下将用概念整合理论分析 Clark 的思维风格。

Clark 与 Flora 的关系可以被看做源输入空间,此心理空间来源于 Clark 概念结构中的 Flora 域。目标输入空间是 Clark 与 Carla 的关系,此心理空间来源于 Clark 概念结构中的 Carla 域。每个输入空间内部都具有一定的联系,这种联系是被概念地、经验地激发出来的(Fauconnier & Turner, 2002),且输入空间都从属于一定的环境(context-dependent)(Ungerer & Schmid, 2008:261)。在小说交代的社会环境下,弱势的 Carla 对于强势的 Clark 是妻子、伴侣、性对象等,温顺的 Flora 则是 Clark 的家畜、附属品、玩物等,这两个输入空间之间存在部分跨空间的映射,具有一定的识别关系。

如图1所示,Clark 作为 Carla 的丈夫与作为 Flora 的主人相对应;Carla 和 Flora 相对应;Clark 与 Carla 度过的一段婚后快乐时光,相当于在集市购买 Flora 一段时间后,Flora 成为了他的宠物;而后,Carla 逃离了 Clark,这个过程与 Flora 莫名消失了一段时间相符;Carla 后来的回归,又与 Flora 不明原因地出现在一个浓雾的夜晚相吻合。然而最后,Clark 为了达到对 Carla 的完全控制,杀害了 Flora 并将其抛尸野外。而对 Carla,一个有血有肉的人却不能同样对待。

这两个输入空间之间的对应关系源自 Carla 与 Flora 之间的隐喻关系,然而,源输入空间对于 Flora 的解决方法是暗杀并抛尸荒郊野外。目标输入空间却不同,这种解决方法不适用,因为 Carla 是具有社会属性的人。因此,Clark 对 Carla 的态度更像是精神上的束缚,设置精神和身体的藩篱。他封锁 Flora 回来过的消息,不准 Sylvia 再与 Carla 见面,这不同于杀害 Flora 的身体,但无异于残害 Carla 灵魂。

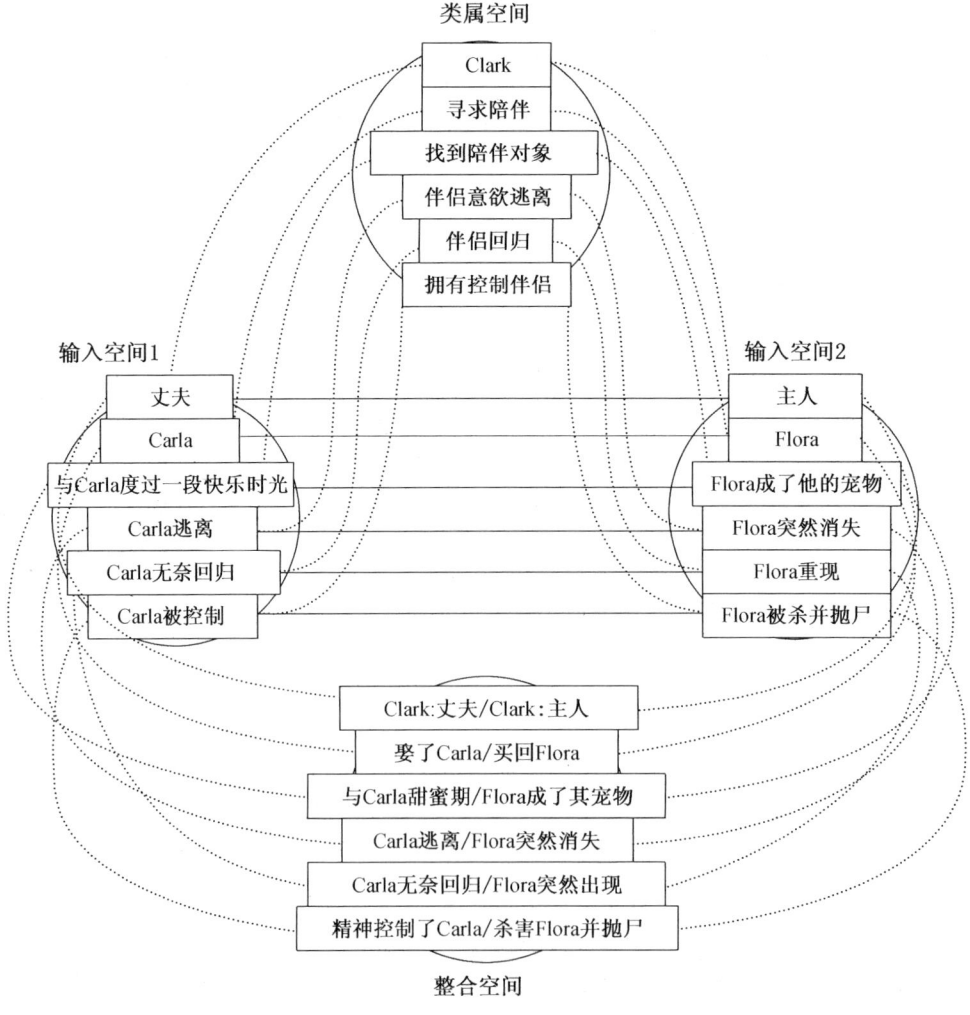

图1　Clark 的概念网络示意图

第三个是类属空间,这是一个抽象的情景域,由这两个输入空间的基本结构组成,只是在拥有并控制伴侣上,Clark 对 Carla 和 Flora 采取了不同的处理方式。

第四个空间,即整合空间,在跨空间的对应关系以及他们共同的类属结构基础上,(图 1 中,四个空间的对应关系用虚曲线表示)把两个输入空间融合成一个单独的情景域。整合的一个重要目的是消解输入空间之间的冲突,并解决其中的问题(Fauconnier & Turner, 2002)。在整合空间中,对 Carla 的处理方式异于 Flora。由于 Carla 具有社会属性,Clark 不能像通过杀害 Flora 达到对她的绝对控制,而是通过控制她的精神和灵魂达到此目的,将她逃离的想法扼杀在摇篮之中,即封锁 Flora 回来过的消息,不许她再见 Sylvia 等,这就使整合后的空间更具合理性。Carla 的最终结果是精神和灵魂失去了自由,这与 Flora 被抛尸荒野一样让人感到凄凉和绝望,也注定了 Carla 日后生活的悲剧性。

小说中,在那个特定社会环境下,Clark 将温顺但神秘的 Flora 与弱势但有一些自由意识的 Carla 视作同一体。概念整合理论解释了两个输入空间,即 Clark 与两者之间的关系,如何有选择地进行了映射,以及 Clark 在特殊情境下对 Carla 不同于 Flora 的处理方式,这些表现预示了女主人公 Carla 的悲剧结局。

5 结 论

本文运用系统功能文体学、话语文体学以及认知文体学的相关理论对短篇小说《逃离》进行了文体学分析,主要围绕着男主人公 Clark 与妻子 Carla 的对话、与邻居 Sylvia 的交谈、Clark 对待妻子与山羊 Flora 的态度和方式展开的分析。通过分析,男主人公 Clark 霸道强势的大男子主义形象以及 Carla 顺从柔弱的形象跃然纸上,同时,Clark 对妻子 Carla 的绝对控制权也通过会话分析体现得淋漓尽致,这解释了女主人公 Carla 逃离的必然性;Clark 对 Carla 的精神控制犹如残杀山羊 Flora 并抛尸野外,即使没有对 Carla 设立现实的藩篱,Clark 设置的精神藩篱也是 Carla 无法逃脱的,这预示了 Carla 日后生活的悲剧性。

门罗对加拿大郊区小镇上普通男女的生活进行了描述,霸道强势的 Clark,柔弱顺从的 Carla,还有女性主义先进思想的代表 Sylvia。Carla 可以说代表了这一类女性形象,她们有一定的道德标准和追求自由的意识,饱受霸道强势丈夫的控制,需要像 Sylvia 这样的社会群体对其关注和帮助,才能摆脱不幸婚姻的束缚,寻找自我。但是她们又具有惰性和依赖性,Carla 选择逃离后又回归就说明了这一点,因此她们仍然很难摆脱自己设置的精神藩篱。

参考文献

[1] Fauconnier, G. 2010. *Mappings in Thought and Language* [M]. Beijing: World Publishing Corporation.

[2] Fauconnier, G. & M. Turner. 2002. *The Way We Think: Conceptual Blending and the Mind's Hidden Complexities* [M]. New York: Basic Books.

[3] Halliday, M. A. K. Revised by Matthiessen, C. 2008. *An Introduction to Functional Grammar* (3rd ed.) [M]. Beijing: Foreign Language Teaching and Research Press.

[4] Halliday, M. A. K. & R. Hasan. 1976. *Cohesion in English* [M]. London: Longman.

[5] Munro, A. 2004. *Runaway* [M]. New York: Vintage International.

[6] Sacks, H. & E. A. Schegloff. 1979. Two preferences in the organization of reference to persons and their interaction [A]. In G. Psathas (ed.). *Everyday Language: Studies in Ethnomethodology* [C]. New York: Ivrington Publishers, 15 – 21.

[7] Ungerer, F. & H. J. Schmid. 2008. *An Introduction to Cognitive Linguistics* (2nd ed.) [M]. Beijing: Foreign Languages Teaching and Research Press.

[8] Wardhaugh, R. 1986. *An Introduction to Sociolinguistics* (2nd ed.) [M]. Oxford: Basil Blackwell.

[9] 陈思,2014.爱丽丝·门罗的《逃离》与女性主义批评研究[J].佳木斯职业学院学报,(10):24 – 25.

[10] 封宗信,2002.《文学语篇的语用文体学研究》[M].北京:清华大学出版社.

[11] 傅琼,2011.叙事文体学视阈下《逃离》中的叙事视角与人物话语分析[J].外语与外语教学,(3):94 – 97.

[12] 高迪,李奇志,2020.《逃离》的空间叙事与加拿大的民族性[J].外国文学:文学教育,(1):67 – 69.

[13] 胡恩璇,2018.论《逃离》中悖论式的"自由选择"[J].文学评论·外国文学,132.

[14] 李亚莉,2015.艾丽丝·门罗短篇小说《逃离》中的隐喻解读[J].长春大学学报,(5):66 – 69.

[15] 梁艳,2012.逃往何处——艾丽丝·门罗的《逃离》中的"逃离"主题探析[J].吉林省教育学院学报,(4):120 – 121.

[16] 刘金萍,2015.艾丽丝·门罗《逃离》的女性主义解读[J].视界:外国文学研究,63 – 64.

[17] 刘世生,2016.什么是文体学[M].上海:上海外语教育出版社.

[18] 刘世生,宋成方,2014.关于功能文体学的发展[A].苏晓军(编),《文体学研究:实证认知跨学科》[C].上海:上海外语教育出版社.

[19] 刘娜,2019.态度系统视角下的《逃离》分析[J].校园英语:文艺研究,(41):255.

[20] 申丹,2009.谈关于认知文体学的几个问题[J].外国语文,(1):1 – 5.

[21] 杨娜,2015.消失的 Flora——对《逃离》中山羊意象的分析[J].文学评论·外国文学,90 – 91.

[22] 杨司桂,2016.无法逃遁的精神之围——评爱丽丝.门罗的逃离[J].全民阅读,90 – 91.

[23] 谢格罗夫,2013.对话中的序列组织(马文译)[M].北京:北京大学出版社.

[24] 于艳平,2011.《逃离》的背后:女性意识的觉醒与成长[J].郑州大学学报(哲学社会科学版),(3):109 – 112.

[25] 王雪玲,2014.逃离:女性自我解放意识的表征[J].中华女子学院学报,(5):70-75.

[26] 王云侠,2015.门罗短篇小说集《逃离》的空间叙事研究[J].伊犁师范学院学报:社会科学版,(2):98-100.

[27] 张亚娟,2019.《逃离》中的动物隐喻解读[J].三峡大学学报(人文社会科学版),(1):108-111.

[28] 章芸,2017.《逃离》:女性的自我探寻与成长[J].菏泽学院学报,(3):36-39.

[29] 周庭华,2014.逃离抑或回归[J].国外文学,(3):119-126.

[30] 周雪,2019.《逃离》中女性成长的历程和女性关系的别样书写[J].外国文学.文学教育,36-37.

神话中的觉醒
——《野猫精》中的反乌托邦思想解读*

南京大学 赵 杨**

摘要：塔·托尔斯泰娅是俄罗斯后现代主义文坛最具个性的女性作家之一，她在创作中为我们展现了光怪陆离、五彩缤纷的童话氛围及神话世界，同时也表达了具有警示意识的反乌托邦思想。长篇小说《野猫精》以独特的后现代艺术表现手法创造了一个荒诞的"百科全书"式的神话世界，小说作为人类发展的一部灾难性预言，其中的反乌托邦思想是不言而喻的。本文以此作品为例分析了作家的艺术特色，指出，作家不仅展现了生活的悲剧性因素，同时将俄罗斯后现代主义文学所具有的"绝望的戏谑"精神赋予苦难的俄罗斯民族一剂乐观的"良药"，这不仅帮助俄罗斯人免除不切实际的幻想，对于全人类抵抗一切乌托邦式的诱惑也颇有启发意义。

关键词：童话；神话；反乌托邦主义

Title: The Awakening in the myth: The Idea of Dystopia in T. Tolstay's Novel Keis

Abstract: T. Tolstay is one of the most distinguished female writers of Russian postmodernism. She not only shows us a world of fairy tales and myths bearing bizarre and colorful atmosphere in her works, but also conveys the thought of dystopia with the awareness of warning. Moreover, Tolstay creates a fantastic encyclopedic world of myths with more distinctive postmodern artistic devices in the full-length novel *Keis*. As a disastrous prophecy of human development, the thought

---

* 本研究是江苏省社科基金项目"当代俄罗斯小说中的'文化重塑'与俄罗斯文学传统的关系研究"（编号：18WWB007）的部分成果。

** 作者简介：赵杨，南京大学外国语学院副教授，研究方向：俄罗斯文学。电子邮箱：yangyang.els@163.com。

of dystopia contained in this novel is self-evident. This paper takes these two masterpieces as an example to analyze the writer's artistic characteristics. In the analysis, the author points out that Tolstay not only reveals the tragic elements of life in her works, but also provides a best positive medicine for the miserable Russian people by virtue of the spirit of "desperate banter" in the Russian postmodern literature. This medicine is helpful in freeing the Russians from unrealistic fancies and enlightening for the humans to resist all utopian temptation.

Key words: Fairy tales; myths; dystopia

"乌托邦"本是托马斯·莫尔为人类社会设计的一个"美丽新世界",尽管因其纯粹的幻想性而演变成"不切实际、虚幻"事物的代名词,可古往今来,"乌托邦"一直是文人志士们内心不断追求的理想。因此,在哲学著述抑或是文学作品中,总能或多或少折射出他们所具有的"乌托邦思想"的激情。遗憾的是,这种寄托了知识分子崇高理想的个人话语一度成为了迷惑人心的麻醉剂,使人类社会蒙受巨大灾难。对此,苏联作家扎米亚京、英国作家赫胥黎以及乔治·奥威尔早在自己的不朽名著中有所预见,"反乌托邦文学"亦从此萌芽。

俄苏文学中的反乌托邦文学一直贯穿整个俄苏文学史,而俄罗斯后现代主义文学作为俄苏文学中"反乌托邦文学"的一个重要分支,对于颠覆人类一切乌托邦式的幻想、挖掘人性本质都发挥了极大作用。它在俄罗斯大地的诞生不仅仅是由于西方后现代主义文化思潮的影响,同时也是苏联文学发展的必然结果,其开山之作——《从莫斯科到彼图什基》《普希金之家》以及《与普希金一起散步》等都不同程度地表达了作家们解构权威、颠覆传统经典的反乌托邦主义思想,因而可以说,俄罗斯后现代主义文学从开始便具有反乌托邦主义的天然本性。然而这种创作特质在许多俄罗斯后现代作家的作品中却又体现着各不一样的风景。譬如,哈里托诺夫以俄罗斯知识分子的"命运线"勾勒出特定历史阶段苏联社会的面貌,柳·彼特鲁舍夫斯卡娅所描绘的一幅幅"绝望人生"的晦暗图画揭示了生活不可避免的悲剧性,维·佩列文的作品中始终贯穿着"追求精神自由"的主题,而塔·托尔斯泰娅则以幽默的童话语言、睿智的喜剧精神表达了对权威文化的抗拒和反叛。

塔吉娅娜·托尔斯泰娅(1951—)作为当代俄罗斯文坛最具鲜明个性的女性作家之一,早在上个世纪80年代初登文坛时便已引起评论界关注。如今很多评论家将其归于后现代作家,也有研究者认为她的创作观念及人物体系只是符合了后现代的传统。此外,也有人将其作品归为当代"女性文学"之列,因为她的作品表达了对人之存在、对孤独感以及理想与现实的幻灭等主题的关注。尽管仁者见仁,但倘若抛开了关于流派的纷争,从作家整体创作的艺术本质上来看,我们可以发现,作家的一系列作品,譬如《喜欢——不喜欢》《坐在金色的台阶上》《与小鸟约会》《云游者》等等短篇故事均不同程度地凸显了一种"具有反叛意识的童话性和神话色彩"。换言之,在作家所展现的光怪陆离、五彩缤纷的童话氛围以及神话世界里我们都可以看到一种具有警示意义的反乌托邦思想。作家唯一的一部长篇小说《野猫精》便是以独特的叙事手法表达了作家内心深处独特的反乌托邦精神。

1 反乌托邦思想在体裁上的体现

对于《野猫精》的体裁问题学界一直存在很大争议。同许多评论家一样,作家本人将之界定为长篇小说,而有些人则认为该小说是脱离了体裁界定的难以捉摸的中篇故事,还有些学者认为《野猫精》的叙事规模远超过中篇小说,因为它融合了各种体裁因素,是新神话学派与寓言式童话、社会讽刺与反乌托邦特征的结合体。从小说所具有的醒世作用来看,它似乎更接近于寓言小说,因为它们都涉及到了道德规范、真理的寻觅以及"受社会制约的自然人的心理特征"。而寓言的本质特征是要借助文本的创造性想像来实现的,也就是须生成引喻和激发读者对典故的追忆和联想。然而,寓言却又排除了描述性,它的主人公们通常不具备外部及内在特征,他们不是叙事的客体,而是作为伦理学意义上的行为主体而存在的。这些特点在《野猫精》里均不明显,因而寓言并非是该小说完全意义上的体裁模式。

但有一点毫无疑问,这是一部反乌托邦小说,而且不是传统意义上的"反乌托邦"。学者伊·伊万诺娃指出,"托尔斯泰娅书写的不是以往的反乌托邦,而是对它的戏仿……作家将属于知识分子的乌托邦话语与俄罗斯民俗文化及童话结合在了一起"。这种说法似乎与近年来俄国文学中出现的一种新的叙事体裁有很大相似之处。这种新的形式打破了以往各要素之间的平衡,使得传统体裁要素所建构的主题思想变得模糊,最终导致在这种残缺性的要素之间产生了新的变体,从而使作家重新建构出个性化的创作观念。作家所注重的不只是个人的世界观,而是将个人意志置于"体裁的记忆"(巴赫金语)之中并与之和谐相处。确切地说,作家并非无视传统的体裁特征,而是有选择地使用了那些能恰当反映自己思想的要素,从而建构自己的叙事体裁。类似的体裁往往具有"宏大的故事和情节的多面性",这一点在《野猫精》中可见一斑。

作家用自己一贯的童话意识表现手法创造了一个荒诞的"百科全书"式的神话世界,小说的每个章节都以古俄语字母表中与文本情节有着密切相关含义的称谓命名,而且,评论家鲍·巴拉莫纳夫认为,"塔·托尔斯泰娅创造了一个当代俄罗斯历史、文化的典型模式,一个微型宇宙"(Парамонов,2010)。而评论家斯捷潘尼扬认为,"作品无论在思想上还是在结构上都体现了作家的反乌托邦思想,此外,对国家历史以及公认的典型个人的冷漠嘲讽,对国家辉煌过去的回忆的平淡语调也明显说明了这一点"(Степанян,2001)。

的确,小说的整个情节是超乎想像、近乎荒诞的,是蕴含着对现实嘲讽的寓言式反乌托邦神话:莫斯科发生了毁灭性的大爆炸,灾难过后,幸存下来的人类与新生人类重新组合成了一个社会群体,他们在莫斯科原地建立了新的城市,城市的名称与城市的统治者费多尔·库兹米奇的名字同名——费多尔-库兹米奇斯克。城市的居民在费多尔·库兹米奇的独裁统治之下,分为两种人。一种是新生人类,这些人整体上被称作"戈卢布奇克",他们绝大多数完全崇拜并迷信统治者的意志,完全丧失了自我。而另一种人则是在灾难中留下来的居民,他们都是活了几百岁的老人,是古老文明传统的代表,无论在思想还是生活方式上都与新生人类格格不入。这两种人虽迥然不同,但他们有一个共同的特点,毁灭性的大爆炸给他们每个人都带来了不同程度的后遗症:"戈卢布奇克"们出现了"返祖现象",有人长出了尾巴,有人长出尖利的爪子,有人长出浓密的体毛;而老一代人竟然有了"特异功能",主人公之一尼基塔·伊万内奇就能口吐火焰,自取火种。小城居民们主要以老鼠和各种小动物为食,他们被禁止读书,禁止接触古老文化,在统治者的专制意志下文明遭到践踏和毁灭,道德和语言正在堕落和退化,鲜明的等级制度及奴隶制度盛行,"大穆尔扎"和"小穆尔扎"界限分明,野蛮、贫穷与无知笼罩着整个城市。

2 反乌托邦思想在主题思想上的体现

小说以主人公别涅季克特的回忆录般的叙述语调写成,中间亦夹杂着叙述者的语言,整部小说充满了调侃、戏谑色彩。小说主人公别涅季克特是新生人类的一员,也是费·库兹米奇建立的虚假的"神话世界"的掘墓人。他曾是费·库兹米奇旗下的一名抄写员,专门负责抄写费·库兹米奇创作的诗歌、发布的命令及告示等。直到有一天,当他第一次亲眼目睹了费多尔的真面目并意识到了这个统治者的虚伪本性之后,血气方刚的年轻人终于开始觉醒,他的自我意识因其内心对知识的源泉——书的渴求以及在他的精神导师、老一代人的代表尼·伊万内奇的引导下慢慢复苏。然而,别涅季克特寻找真理、追求内心宁静的渴望并未使其最终建立一个真正和谐的理想乌托邦社会。为了接近梦寐以求的书籍,他处心积虑与同是抄写员的奥莉娅结婚,以此成为拥有大量藏书的库·库杰雅罗维奇的女婿。大量如饥似渴的阅读不仅没有使他找到生活真谛,反而使他变得愈加贪婪。为了获得更为重要的"宝书",他不惜铤而走险来到藏书禁地"红楼",还用铁钩杀死了一名无辜的"戈卢布奇克"。别涅季克特成功推翻了费·库兹米奇的专制统治,然而,权力的欲望使他不禁重蹈覆辙,导致他所统治的城市在一场大火中最终被毁灭。一个统治者被另一个统治者取代,极权主义悲剧的不断重复上演,生与死、善与恶的永恒存在似乎在告诫人们:不要对现实抱有天真的乌托邦式的幻想,改变生存状态的唯一途径是继承古老的传统文明,提升人类自身的道德修养。这也正是作家在小说中所要表达的反乌托邦思想的精髓所在。

而在小说的另一位主人公尼·伊万内奇的身上,恰好体现了作家从本质上改变人类生存状况的这一主导思想。尼·伊万内奇是老一辈人的代表,睿智而富有思想,是塑造人类灵魂的工程师。他为了实现保存人类古老文明的愿望,不断用传统文化教导、启迪别涅季克特对知识、对真理的渴望。当他第一个发现了别涅季克特的秘密——背后长出的白色长尾巴时,他明智地提出警示:"的确,尾巴从某方面来说具有一定作用,在远古时代这是正常现象无可非议……可如今这是返祖现象。令我担心的正是这种突然性的肢体增生。这说明了什么?我们所有人都在向非人性退化,我们已经成为一个野蛮的社会"(Толстая,2007:142)。而别涅季克特并未真正理解导师挽救真理的良苦用心,出于对个人社会地位与权力的追逐才被迫同意将尾巴割掉。尼·伊万内奇第一个发现了别涅季克特身上的不凡之处,但是,他也最终清醒地意识到了自己的努力全都会付诸东流,因此他毅然决定与别涅季克特断绝关系。然而,由于别涅季克特的出卖,他最终被判处死刑。临刑前,当别涅季克特突然想起自己还没有明白生活的真谛,便追问昔日导师:"在哪里能找到你说的那本书!它藏在什么地方?……在哪里写着,怎么生活!"而老人如此答道:"学习字母!字母!我说了多少遍了!没有字母你就不可能读书!"(Толстая,2007:322)由此,作家对于人类古老文化的遗失所表露出的遗憾,对于人类只耽于乌托邦式的空想而非进行实质性自身改变的痛心,在人物尼·伊万内奇身上可见一斑。

此外,小说中古典与当代作家的引文贯穿前后,其中普希金的名字与形象占据重要地位,作为俄国传统文化的经典标志,他失去了往日光环竟成为主人公戏讽的对象。对于别涅季克特来说,"普希金"不过是个由字母书写而成的普通名词,是个他用木头刻成的具有"大骨节的"、"六个手指"的"木偶、笨蛋、蠢货"(Толстая,2007:316)。因此,不无讽刺意味的是,在女主人公之一瓦·鲁基尼什娜临终时别涅季克特将画好的"普希金"侧面像作为神像塞进她的手里;当别涅季克特在追求理想而深感无助时,他面对自己的木刻杰作——"普希金"自言自语道:"你,普希金,你说!怎么生活?……不错,你是我的'大骨节',我的'秃后脑勺',你手指不正常,还没有腿。……本来就是这样嘛,忍着点吧,小笨蛋——我们是,而你也是!"(Толстая,2007:269)。在小说最后,"普希金"的脸和手在火灾中被烧毁,成为"野猫精"世界里人类文化贫乏的象征。

3 反乌托邦思想在神话意象上的体现

　　如果小说中以别涅季克特为代表所反映的是现实层面的"神话世界",那么,伴随这个现实"神话世界"存在的还有两个虚无缥缈的"神话形象":野猫精与孔雀公主。在小说中"野猫精"源于老人们的传说:在离费多尔-库兹米奇斯克城不远处有一座茂密的森林,那里住着一只凶猛的野兽——野猫精,它总是蹲在浓密的树枝上发出恐怖的怪叫:克—斯!克—斯!但是,谁也看不见它。"野猫精"具有某种魔力,城里的居民几乎都怕它并把其视为不祥之兆。主人公别涅季克特同样对它充满恐惧,在他不断追求人间天堂、思索人生的过程中,他时常觉得这只猛兽正在背后看着他,每当这时他总是浑身发抖,慌忙四顾并自言自语:"我是什么?我是谁?……啊哈……这就是我"(Толстая,2007:59)。主人公努力驱逐"野猫精"对其内心的纠缠,但事实上,"野猫精"与别涅季克特一直如影相随并对其人生的每一步决定都产生了重要影响。

　　与"野猫精"的第一次"会面"使别涅季克特做出向奥莉娅求婚的决定;第二次"会面"他决定开始阅读禁书……最终别涅季克特手持铁钩来到"红楼"杀死了一个"戈卢布奇克",后来又成为岳父的帮凶,以治病为由抢夺别人收藏的禁书。从此,"野猫精"与主人公的关系发展走入了新阶段。当别涅季克特得知,"红楼"里藏着的正是他生活的支柱——书时,他不禁发出与其说是表达人的兴奋不如说是"野猫精"的恐怖怪叫:"斯—斯—斯!!!"当主人公推翻了极权统治对"大穆尔扎"进行惩罚时,他再次表现出酷似"野猫精"的举动:"灵敏地跳上桌子……闭上眼睛脑袋摆来摆去,捂上耳朵,鼓着鼻孔——嗅着空气"。至此,主人公与"野猫精"已完全融为一体。评论家拉多欣认为,"'野猫精'是人类灵魂的一部分……它代表着人类的自私,而非动物的……它是一种人类现象,善于为杀人找到冠冕堂皇的理由,它象征着对过去、对前辈经验的遗忘,它永远闪烁着贪婪、凶恶的目光"(Ладохин,2002)。而科罗斯捷列瓦娅的观点则更为精辟:"结论也许是,'野猫精'并非在那茂密的森林里,而是在人类深奥的心灵中"(Коростелева,2002)。由此可见,小说的名称"野猫精"与主人公心灵的发展是密不可分的。别涅季克特预感到,只有明白自己的内心本质才能获得生活的真理。然而他并未成功,因为他忽视了与老一代人心灵上的交流,当他离他们愈来愈远时,"野猫精"却离他愈来愈近。可以说,小说的名称"野猫精"具有多重象征性含义,它象征着人类的无知、自私、心灵简单化、不会从老一代人那里获取文化经验而达到自我发展与完善;象征着狭隘、愚蠢、思想的笨拙,不会脱离自我情感的圈子冷静地旁观自我;象征着对周围人的妒忌和冷漠,自负、自我满足,只求索取不求奉献。

　　小说中与"野猫精"相对立的另一个神话形象便是象征着爱情与幸福、心灵之纯洁、世界之宁静的"孔雀公主"。对于俄罗斯人来说"孔雀公主"的神话故事永远表达着心中朝夕思慕的梦想,因此小说中它只出现在别涅季克特的幻想与梦境中。它不断激励主人公奔向美好的未来,给他以生存的力量。别涅季克特不止一次地想像着,森林中的空地上铺满了红色郁金香,那里生活着一只美丽的孔雀,它对他说:"你好,别涅季克特,英俊的年轻人,你来问候我了?……我是没有危害的,这你知道,过来吧,让我们亲吻一下……"(Толстая,2007:59)主人公第一次回想起"孔雀公主"的故事是在他初次去"红楼"杀死一个无辜的"戈卢布奇克"而悔恨不已的时候。但他最终还是为自己找到了一个最好的借口:这是为了挽救"书",为了驱逐黑暗,开辟光明,而那里有能给人以宁静和爱的"孔雀公主"。而小说结尾"书"和"孔雀公主"形象的同时出现再次证明,二者象征着不可分割的人类心灵力量的源泉。当别涅季克特开始读"书"时,他觉得自己与"孔雀公主"越来越近;而当他准备放弃岳父的图书馆和赚钱的职业而去寻找梦寐以求的"孔雀公主"时,他又觉得一切都是徒然的:"穿过一座小桥,进入密林深处……那里隐藏着一块空地,一只白色的鸟儿在和风中休憩……突然一个念头涌入脑海:白费劲,既没有空地也没有鸟儿。什么"孔雀公主",早被人用绳索逮走了"(Толстая,2007:314)。

显然,"野猫精"与"孔雀公主"作为两个具有一定文化语义的神话形象,象征着人类心灵的不同层面:善与恶,生与死。它们在主人公别涅季克特的心灵深处彼此对立,同时又相互依存:一方面是令其恐惧的"野猫精",一方面是象征梦想的"孔雀公主"。"别涅季克特——野猫精","别涅季克特——孔雀公主",这两种个性模式在整个小说中不断互相施以影响。可以说,主人公个性的发展是建立在"孔雀公主"形象的变形和"野猫精"形象的脱冕基础之上的。然而在主人公灵魂轨迹的发展中,"孔雀公主"最终被"野猫精"所打败,别涅季克特身上所具有的人性,最终被代表无知、野蛮与精神贫乏的"野猫精"所取代。作家在这里所要表达的对年轻一代乃至整个人类社会的失望情绪不言而喻。由此,小说的名称"野猫精"不仅给人带来多重遐想,也蕴含着作家高度的哲理性思索:人类灵魂中善与恶的永恒存在以及人类的堕落终将导致自我解体与自我毁灭。

显然,托尔斯泰娅以自己形式独特、内涵丰富的艺术创作展现了生活的悲剧性因素,同时又将俄罗斯后现代主义文学所具有的"戏谑"精神赋予苦难的俄罗斯民族一剂乐观的"良药"。与苏联文学中现实主义作家的创作相比,托尔斯泰娅作品中的反乌托邦思想具有浓厚的文体意识和解构意识,作家不再像以往大多数苏联作家那样执著于表现鲜明的政治—历史—社会观念,而是将反乌托邦主义思想融入自身的艺术形式探索中,从而在文化立场的高度而不是在政治—意识形态立场的高度实现了对乌托邦主义的反动,其作品中透出的怀疑主义与对荒诞的冷峻感悟克服了传统现实主义文本的单纯的理性主义激情。因而可以说,作为俄罗斯后现代主义文学的一部重要作品,《野猫精》中的反乌托邦思想也更具普遍性和彻底性。

4 结 语

　　值得一提的是，小说《野猫精》写于1986至2000年，正值苏联解体前后俄罗斯社会转型的动荡时期。旧的体制刚刚瓦解，新的体制下社会问题丛生。小说《野猫精》在此过程中完成，可以说，它恰恰侧面反映了当代俄罗斯在经济、政治、道德领域上所遭遇的精神危机，俄罗斯在国际社会角色的转换，古老文化传统的遗失。正如拉多欣所公正指出的："在整个小说的撰写过程中既有个人的发展，也有国家的发展，既有幻想的破灭，也有理想的获得"（Ладохин，2002）。昔日"帝国"俄罗斯在新时期的社会转型过程中何去何从，模仿西欧的当代社会模式还是以俄罗斯民族精神为归宿，这种始自19世纪四、五十年代斯拉夫派与西欧派之间的两难抉择在当代作家塔·托尔斯泰娅的小说《野猫精》里与其说不难找到相似的影射，不如说演变为了一种理性主义精神的高度升华。新斯拉夫主义者索尔仁尼琴曾在其"政论三部曲"之一的《倾塌的俄罗斯》（1998年）里指出，"俄罗斯正处在一个全面'倾塌'的过程中，分崩离析的国家体制和民族意识，将最终导致俄罗斯民族的衰落甚至消亡……"（转自刘文飞，2006：369），而托尔斯泰娅在《野猫精》里创作的毁灭性爆炸之后的莫斯科"神话"可谓是对索尔仁尼琴思想的别样阐释。作家以自己的方式表达了反乌托邦思想的清醒意识，同时将民族出路的诸多问题上升到全人类的高度，从人类存在的视角出发为我们提出了文化对于文明发展的重要意义。如果说民族精神的认同对于一个民族而言是一种广义的"乡土意识"，那么托尔斯泰娅对于"古文化"的倡导无疑是寓意更为宽广的人类整体文化层面上的"乡土意识"。简言之，《野猫精》作为人类发展的一部灾难性预言，在号称文明、飞跃进步的新世纪对人类灾难的提醒，对于我们将是一种道德上的启迪。

参考文献

[1] Парамонов, Б. 2010. Русская история наконец оправдала[J]. себя в литературе 10. (14)：12-15.

[2] Степанян, К. 2001. Отношение бытия к небытию[J]. Знамя (3)：215-217.

[3] Толстая, Т. 2007. Кысь[M]. Москва：Эксмо.

[4] Ладохин, П. 2002. Кыш, Кысь, кыш! [J]. Русская словесность (1)：40-43.

[5] Коростелева, Т. 2002. В лесах, где живет Кысь[O]. из http://www.pr.azov.net/archiv/2002/No_174/kni.htm.

[6] 刘文飞，2006.《伊阿诺斯，或双头鹰：俄国文学和文化中斯拉夫派和西方派的思想对峙》[M]. 北京：中国社会科学出版社.

翻译研究

"被××"反讽句的跨文化阐释及英译*

上海财经大学 姚 俊**

摘要:本文从反讽认知的角度考察了"被××"反讽结构的语义特征,比较了汉英两种语言中有标记被动句的异同。我们发现,"主语作为受事直接受损害"是原型汉语被动句的语义特征。英汉被动句的差异在于人们对施事与主语之间产生影响程度的容忍度不同。表"受益"义的被动句在英汉两种语言中都是有标记的;无所谓"受损"和"受益"的被动句,在英语中是无标记的,在汉语中却是有标记的。基于此差异,本研究根据Chakhachiro的反讽翻译模式,通过语料分析,提出了"被××"反讽句在不同语义类型下的英译策略。

关键词:"被××"反讽句;语义特征;有标记被动句;翻译策略

Title: The Cross-cultural Explanation and Translation of Ironical Chinese *Bei*-passives

Abstract: The paper examines the semantic features of ironical Chinese *bei*-passives from the perspective of irony identification. In addition, it compares the semantic features of marked passives between Chinese and English. It is found that the semantic property of prototypical Chinese *bei*-passives is that the subject is acted upon in an adverse way. The difference between Chinese *bei*-passives and English passives lies in people's "tolerance" toward evaluative meaning of "being neutral" and

---

* 本研究是2018年国家公派访问学者项目"中英跨文化沟通语用研究"(编号:201806485010)的部分成果。

** 作者简介:姚俊,上海财经大学副教授。研究方向:语用学、对比语言学和话语分析。邮箱:virginiayj@126.com。

degrees of "indirectness" in terms of the correlation between the causer and the affected entity. Passives with the subject being positively affected are marked both in Chinese and English. However, passives with the subject being neither negatively nor positively affected are unmarked in English and marked in Chinese. Based on the findings of the comparison and the data analysis, several strategies of translating Chinese ironical *bei*-passives into English are suggested corresponding to different semantic categories with Chakhachiro's irony translation model as an application tool.

Key words: ironical Chinese *bei*-passives; semantic feature; marked passives; translation strategies

1 引 言

"被××"反讽句自2009年以来风靡已久。各种新奇的"被××"结构,如"被就业、被涨薪、被代表、被自杀、被和谐"等等至今仍然频频出现在报纸、杂志、网络新闻中,这些结构充分表达了人们对媒体报道的失实、权威机构公布的虚假数据、迫于权势而实施的行为等"别扭的被动现实"的无奈与失望。"被××"结构如何能够反映这些社会现象并得到中国公众的广泛认可?作为频繁出现在新闻媒体上的语言,它如何被读者解读?在跨文化交际中我们怎样让非汉语背景者领悟这种特殊的反讽表达?本文将考察"被××"结构作为反讽的认知,比较汉英两种语言的被动句语义特征,在此基础上,借鉴Chakhachiro(2011)的反讽翻译原则,结合语料分析,提出该结构在主要语义类型下的英译策略。

2 "被××"结构作为反讽的认知

反讽的认知除了语境的作用外,往往是该语言结构的使用偏离了人们在日常生活中形成的固定模式,从而引导读者解读作者的反讽意图(Yus,2000)。这种现象被称为反讽暗示(ironic cues)。"被××"反讽句也是如此。除了引号产生的暗示外,一些"被××"结构的使用偏离了汉语被动句的基本语义特征,从而导致读者探寻作者的反讽意义。

2.1 汉语被动句的基本语义特征

汉语被动句的"被动意义"多是表达不如意或者不企望的事情(王力,1957)。这种观点为很多汉语学者所接受。其中,李宗江(2004)从历史、认知和语言类型学的角度进一步论证了这一汉语被动句的语义特征。他考察了古汉语、现代汉语叙事性文学作品以及报刊语言中的被动句,经统计发现大多数的被动句都具有"有损"的语义倾向。据此,李宗江提出原型汉语被动句的语义特征是表达主语受到了直接的损害。围绕这个原型,他从主语受影响程度出发归纳了三个层次的语义特征,即作为受事直接受损害、受负面影响、间接受负面影响。

主语作为受事直接受损害的被动句中,"被"字后的谓语动词具有"损害"的语义特征,主语作为动词的受事直接受损害。"被杀""被抢""被灭""被抓"等被动结构都是典型的原型汉语被动式的例子。

主语受到负面影响的被动句中,主要动词没有"损害"的语义特征,但整个谓语对主语来说有负面影响,或者是主语不情愿、不企望的事情。例如:他没料到被老王认出来了。

第三类被动句的主语不是谓语动词的受事,主语与主要谓语动词没有直接的语义关系,只是整个由"被"参与构成的句子对主语或者某个句中或句外的相关对象构成不利影响,是主语或者某个相关对象所不情愿或者不企望发生的。例如:贾政还要打时,早被王夫人抱住板子(《红楼梦》33 回)(李宗江,2004:8)。

上述三个层次的语义特征中,"主语作为受事直接受损害"是原型汉语被动句的语义特征,另外两个层次在汉语背景者看来也是自然的,无标记的。

2.2 "被××"反讽句的反讽语义暗示

为了考察"被××"反讽句的语言暗示形式,笔者从 2009 年 8 月到 2010 年 8 月的网络报刊新闻中收集了 140 个"被××"反讽句的例子。分析发现,一些有标记汉语被动句往往能够暗示作者的反讽意图。

本文提到的有标记汉语被动句是指不符合汉语背景者在日常生活中使用被动句的常用模式,对汉语背景者来说是不自然的被动句。从语义特征来看,根据主语受影响程度,主语作为受事直接受损害是原型,主语受到负面影响以及间接受负面影响都是可接受的,是无标记的。但是,如果被动句的主语没有受到被动句所涉事件的负面影响甚至从该事件中"受益",这就不符合汉语背景者使用被动句的习惯,这种被动句便是有标记的。这种有标记性往往促发读者识别作者的反讽意图。

汉语被动句的标记性主要体现在情感意义上。虽然主语受影响程度不同,但是只要表示"有损"义,都是无标记的。如果被动句表达的情感意义无所谓受损或者受益,或者表达"受益"义,这些被动句都是非典型的、有标记的。正因为无标记被动句的"有损"

义特征,汉语背景者能够迅速觉察"被××"反讽句的语义异常,并结合语境,解读作者的反讽意义。例如:

(1) 最热夏天:预报和实际感受差距大 市民怀疑"被清凉"

(新华网 2010 - 08 - 10)

(2) 福州"被宜居"了? 宜居福州讨论持续升温

(福州要闻 2010 - 07 - 08)

(3) 于是,那些原本在小康水平之下的群众,一夜之间就"被小康"了。

(重庆日报 2010 - 03 - 04)

(4) 半数孩子的暑期"被计划" 平均培训 23.7 天

(深圳新闻网 2010 - 8 - 6)

例(1)中的"清凉"、例(2)中的"宜居"和例(3)中的"小康"都表达了人们受益的概念,这与典型的"有损"义被动句不一致,有明显的标记性。例(4)的"计划"是一个中性词,无所谓受损或受益。因此,这一被动句也是有标记的,它的标记程度介于受损义与受益义之间。

但是,并非所有的"被××"反讽句都是在语义上有标记的被动句,正如并非所有的反讽都存在语言暗示一样,语境对反讽的认知起着决定性作用(姚俊,2008)。尽管如此,语义上有标记的被动句代表了相当一部分"被××"反讽句。

2.3 "被××"反讽句的深层语义结构

曹道根(2009)分析了汉语被动句事件结构的句法映射过程,提出非直接短被动句的句法模式:受影响者/主语+被动标记和转指成分"被"+隐性主要谓语(标记对象和转指对象)+次要谓语。从表层结构来看,"被××"似乎归属非直接短被动句。但是,通过对 140 个"被"字反讽句的分析,我们发现这些"被"字句由间接长被动句演变而来,它们均表达了某种使役意义,都存在一个缺乏语音形态的使役动词或者处置式动词,其深层句法模式可归纳如下:

受影响者/主语+被+(使役者)+(隐性主要谓语)+显性次要谓语

上述模式中,使役者与主要谓语常常省略,构成最常见的"受影响者/主语+被+显性次要谓语"结构。在"被××"反讽句中,主要涉及两个事件参与者:受影响者与使役者,反讽的对象往往是使役者。尽管使役者未在表层结构中出现,读者仍然能够通过语境确认使役者身份。我们发现,"被"字反讽句的使役者及隐性主要谓语在语义上具有一定的规律性。使役者通常是这个主要谓语的施事,往往享有某种特权或者处于强势地位。隐性主要谓语表达使役者实施的特权行为。

3 "被××"反讽句的跨文化阐释

"被××"结构使用的标记性作为反讽暗示被汉语背景者识别。那么,在跨文化交际中我们怎样阐释,让非汉语背景者领悟这种特殊的反讽表达？我们先讨论有标记汉语被动句与英语被动句在语义特征上的差异。

3.1 有标记汉语被动句与英语被动句在语义特征上的差异

李宗江(2004)指出,表"有损"义的被动句在任何语言里都是最典型的,是无标记的,不同语言的区别是对非"有损"义的宽容程度。就汉语与英语而言,表"受益"义的被动句在两种语言中都是有标记的;无所谓受损和受益的被动句,在英语中是无标记的,在汉语中却是有标记的。这种差异缘于英语中 be 型被动句与 get 型被动句的并存。Huang (1999)明确指出,be 型被动句通常不表"有损"义而 get 型被动句在很多情况下都表"有损"义。所以,有标记英语被动句仅限于表"受益"义的被动句,而有标记汉语被动句则包括表"受益"义和无所谓受损和受益义的被动句。

3.2 "被××"结构作为反讽的语义阐释

当被动句表"受益"义时,两种语言背景的人都能领悟该语言结构的标记性,能够结合语境探悉作者的反讽意图。但是,当"被××"结构表达无所谓受损和受益义时,英语背景者将如何理解这种反讽暗示？他们需要知道两点:首先,汉语的无标记被动句仅限于表"有损"义,表"受益"义或者无所谓受损和受益义的被动句都是有标记的,违背了汉语背景者使用被动句的固定模式,从而作为反讽暗示引起读者的注意。

此外,"被××"反讽句的深层语义模式为:受影响者/主语＋被＋(使役者)＋(隐性主要谓语)＋显性次要谓语。反讽的对象往往是未出现在表层结构中的使役者。主语与"被"后面的动词存在一定的语义关联,这种语义关联实际上是一种使役事件造成的结果。

在跨文化交际中,如何将"被××"反讽句的隐含意义传达给英语背景者,同时保留原文的反讽色彩,这无疑是个翻译的难题。

4 反讽的翻译原则

反讽作为一种与语境密切相关的语用现象,具备其特有的交际功能和修辞意义。

Chakhachiro(2011)指出,反讽的翻译必须兼顾其交际功能和文本的修辞意义。他归纳了反讽在议论文体中的四大交际功能:1) 向读者表明态度和立场;2) 表明对反讽对象(个人,政府,政治党派,情景等)的态度;3) 传达一个具体的信息;4) 确保读者介入、维持与读者的和谐关系。同时,他借鉴 Crystal 和 Davy (1973)的三个情景维度概括了文本的修辞意义。这三个维度是态度(attitude)、介入程度(participation)和话题范畴(province)。态度涉及作者的观点、文本的语气以及作者偶尔表现的特有语言特征。介入程度指作者与读者、作者与反讽对象、作者与间接话语参与者的社会角色关系。话题范畴涉及不同文本类型特有的语言文化策略、互文性以及情境语境。Chakhachiro(2011:90)提出了反讽翻译的原则:首先找出原文的反讽手段(ironic devices),然后结合其交际功能分析文本的修辞意义,最终选择目标语与原文功能对等的反讽手段以确保译文与原文的修辞意义和文本展开策略保持一致。

5 "被××"结构在主要语义类型中的英译策略

根据 Chakhachiro 的反讽翻译模式,首先需要找出原文的反讽手段。就本文而言,"被××"结构就是汉语的反讽手段。这种反讽形式借助被动句来实现,是汉语特有的语法类反讽手段,在英语中没有完全对应的反讽形式。因此,我们只能找出英语中在类似语境下,实现类似交际功能的反讽手段。Chakhachiro(2011:211)的语料分析显示,英语议论文中常用的反讽手段包括:1) 词汇手段:系动词、对人物的称呼、表达观点的时间与数量副词,情态动词、复合名词、特定形容词以及习语等等;2) 语法手段:省略、分裂句、第二人称单复数、祈使语气、总结性状语、后置修饰语、指称;3) 副语言手段:斜体。Chakhachiro 指出,英语最典型、最常见的反讽形式是表达观点的标记词(opinion markers)的应用。

其次,我们需要分析"被××"结构作为汉语反讽手段所具备的特定交际功能和修辞意义。"被××"结构通常出现在报刊、网络的时事评论中,属于议论文本。该结构往往含蓄地揭示了弱势群体遭遇强权,遭受某种侵害的事实。前面我们探讨了该结构的深层语义模式,它反映了一种使役事件结构,由于主语受到使役者不同程度的影响,文本传达了不同类别的信息。下面,我们根据不同类别信息,探讨相应的英译方式。

根据"被××"结构中的隐性主要谓语类型与主语受影响程度,我们把该反讽句分为三类:伪造假象类、胁迫行为类以及诬蔑冤枉类,针对这三种类别,相应的翻译方法为:直译法、语义对立法以及观点评述法。

5.1 直译法

伪造假象类所叙事件的使役者往往是媒体、职能部门或者权威机构,他们报道或者发布虚假信息,瞒报甚至歪曲事实,为了炫耀政绩或者获取某种利益,制造美好假象,使公众受到蒙蔽。公众作为受影响者,就其受影响程度而言,这一类最轻。作者往往站在公众的立场,用自嘲的语气表达人们面对信息不透明的社会现象的失望与无奈。这类"被××"结构从字面上常常表达主语"受益"义,是有标记汉语被动句。在译成英语时,由于表"受益"义的被动句在英语中也是有标记的,英语背景者很容易识别原文的反讽意图。由于两种语言在这一点上语义与形式对等,我们不妨采用直译法,用被动句式"be reported/be said"把"被××"深层语义结构中的隐性主要谓语译出来,同时使用斜体或者引号即可(例5和例6)。

(5) 最热夏天:预报和实际感受差距大 市民怀疑"被清凉"
The hottest summer: there was a big difference between the weather forecast and the real feeling. Citizens suspected that they "were reported to feel cool"

(6) 福州"被宜居"了? 宜居福州讨论持续升温。
Has Fuzhou "been said to be liveable"? A discussion about a liveable Fuzhou continues to heat up.

当然,"被××"结构中的隐性主要谓语也可以用不同词性翻译出来,暗示反讽对象,原文的反讽效果依然存在。例如:

(7) 于是,那些原本在小康水平之下的群众,一夜之间就"被小康"了。
Consequently, those who originally lived below the level of moderate prosperity "were statistically known as being moderately rich".

此类语义中,我们可以采取类似的翻译方法,如"被第一"(to be said to rank first)、"被强大"(to be said to be strong)、"被就业"(be said/reported to be employed)"被涨薪"(be statistically/reportedly known as getting a raise) 等等,都可以保留原文的被动句式,借助隐性主要谓语的现身暗示反讽对象,达到译文的反讽效果。

5.2 语义对立法

胁迫行为类的使役者是享有特权的机构或者个人,他们利用特权施加压力,迫使受影响者实施违心的行为。这类结构的隐性主要谓语都含有逼迫、威胁的意思,描述了一种弱势群体受强势权力摆布的不自由状态。就受影响程度而言,这类事件介于其他两类之间。此类"被××"结构字面上表达主语"受损"义或者无所谓受损受益的情形较多,在英语中都是无标记被动句。翻译时,直译法无法让英语背景者领悟反讽的存在。因此,我们采用英语的反讽手段——语义对立法(传统修辞学称作"矛盾修饰法Oxymoron")进行翻译。首先用被动句式"be pressured /be forced"译出"被迫、不情愿"的意义,再利用与其语义相矛盾(例8和例9)或者不匹配(例10和例11)的形容词或者副词,造成明显的语义异常,使英语背景者迅速领悟原文的反讽意义。

(8) 河南镇平拟投2.3亿建高中 居民抱怨"被捐款"

(中国新闻网 2010-05-27)

Zhenping County in Henan Province planed to raise fund of RMB 230,000,000 to build high schools and the citizens there complained that they "were pressured to donate willingly".

(9) 青州公务员"被自愿"加班?宣传部称系自发

(羊城晚报 2010-08-07)

Civil servants in Qingzhou were forced to overwork "voluntarily"? Publicity Department claimed that they volunteered to do so.

(10) "被参加"广州亚运会,对刘翔来说,究竟是福还是祸?

(钱江晚报 2010-08-03)

"Being forced to actively take part in" the Guangzhou Asian Games, is it a fortune or a misfortune to Liu Xiang, the 110 metre hurdles champion in the 2004 Olympic Games?

(11) 端午节成"相亲节""80后"无奈"被相亲"

(新华网 2010-06-16)

The Dragon-Boat-Festival becomes "Blind-date Day" and the Post-80s Generation "were pressured to have a happy blind date"

例8与例9译文的语义对立十分明显,"willingly"和"voluntarily"与"are pressured"和"are forced"形成鲜明对比,英语背景者一目了然。例10与例11中,"actively"和"happy"与"被迫、不情愿"在语义上基调不一致、不匹配,这两个词是译者特意加入译文的,旨在暗示原文用词异常,这种异样有助于英语背景者洞察原文的反讽意图,保留原文的反讽风格。

5.3 观点评述法

诬蔑冤枉类中受影响者被某些个人或者机构利用、冤枉,其权益往往受到严重侵害。就受影响程度而言,受影响者遭受的危害程度最大。此类"被××"结构中的隐性主要谓语语义范围十分广泛,字面上主语受损或者受益的情况都存在。因此,翻译时译者应当在译文中添加表达观点的词汇,这样既应用了英语最典型的反讽手段表达文本修辞意义,又明确了原作者的态度,确保了原文反讽交际功能的实现。一些表达观点的词汇,如"allegedly, so-called, scandal, assumed, presumed",或者具有评判意义的构词成分,如"mis-, -gate",都可以巧妙应用到译文中。

(12) 这次孙红雷得知自己"被传记"的消息也很无奈。

(西安晚报 2010 - 07 - 21)

This time when Sun Honglei got to know that he "had a so-called biography published", he said he had no alternative but to live with it.

(13) 父女"被梅毒"治疗花 120 万 "专家"被拘竟不识字

(南宁晚报 2010 - 06 - 17)

Father and daughter "were misdiagnosed with so-called syphilis" and it cost them ￥1,200,000 RMB for the treatment. However, it turned out that the arrested "expert" was an illiterate.

(14) 65 岁的中国科学院院士、北京大学教授丁伟岳表示自己"被委员"。

(两会盘点之走红群体——被一族,广州日报 2010 - 03 - 14)

65-year-old academician of the Chinese Academy of Science, Professor Ding Weiyue at Beijing University suggested that he "was allegedly known as a committee member".

(15) 白岩松网上"被自杀"回应称"生活还那样"

(来源:tom 娱乐 2009 - 10 - 29)

Bai Yansong who "was officially assumed to have committed suicide" online responded by saying "Life goes on the same way".

一些常见的媒体八卦新闻,如"被分手"(split scandal)、"被结婚"(marriage scandal)、"被失踪"(to be presumed to have disappeared)、"被潜规则"(to fall victim to the so-called unspoken rules)、"被怀孕"(pregnancy-gate)等等,都可以采用类似的翻译方法,确保反讽意义的传达。

6 结　语

本文从反讽认知的角度探讨了"被××"结构作为有标记汉语被动句的语义特征。

汉英两种语言中有标记被动句的差异在于汉语有标记被动句包括表"受益"义和无所谓受损和受益义的被动句,而英语有标记被动句仅限于表"受益"义的被动句。基于这一差异,在翻译"被××"反讽句时,针对不同的文本,我们应当采取不同的翻译策略。本文根据 Chakhachiro 的反讽翻译模式,按照"被××"结构的语义类型分类,提出了直译法、语义对立法以及观点评述法三种针对"被××"反讽句的翻译策略。本研究作为反讽翻译研究的补充,一方面验证了翻译研究中语言对比分析对翻译的重要性,另一方面为反讽研究提供了一个新的视角。

参考文献

[1] Chakhachiro, R. 2011. *Translating Irony: An Interdisciplinary Approach with English and Arabic as a Case in Point*[M]. London: Sayyab Books Ltd.
[2] Crystal, D. & D. Davy. 1973. Stylistic analysis[A]. In J. P. B. Allen & S. Pit Corder (eds.). *Readings for Applied Linguistics*[C]. London: Oxford University Press, 69–90.
[3] Huang, J. 1999. Chinese Passives in Comparative Perspective[J]. *Tsing Hua Journal of Chinese Studies*, 29: 423–509.
[4] Yao, J., J. Song and M. Singh. 2013. The ironical Chinese bei-construction and its accessibility to English speakers[J]. *Journal of Pragmatics*, 55: 195–209.
[5] Yus, F. 2000. On reaching the intended ironic interpretation[J]. *International Journal of Communication*, 10 (1–2): 27–78.
[6] 曹道根,2004.反语隐性展示理论的心理空间模式[J].外语与翻译,(1):1–7.
[7] 曹道根,2009.汉语被动句的事件结构及其形态句法实现[J].现代外语,(1):1–12.
[8] 邓思颖,2004.作格化和汉语被动句[J].中国语文,(4):291–301.
[9] 李宗江,2004.汉语被动句的语义特征及其认知解释[J].解放军外国语学院学报,(6):7–11.
[10] 刘飞兵,2007.反语使用的认知与心理动机[J].外语学刊,(4):82–85.
[11] 邵敬敏,赵春利,2005."致使把字句"和"省隐被字句"及其语用解释[J].汉语学习,(4):11–18.
[12] 石定栩,2005."被"字句的归属[J].汉语学报,(1):38–48.
[13] 王力,1957.汉语被动式的发展[J].语言学论丛第1辑,1–16.
[14] 文旭,2004.反讽话语的认知语用研究[M].北京:中国社会科学出版社.
[15] 熊仲儒,2003.汉语被动句句法结构分析[J].当代语言学,(3):206–221.
[16] 姚俊,2008.反讽暗示的形式与功能[J].中国外语,(2):22–26.

前沿动态

基于 CiteSpace 的国外语言学领域立场研究*

江苏科技大学/南京大学　夏　秸　南京大学　陈新仁**

摘要:本研究基于 Web of Science(WoS)数据库,借助 CiteSpace 软件对国外语言学领域 1980—2017 年间的立场研究英文文献进行统计分析。研究内容包括:(1) 立场的年度发文趋势;(2) 立场的研究对象,主要涉及研究话题、立场类别、语体和体裁等方面;(3) 立场的高被引文献、高被引作者和高被引期刊。研究发现:立场的年度发文 2000 年起逐年递增;立场涉及的研究话题呈现学科互补和议题交叉的特征,情感立场的研究有待加强,研究语体以口语语体为主,体裁涉及日常会话及多种机构话语;高被引文献以互动路径下的研究为主,高被引作者呈现多学派特征,高被引期刊反映了立场研究的多种属性。本研究有利于帮助国内学者把握国外语言学立场研究的前沿和发展趋势,促进国内语言学立场研究的发展。

关键词:立场;CiteSpace;议题;趋势

Title: A Citespace-based Analysis of Linguistic Stance Research Abroad

Abstract: Based on the database of Web of Science (WoS), this study conducts an analysis of linguistic stance research abroad from 1980 to 2017 by using CiteSpace. The study examines the following three aspects: (1) the trend of published works in stance research; (2) the research issues in stance research, including research topics,

---

* 本文系江苏科技大学 2017 年在职攻读博士学位科研启动基金项目"师生学术指导问答话语中的身份建构"(编号:1072931703)的阶段性成果。

** 作者简介:夏秸,江苏科技大学讲师,南京大学博士。研究方向为语用学理论与实践。邮箱:xiajie132@163.com。陈新仁,南京大学教授、博士生导师。研究方向为语用学理论与实践。邮箱:chenxr1010@163.com。

stance types, registers, and genres; (3) the most frequently cited references, authors, and journals. It is found that there has been a steady increase in the number of published works on stance since 2000; the research issues on stance research are characterized by interdisciplinary studies and intersectional studies; studies on affective stance need further investigation; stance research in spoken registers is the focus of current studies; and stance research involves either daily conversations or institutional discourse; the most frequently cited references follow the interactional approach of stance; the most frequently cited authors come from different schools of linguistics; and the most highly cited journals reflected the multifaceted nature of stance. This study can help Chinese scholars to grasp the trend of international linguistic stance research, which helps to promote linguistic stance research in China.

Key words: stance; CiteSpace; issues; trend

1 引言

立场是交际者参与者主体性的表达，其蕴含着主体对客体的态度、情感及认识。作为交际的重要特征之一，它受到语言学界的广泛关注。近三十年来，研究者从语言学的不同视角对其进行研究，产生大量的研究成果。

对立场研究文献的分析可以帮助学者把握研究现状和趋势，从而找到研究空白，助力立场的创新性研究。目前，国外学者从主体性和主体间性的视角梳理了语料库语言学、系统功能语言学以及互动路径下的立场研究（Haddington，2013）。国内学者总结了语法—语义、功能和互动视角下对立场的不同概念界定及研究模式（罗桂花，2014），发现立场经历了语料库语言学视角、系统功能语言学视角和社会学视角的演进（柳淑芬，2017）。以上研究梳理了立场的研究路径，有助于我们从宏观上把握立场研究的视角和认识论发展趋向。然而，不同研究路径之间并不是孤立的，而是密切联系，互为补充的。同时，立场本身具有复杂性和多层面性（Englebretson，2007），是一种复杂的语言、认知和社会现象（Haddington，2013）。因此，对于立场的研究者而言，为了更精准地把握立场研究的现状及趋势，确定研究选题，还需要从微观角度从对于立场研究特征进行多层面的具体分析。

关于立场研究，我们至少还需关注以下几个问题：首先，迄今为止的立场的研究是否具有阶段性发展特征？其次，虽然不同路径对于立场的研究界定不尽相同，但是立场作为交际的重要特征之一,它与哪些语言学领域的热点研究话题密切关联?这些研究话题涉及哪些立场类别、语体和体裁?再次,立场研究领域涉及哪些影响力的文献和研究者?最后,立场研究相关的论文在哪些期刊发表?把握立场研究的阶段性特征有助于研究者知悉立场研究的发展规律,从而对自己的研究进行合理定位;了解立场研究相关的热点话题有助于研究者找到研究切入点,将立场研究与当前语言学领域的研究热点对接。这样可以凸显立场对于相关议题的研究价值,同时也推动对于相关研究议题的进一步研究;通过了解立场研究的重要文献和主要研究者,可以减少文献阅读的盲目性,基于有影响力的研究者的重要文献开展创新性研究;熟悉立场研究论文国际期刊发表的阵地,可以帮助研究者及时掌握国际立场研究方面的最近成果动态,同时也为该议题论文的国际发表提供目标期刊方面的参考。

随着文献检索技术的发展,以往基于文献数据库人工搜集、整理文献的方式被更先进的文献分析软件所取代。CiteSpace 文献分析软件则是一款功能强大的文献被引分析软件,它能够帮助学者更准确地把握某一研究领域或研究话题的发文趋势、研究议题特征及文献、作者和期刊共被引情况。迄今为止,语言学研究者(李民、肖雁,2015;袁周敏、刘环环,2017)借助该软件对语言学领域的多个议题进行了文献分析,为相关议题的研究提供指导。为解决上述关于立场研究现状的相关问题,深化对立场研究特征的认识,帮助国内学者更好地把握国外语言学领域立场研究的现状及趋势,本研究基于 Web of Science(WoS)数据库,借助 CiteSpace 软件对国外语言学领域 1980—2017 年间的立场研究文献进行统计分析。拟通过统计以下几个方面的指标解决本文的研究问题:一、立场研究的发文趋势;二、立场研究的主题词被引情况;三、立场研究的文献共被引情况;四、立场研究的作者共被引情况;五、立场研究的期刊共被引情况。

2 研究方法

2.1 研究工具

本文的研究工具是 CiteSpace 5.1 R8. SE 版本的可视化分析软件。CiteSpace 是一款在科学计量学、数据和信息可视化背景下逐渐发展起来的一款引文可视化分析软件(李杰、陈超美,2016)。本研究使用其相关功能进行文献检索和分析。

2.2 数据来源和处理方法

为提高文献的权威性,本研究的文献来自 WoS 核心数据库中人文社科领域的两大权威文献数据库——SSCI 和 A&HCI 数据库,检索时间段设定为 1980 年到 2017 年,以 stance（立场）为检索词①，以"主题词"为检索项。

首先，我们在 WoS 数据库内对 stance（立场）进行主题检索，不限定学科，语种选择"英语"，文献类型选择"文章"，得到立场相关文献在 WoS 的一百多个学科门类的数量分布情况。然后，使用 WoS 的精炼功能，学科类别选择"语言学"和"语言语言学"两个类别，数据类型为"文章"，语种选择"英语"，共检索到 895 条记录；然后，分别选择相应的选项分析关键词共现情况、文献共被引、作者共被引和期刊共被引情况，生成关键词共现以及文献、作者和期刊共被引情况的可视化图谱及相关数据统计总表。

3 研究结果分析及讨论

3.1 语言学立场的发文趋势

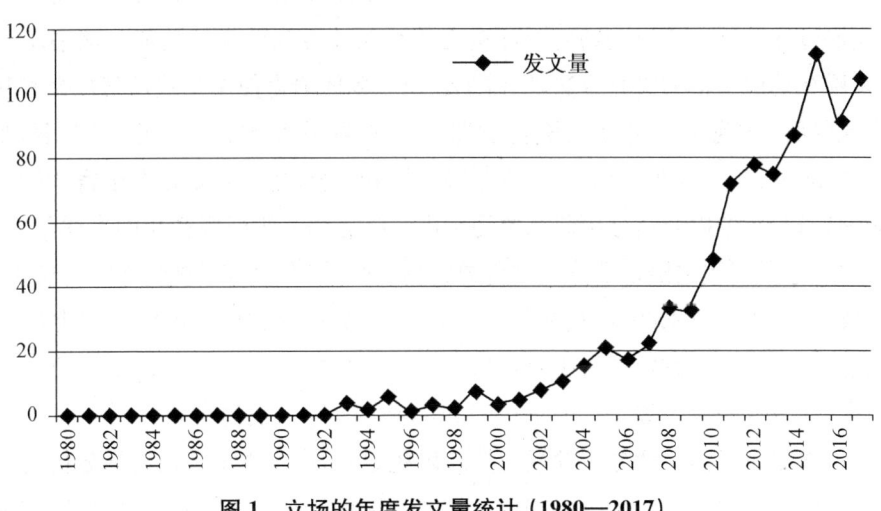

图 1 立场的年度发文量统计（1980—2017）

由图可见，立场研究发文量的总体发展趋势：自 1980 年开始到 2000 年期间，发文量较少，且没有显著变化。但从 2000 年开始，发文量稳步增加，至 2015 年达到最高值（112 篇）。可见，近二十年来立场逐步成为话语分析的热点议题（柳淑芬，2017），同时也是语言学领域的热点议题。

根据发文量我们可以大致将近三十年来的立场研究分为三个时期：早期（1989—1999 年）、发展期（2000—2009 年）和鼎盛期（2010—至今）。首先，在研究早期，立场研究以语法—语义视角为主。该路径认为语言是立场的编码手段，立场通过言语或非言

---

① 一些术语如"evaluation"、"appraisal"等与立场有相似之处，但研究路径和术语的内涵有所差异，为避免术语混乱，同时增加检索结果的相关性，这里仅使用 stance 作为检索词。

语的表征形式实现。主要采用语料库方法，基于语料库考察不同语义类型的立场语言实现形式以及不同体裁的立场标记特征。最早的研究出现在 1990 年前，比如 Biber & Finegan(1988，1989)基于语料库分析了立场的词汇和语法标记特征及其所呈现的不同言语风格。由于立场是通过语言表征的，对立场语言实现手段的研究为后续功能路径和互动路径的立场研究奠定了基础。其次，在发展期，立场研究主要是互动语言学的研究。长期以来，在话语分析领域，学者从话语功能视角探讨语言使用中语法形式和结构的功能动因。20 世纪 90 年代以来，学者越来越认识到对语言使用特征的研究离不开对社会互动模式的研究(Ford & Wager, 1996)，因此在话语国内分析的基础上借鉴会话分析的研究方法和成果，对互动中的语言使用进行分析（Couper-Kuhlen & Selting, 1996；Ford & Wagner, 1996；Selting & Couper-Kuhlen, 2001；Ford, Fox, & Thompson, 2002），探讨互动对于句法的塑造作用，以及句法形式对于互动实践的限制作用。该方法被称为互动语言学的分析方法。然而，一直以来，立场的互动研究并没有受到较多关注。Kärkkäinen(2003)在其专著中指出认识立场是口语互动中普遍存在的表达，应探讨在会话中认识立场的语言模式及其在社会互动中的功能。该书基于实证分析，采用互动语言学的研究方法，探讨了认识立场的语言使用模式及其社会和互动功能。自此以后，出现了大量互动语言学路径下立场研究的论文(集)和专著，如 Wu(2004)、Englebretson(2007)等。最后，鼎盛时期的研究主要包括社会语言学和会话分析视角的研究，其中以会话分析研究更为突出。随着语言学研究视角的多样化趋势，立场研究同时也受到相关语言学分支学科的影响，比如社会语言学视角下的立场研究，代表性的成果，如 Jaffe(2009)的论文集。同时，会话分析研究的不断深入也促进了立场研究的进一步发展，这方面成果主要是采用会话分析的方法对会话互动中的认识立场进行研究，代表性的成果如 Heritage(2012a，2012b)等。随着会话分析中立场研究的深入，认识立场也成为会话分析领域的热点议题之一，产生大量采用会话分析的方法进行立场研究的论文及专著。因此，2010 年到 2017 年立场的发文量最大，且呈现持续快速增长的趋势。

由以上分析可以看出，立场作为语言学领域的研究话题，其发展趋势受到语言学领域本身研究路径发展的影响，其中互动语言学和会话分析对于立场研究的影响较大，分别产生了 2000 年以来的互动语言学研究以及 2010 年以来会话分析的研究高潮。这些研究也增进了对于立场本质属性及其功能的认识，推动了将立场作为孤立语言形式的研究转向会话互动中立场作为互动行为的研究，从关注立场话语功能逐渐发展到关注其社会及互动功能的研究。因此，当前研究者对于立场的研究应该考虑到语言学研究领域的发展现状，推动当今互动语言学和会话分析研究的深入研究，同时考虑从新兴的研究视角来研究立场研究中尚待解决的问题，这必将为立场研究注入新的活力，进一步推动立场的研究。

3.2 主题词被引情况

对检索到的895条记录进行主题词分析,选择 terms(术语)和 keywords(关键词)选项,生成图2。

由图2可见,以主题词 stance(立场)为中心,周围凸显出的关键词有 language(语言),discourse(话语),conversation(会话),English(英语),talk(谈话),organization(组织),identity(身份)以及 conversation analysis(会话分析)。为进一步分析立场研究的主题词特征,本研究使用 CiteSpace 自带的数据输出功能,得到关于主题词相关的频次和中心性的统计数据。频次和中心性都是分析关键词研究状况的重要指标。高频关键词体现与研究对象相关的热点议题,而中心性是衡量网络结构中节点重要性的指标之一,中心性越大,表明其连接的信息

图2 立场研究主题词可视化图谱

越多,在网络结构中占据的位置越重要(Chen,2006)。比如袁周敏、刘环环(2017)基于主题词的频次和中心性(≥0.1)排名前十位的关键词,分析与研究对象相关的主流研究话题。但是,如表1所示,本研究中频次居前十位的主题词如 stance,conversation 和 language 以及中心性大于等于0.1的关键词如 conversation(会话)(0.14),discourse(话语)(0.18)和 performance(交际行为)(0.16)多属于比较泛化的关键词(俞琳、李福印,2016),不能够反映立场研究相关的具体研究话题。为了获取更多体现与立场研究相关的具体研究话题,本研究将频次统计范围扩大到频次居前40位,主要对其中非泛化的高频关键词进行分析。

表1 频次前四十位的立场共被引关键词频次及中心性

序号	频次	中心性	关键词	序号	频次	中心性	关键词
1	183	0.08	stance	7	65	0.08	identity
2	118	0.14	conversation	8	54	0.07	talk
3	105	0.07	language	9	40	0.06	conversation analysis
4	98	0.18	discourse	10	26	0.05	speech
5	87	0.05	English	11	24	0.09	ideology
6	69	0.09	organization	12	22	0.07	narrative

(续表)

序号	频次	中心性	关键词	序号	频次	中心性	关键词
13	21	0.02	construction	27	15	0.02	Spanish
14	19	0.03	knowledge	28	14	0.02	perspective
15	19	0.02	style	29	14	0.01	information
16	19	0.01	epistemic stance	30	14	0.00	sequence
17	18	0.05	language ideology	31	14	0.03	academic writing
18	17	0.07	evaluation	32	13	0.03	multimodality
19	17	0.06	participation	33	13	0.02	politeness
20	17	0.04	discourse analysis	34	12	0.06	classroom
21	17	0.10	communication	35	12	0.03	gender
22	17	0.16	performance	36	12	0.05	acquisition
23	16	0.02	metadiscourse	37	12	0.00	emotion
24	15	0.08	grammar	38	12	0.09	discourse marker
25	15	0.04	research article	39	12	0.04	repair
26	15	0.02	student	40	11	0.01	humor

下面根据频次情况对主题词进行多角度分析。

1. 研究话题：从研究议题来看，identity(身份)(65次)在立场研究中是一个研究较多的话题。立场作为社会行为和社会身份的核心意义成分，是语言社会化重要的语言资源(Ochs,1993)，是社会文化语言学视角下身份建构的指示方式之一(Bucholtz & Hall,2005)，也是社会语言学视角下立场研究的重要议题(Jaffe,2009)。近年来，学者探讨立场在身份建构中的作用，比如Jacknick & Avni(2017)通过会话分析方法，探讨在线论坛中的参与者通过话语动态建构认识立场从而实施身份工作；Fuoli(2017)则基于语料库的方法，分析企业年报和社会责任报告中的认识立场和态度立场表达建构可信的企业身份；Cekaite(2012)分析了教师与学生之间的互动会话中的情感立场，探究情感立场如何作为资源指示机构身份的。由于身份研究日益成为语言学领域的热门话题，从立场表达的角度切入，可以推动身份建构具体路径的研究，同时也可以从身份角度解读立场表达及管理的语用动因。此外，语用学的经典话题politeness(礼貌)(13次)也是立场研究的对象之一，如对言据性和礼貌(Kamio,1997)、评价和礼貌(Ferenčik,2017)之间关系的探讨。Evaluation(评价)(17次)是立场的重要功能之一，也是系统功能语言学评价理论(Martin & White,2005)中的核心概念。

2. 立场类别：从立场的类别来看，knowledge(知识)，epistemic stance(认识立场)的频次分别为19次，information(信息)(14次)，以上三个关键词都与认识立场相关，可见认识立场是立场研究的主要类别。emotion(感情)出现频次为 12 次,affect(情感)和 affective stance(情感立场)的频次分别为 7 次,可见,立场研究涉及的另一类别是情感立场,与认识立场相比,研究相对较少。尽管有学者较早指出情感在语言交际中的作用(Ochs & Schieffelin,1989),但相对于交际学而言,情感因素在语言学和语用学领域尚未得到足够重视(Langlotz & Locher,2012)。由于情感本身具有多面性和多阶段性(Alba-Juez & Thompson, 2014),尽管人们对于人类情感做了多个视角和多学科的研究,但是它仍然是一个具有复杂性和神秘性的现象。正如 Damasio(2018)指出,虽然情感在人类生活中是无处不在的,但是长期以来科学研究却忽视了对于情感的研究。而认识立场与知识相关,在 1989 年之前已有大量关于认识立场相似概念的语言学研究,如认识情态(Lyons,1977;Palmer,1986)和言据性(Chafe & Nichols,1986)等,这些研究为后续不同路径下认识立场语言表征的识别奠定基础。此外,会话分析领域已有大量关于认识立场的研究,形成了认识状态和认识立场等相关的术语和分析方法(Heritage,2012a,2012b),而情感立场方面的相关成果还比较有限。因此,应该对情感立场作进一步研究,尤其是情感立场的语言表征方式及其动态性和主体间性的研究(Alba-Juez & Mackenzie,2019)。

3. 语体和体裁:在语体形式方面,由表 1 可见,conversation(会话)(118 次)和 discourse(话语)(98 次)是立场语篇的主要形式,是立场研究的主体,其中以会话居多,因此侧重研究口语体。同时,由下表中同样居于前十位的 talk(言谈)(54 次)和 speech(言语)(26 次)的频次来看,相对于书面语篇而言,立场主要研究的是口语语篇。立场在日常口语互动中是普遍存在的。在口语交际中,说话者不仅表达态度、评价和情感,还表达自己的认识立场(Biber, et al,1999)。从研究涉及的体裁来看,我们由表 1 可以看出,在频次前 30 名的关键词中,conversation(对话)(118 次)居首位,其次是 narrative(叙事语篇)(22 次),另外,research article(研究论文)和 academic writing(学术写作)的频次分别为 15 次和 14 次,这表明除了会话语篇之外,学术语篇中的立场也得到较多研究。学术语篇中作者不仅要向读者传达信息,同时也要表达自己的立场和观点,与读者协商意义(Hyland,2005)。同时,由于学习者语言能力的限制,二语学术写作中的立场表达既是学习的难点,也是二语学术话语习得的重点(徐昉,2015)。因此,国内外学者对学术语篇中的立场标记做了大量研究,包括跨语言、跨学科的立场对比研究,以及二语学习者的立场使用研究(钟兰凤、郭晨璐,2017)等。student(学生)(15 次),classroom(课堂)(12 次),acquisition(习得)(12 次)三个关键词说明立场研究与课堂语境和学生语言习得有着密切关系。比如,Kirkham(2011)探讨可课堂讨论中个人风格与认识立场之间的关系,Gablasova et al.(2017)研究了任务及说话者风格对于学生英语口语表达中立场表达的影响作用。

3.3 文献共被引分析

选择 cited reference(被引文献)选项,对检索到 895 条记录进行主题词分析,生成图 3。

图 3 立场文献共被引可视化图谱

由图 3 所示,该图谱可以分为两大主要阵营,上半部分主要以 Du Bois(2007)为中心,下半部分以 Stivers(2008)为中心,位于中间位置的有 Haddington(2006)和 Goodwin(2007)等。

我们取频次前十位且中心性大于 0.05 的共被引文献。如表 2 所示:

表 2 立场共被引前十位的文献频次及中心性

序号	频次	中心性	被引文献
1	49	0.05	Du Bois (2007)
2	39	0.06	Stivers (2008)
3	30	0.02	Schegloff EA(2007)[①]
4	27	0.10	Goodwin (2007)
5	26	0.15	Heritage & Raymond (2005)
6	23	0.01	Schegloff E (2007)
7	23[②]	0.01	Heritage (2012a)
8	22	0.01	Heritage (2012b)
9	21	0.01	Jaffe (2009)
10	20	0.05	Kärkkäinen (2006)

---

① 根据数据结果呈现的信息,此处 Schegloff EA (2007)和下面频次位于第 6 位的 Schegloff E (2007)是同一作者,对应的文献也是相同的,这可能是由于不同出版物的参考文献格式不同。为客观呈现文献统计结果,这里忠实于软件输出的结果。

② 第 6 位和第 7 位频次和中心性均相同,这里按照二者在输出结果表格中出现的先后排列。

由表 2 可见,频次前十位且中心性大于等于 0.05 的共被引文献有 Du Bois(2007)(0.05)、Stivers(2008)(0.06)、Goodwin(2007)(0.12)、Heritage & Raymond (2005)(0.15)、Kärkkäinen(2006)(0.05)。经过分析我们发现高被引文献以下两个方面的特征:

首先,从研究路径上看,以上高被引文献涉及的语言学研究路径有话语功能语言学(Du Bois,2007)、会话分析(Heritage & Raymond,2005;Heritage,2012a,2012b)和互动语言学(Wu,2004;Kärkkäinen,2006;Haddington,2007;Goodwin,2007)。可见,高被引文献多属于互动路径下的立场研究,且都是互动路径下具有较大理论贡献的文献。其次,从该研究内容上看,以上高被引文献大多是在理论、研究视角、研究对象或者研究方法方面有重大创新意义的文献:在理论创新方面,Du Bois (2007)从话语功能语言学视角,将立场定义为实施评价、定位和结盟三个方面功能的公共行为,提出了立场三角理论。该理论区别于以往对于立场的类别划分,将立场视作一个整体性的概念,强调立场的主体性和主体间性的特征,建构了立场表达不同主体和客体之间相互关系,推动了立场研究的理论创新,为后续立场的互动研究奠定重要的理论基础。同时,该理论使用对话句法的理论和分析方法,为分析交际互动中参与者立场表达提供可操作的分析方法;Heritage & Raymond (2005)对会话中认识权力管理的分析以及 Heritage (2012a,2012b)将认识立场引入会话分析,研究会话双方在交际中的实时认识立场变化。他所提出的认识状态和认识立场等概念,是会话中的认识立场研究的理论基础,催生了后续不同会话场景中认识立场动态性的大量研究。在研究视角方面,Kärkkäinen(2006)提出立场不是内在的心理状态,而是在对话互动中浮现的,是交际双方共建的产物。从多个语言层面探讨了立场从主体性到主体间性的转变,成为互动语言学视角立场研究的典型文献之一。在研究对象和方法创新方面,Stivers(2008)对故事讲述话语中的立场进行研究,考察了听故事者在听故事的过程中如何使用言语和非言语手段作为交际资源来表现与讲故事者一致的立场,从而实现关系上的联结。该研究对于故事讲述这一话语类型的研究有深远启示意义,随后又大量关于故事讲述话语中的语言使用及会话分析研究;Goodwin (2007)通过对眼神、手势等多模态资源的分析,研究了日常家庭对话组织中的参与、立场和情感,说明立场是如何在日常对话中实现的。该研究对于会话中立场的多模态的分析方法,对会话中多模态资源分析的方法具有重要参考价值。

分析以上高被引文献的特征对于提高学术研究成果的影响力有重要借鉴意义,国内学者可以尝试在理论、研究视角、研究对象和研究方法的方面大胆探索,开展立场的创新性研究,提升中国学者的国际影响力。

3.4 作者共被引分析

选择 cited author(被引作者)选项,对检索到 895 条记录进行作者共被引分析,生成图 4。

由图 4 可见,图右侧的作者有 Heritage, Schegloff, Sacks, Jefferson 等会话分析学派的研究者,以及话语功能语言学(Du Bois)、社会语言学(Labov)等学派的学者,左侧是语法—语义学派(Biber)、系统功能语言学(Halliday)及应用语言学派(Hyland)的学者。其中,Biber (1999)对立场表达的语言手段进行系统描述。可见,立场研究受到不同学派研究者的关注,这与立场本身的多层面性和复杂性有关(Englebreston,2007)。

图 4 立场研究作者共被引可视化图谱

突现性是从时间上衡量节点重要性的指标,突现强度根据突现值的大小来判断。输出的数据显示,作者被引频次前 40 位的作者中有四个突现,分别是 Stiver(2010 年,突现值为 8.53),Chafe(2004 年,突现值 4.47),Jaffe(2009 年,突现值 3.83),Schegloff(2010 年,突现值 4.54),这四个突现的相关信息如下表 3 所示。

表 3 立场共被引前十位的文献频次及中心性

序号	频次	中心性	突现值	作者	年份
1	93	0.00	8.53	Stivers T	2010
2	62	0.27	4.74	Chafe W	2004
3	59	0.01	0.01	Jaffe A	2010
4	49	0.00	0.00	Schegloff	2010

认识语义学者 Chafe 是认知学派的语言学家,其与 Nichols 的论文集 Evidentiality: The linguistic encoding of epistemology(《言据性:认识的语言编码》)(1986)对言据性进行了深入研究,而言据性和认识立场有着密不可分的联系。Biber et al.(1999)将言据性表达归入认识立场的语言表征形式,Zuczkowski et al.(2017)则明确提出认识立场本身就包括言据立场。因此,Chafe 对于言据性的研究为立场的言语表征研究提供了重要的参考。会话分析学者 Stiver(2008)对故事讲述话语中的立场实现方式和结盟关系的分析是故事讲述话语中立场研究的重要文献。后来,Stiver 等人于 2011 年编著的论文集 The Morality of Knowledge in Conversation(《会话中的知

识准则》）(Stivers, et al, 2011)探讨了会话互动中的知识状态及协商。会话分析的奠基人之一 Schegloff 的专著 Sequence Organization in Interaction：A primer in Conversation Analysis（《互动中的序列结构：会话分析入门》）(2006)提供的分析会话序列结构的具体方法，成为会话分析路径下立场研究的重要参考文献。社会语言学家 Jaffe (2009)的论文集 Stance：Sociolinguistic Perspective（《立场：社会语言学视角》），从社会语言学角度对立场涉及的社会语言学因素进行了多角度分析，是立场社会功能研究的重要文献。

由以上分析可见，高被引作者主要来自多个研究学派，其中认知语义学派、会话分析学派和社会语言学派的作者出现了被引突现值，主要在于这些作者的著作在推动立场研究方面有着重要贡献。具体而言，认知语义学者 Chafe 对于言据性的研究为立场的语言表征研究提供重要参考；会话分析学派学者 Stivers 对会话中认识立场动态变化的分析推动了 Heritage (2012a, 2012b)对于会话分析路径下的认识立场研究的理论建构，同时，Schegloff 对会话序列结构的分析为立场的会话分析提供了重要的方法论基础；社会语言学家 Jaffe 推动了社会语言学视角下的立场的社会功能研究。

3.5 期刊共被引分析

选择 cited journal（被引期刊）选项，对检索到 895 条记录进行期刊共被引分析，生成图 5。

图 5　立场研究期刊共被引可视化图谱

图 5 是 CiteSpace 生成的共被引期刊的可视化图谱，我们大致可以看出立场研究相关文章发表的主要语言学期刊。

我们选取期刊被引频次大于 100，且中心性大于 0.20 的刊物，得到表 4。

表 4 频次大于 100 且中心性大于 0.20 的立场共被引期刊

次	中心性	期刊来源
375	0.29	*Journal of Pragmatics*
265	0.28	*Language in Society*
194	0.20	*Language*
194	0.21	*Research in Language and Social Action*
185	0.20	*Applied Linguistics*
101	0.24	*English for Specific Purposes*

如表 4 所示，频次大于 100 且中心性大于 0.20 的期刊是 *Journal of Pragmatics*（《语用学研究》）（0.29），*Language in Society*（《社会中的语言》）（0.28），*English for Specific Purposes*（《特殊用途的英语》）（0.24），*Research in Language and Social Action*（《语言和社会行为研究》）（0.21），*Language*（《语言》）（0.20）和 *Applied Linguistics*（《应用语言学》）（0.20），以上分别是语用学、社会语言学、专门用途英语、会话分析、语言研究和应用语言学研究的主流期刊，这里我们也可以窥见立场研究涉及的研究领域包括语用学、社会语言学、会话分析、语言学及应用语言学等，这说明立场不仅具有交际属性和社会属性（Englebretson，2007），同时还具有广泛的应用价值。

4 结 论

本文借助 WoS 文献数据库和 CiteSpace 可视化文献统计和分析工具，对 1980 年到 2017 年间语言学立场研究的文献发文量、主题词、文献、作者和期刊共被引情况进行了统计，分析了立场的学科归属和语言学立场研究的总体发文趋势。

研究发现：(1) 从 1980 年到 2017 年语言学立场研究的年度发文量总体呈增长趋势，且近十年间的发文量达到较高水平；(2) 研究议题上，立场和语言及交际之间有着密切联系，呈现出学科互补和议题交叉的趋势；认识立场是立场的主要研究类别，情感立场研究相对不足；立场研究主要涉及口语语体，体裁主要涉及日常会话以及叙事话语和学术语篇等；(3) 高被引文献以互动路径下的立场研究为主；高被引作者呈现多学派特征，其中社会语言学派、认知语义学派及会话分析学派的领军人物因其理论贡献出现了明显突现值；高被引期刊反映了立场研究的交际属性、社会属性和应用价值。

本研究对文献进行可视化统计分析，呈现了国外语言学立场研究的总体发文趋势、内容特征及被引情况，有利于帮助国内学者把握国外语言学立场研究的前沿和发展趋势，为国内语言学立场研究的理论创新和议题拓展奠定基础。需要指出的是，本研究所使用的文献统计方法是立场文献研究的一种方式,对立场多个研究议题的深入探讨还有赖于对相关文献的仔细研读。限于篇幅,本研究仅选取部分代表性的文献进行分析解读,分析内容也难以做到全面透彻。同时,今后可以综合国内外文献对语言学立场的研究全貌作进一步分析。

参考文献

[1] Alba-Juez, L. & G. Thompson. 2014. The many faces and phases of evaluation [A]. In G. Thompson & L. Alba-Juez (eds.). *Evaluation in Context* [C]. Amsterdam: John Benjamins, 3 – 23.

[2] Alba-Juez, L. & L. Mackenzie. 2019. Emotional processes in discourse [A]. In L. Alba-Juez & L. Mackenzie (eds). *Emotion in Discourse* [C]. Amsterdam/Phaladelphia: John Benjamins, 3 – 27.

[3] Biber, D. & E. Finegan. 1988. Adverbial stance types in English [J]. *Discourse Processes*, 11: 1 – 34.

[4] Biber, D. & E. Finegan. 1989. Styles of stance in English: Lexical and grammatical marking of evidentiality and affect [J]. *Text*, 9 (1): 93 – 124.

[5] Biber, D., S. Johansson, G. Leech, S. Conrad & E. Finegan. 1999. *Longman Grammar of Spoken and Written English* [M]. London: Longman Press.

[6] Bucholtz, M. & K. Hall. 2005. Identity and interaction: A sociocultural linguistics approach [J]. *Discourse Studies*, 7(4 – 5): 585 – 614.

[7] Cekaite, A. 2012. Affective stances in teacher-novice student interactions: Language, embodiment, and willingness to learn in a Swedish primary classroom [J]. *Language in Society*, 41: 641 – 670.

[8] Chafe, W. & J. Nichols. 1986. *Evidentiality: The Linguistic Coding of Epistemology* [M]. Norwood, NJ: Ablex Publishing Corporation.

[9] Chen, C. 2006. CiteSpace II: Detecting and visualizing emerging trends and transient patterns in scientific literature [J]. *Journal of the American Society for Information Science and Technology*, 57(3): 359 – 377.

[10] Couper-Kuhlen, E. & M. Selting. 1996. *Prosody in Conversation: Interactional Studies* [M]. Cambridge: Cambridge University Press.

[11] Damasio, A. 2018. *The Strange Order of Things* [M]. New York: Pantheon Books.

[12] Du Bois, J. W. 2007. The stance triangle [A]. In R. Englebretson (ed.). *Stancetaking in Discourse: Subjectivity, Evaluation, Interaction* [C]. Amsterdam/Philadelphia: John Benjamins, 139 – 182.

[13] Englebretson, R. 2007. *Stancetaking in Discourse: Subjectivity, Evaluation, Interaction* [M].

Amsterdam/Philadelphia: John Benjamins.

[14] Ferenčik, M. 2017. I'm not Charlie: (Im) politeness evaluations of the Charlie Hebdo attack in an internet discussion forum [J]. *Journal of Pragmatics*, 111: 4–71.

[15] Ford, C. , B. Fox & S. Thompson. 2002. *The Language of Turn and Sequence* [M]. New York: Oxford University Press.

[16] Ford, C. & J. Wagner. 1996. Interaction-based studies of language: Introduction [J]. *Pragmatics*, 6 (3): 277–279.

[17] Fuoli, M. 2017. Building a trustworthy corporate identity: a corpus-based analysis of stance in annual and corporate social responsibility reports [J]. *Applied Linguistics*, 39 (6): 846–885.

[18] Gablasova, D, V. Brezina, T. Mcenery & E. Boyd. 2017. Epistemicstance in spoken L2 English: The effect of task and speaker style [J]. *Applied Linguistics*, 38(5): 613–637.

[19] Goodwin, C. 2007. Participation, stance and affect in the organization of activities [J]. *Discourse & Society*, 18 (1): 53–73.

[20] Haddington, P. 2006. The organization of gaze and assessments as resources for stancetaking [J]. *Text & Talk*, 26(3): 281–328.

[21] Haddington, P. 2013. The pragmatics of stance [A]. In C. Chapelle (ed.). *The Encyclopedia of Applied Linguistics*[C]. Oxford: Blackwell/Wiley, 1–7.

[22] Heritage, J. & G. Raymond. 2005. The terms of agreement: Indexing epistemic authority and subordination in assessment sequences [J]. *Social Psychology Quarterly*, 68 (1): 15–38.

[23] Heritage, J. 2012a. Epistemics in action: Action formation and territories of knowledge[J]. *Research on Language and Social Interaction*, 45(1): 1–29.

[24] Heritage, J. 2012b. The Epistemic engine: Sequence organization and territories of knowledge [J]. *Research on Language and Social Interaction*, 45(1): 30–52.

[25] Hyland, K. 2005. Stance and engagement: A model of interaction in academic discourse[J]. *Discourse Studies*, 7(2):173–192.

[26] Jacknick, C. M. & S. Avni. 2017. Shalom, bitches: Epistemic stance and identity work in an anonymous online forum [J]. *Discourse, Context and Media*, 15: 54–64.

[27] Jaffe, A. 2009. *Stance: Sociolinguistic Perspective*[M]. Oxford: Oxford University Press.

[28] Kamio, A. 1997. *Territory of Information*[M]. Amsterdam/Phiadelphia: John Benjamins.

[29] Kärkkäinen, E. 2003. *Epistemic Stance in English Conversation: A Description of its Interactional Functions, with a Focus on I think* [M]. Amsterdam/Philadelphia: John Benjamins.

[30] Kärkkäinen, E. 2006. Stance-taking in conversation: From subjectivity to intersubjectivity [J]. *Text & Talk*, 26(6): 699–731.

[31] Kirkham, S. 2011. Personal style and epistemic stance in classroom discussion [J]. *Language and Literature*, 20(3): 201–217.

[32] Langlotz, A. & M, Locher. 2012. Ways of communicating emotional stance in online

disagreements [J]. *Journal of Pragmatics*, 44: 1591-1606.

[33] Lyons, J. 1977. *Semantics. Vol. 2*[M]. Cambridge: Cambridge University Press.

[34] Martin, J. R. & P. R. White. 2005. *The Language of Evaluation: Appraisal in English* [M]. New York, NY: Palgrave Macmillan.

[35] Ochs, E. & B. Schieffelin. 1989. Language has a heart [J]. *Text*, 9 (1): 7-25.

[36] Ochs, E. 1993. Constructing social identity: A language socialization perspective [J]. *Research on Language and Social Interaction*, 26 (3): 287-306.

[37] Palmer, F. R. 1986. *Mood and Modality*[M]. Cambridge: Cambridge University Press.

[38] Schegloff, E. A. 2006. *Sequence Organization in Interaction: A primer in Conversation Analysis*[M]. Cambridge: Cambridge University Press.

[39] Selting, M. & E. Couper-Kuhlen. 2001. *Studies in Interactional Linguistics*[M]. Amsterdam/Philadelphia: John Benjamins.

[40] Stivers, T. 2008. Stance, alignment, and affiliation during storytelling: When nodding is a token of affiliation [J]. *Research on Language and Social Interaction*, 41(1): 31-57.

[41] Stivers, T., L. Mondada & J. Steensig. 2011. *The Morality of Knowledge in Conversation* [M]. Cambridge, England: Cambridge University Press.

[42] Wu, R.-J. R. 2004. *Stance in Talk: A Conversation Analysis of Mandarin Final Particles* [M]. Amsterdam: John Benjamins.

[43] Zuczkowski, A., R. Bongelli & I. Riccioni. 2017. *Epistemic Stance in Dialogue: Knowing, Unknowing, Believing*[M]. Amsterdam/Philadelphia: John Benjamins Publishing Company.

[44] 李杰、陈超美,2016.CiteSpace 科技文本挖掘及可视化[M].北京:首都经济贸易大学出版社.

[45] 李民、肖雁,2016.国内外体裁核心期刊中语用学研究分析:1980—2015[J].外国语文研究,(2):181-192.

[46] 柳淑芬,2017.话语中的立场:研究现状及发展路径[J].当代修辞学,(5):63-70.

[47] 罗桂花,2014.立场概念及其研究模式的发展[J].当代修辞学,(1):41-47.

[48] 徐昉,2015.二语学术语篇中的作者立场标记研究[J].外语与外语教学,(5):1-7.

[49] 俞琳、李福印,2016.因果关系语言表征研究中的 CiteSpace III 对比分析[J].当代外语研究,(3):9-15.

[50] 袁周敏、刘环环,2017.国际中介语语用学研究动态可视化分析[J].外语教学与研究,(3):453-463.

[51] 钟兰凤、郭晨璐,2017.学术话语中的立场研究述评[J].大学英语教学与研究,(6):43-47.

《劳特利奇语用学手册》与语用学研究前沿*

同济大学　黄立鹤　祝　琳**

A Review of *The Routledge Handbook of Pragmatics* and the Leading-edge Development in qragmatics

Barron, A., Gu. Y. & Steen. G (eds.). 2017. *The Routledge Handbook of Pragmatics*. New York: Routledge.

目前,语用学学科内涵及研究领域日益丰富,正沿着发展与完善理论体系、拓展与延伸应用领域两个方面共同演进。国际上的语用学研究呈现经典命题与新兴议题并存、数据类型与来源多样、研究视野宽阔、跨学科趋势显著等特征。在这样的背景下,多家国际著名出版机构均出版了语用学手册。

作为由国际知名出版社新近出版的语用学研究手册,《劳特利奇语用学手册》是《劳特利奇应用语言学手册》系列中的一本,由三位著名语用学家主编,对目前语用学研究中的研究方法、涉及领域、跨学科研究以及语用学应用等方面进行了详细介绍,具有脉络型、全景式、前沿性等特点。Anne Barron 是德国吕纳堡洛伊法纳大学教授,国际 SSCI 期刊《语用学杂志》及《跨文化语用学》的编委会成员;顾曰国是中国社会科学院语言研究所研究员、北京外国语大学"冠名讲席教授";Gerard Steen 是荷兰阿姆斯特丹大学教授,阿姆斯特丹隐喻实验室发起人及主任。

本文主要基于《劳特利奇语用学手册》的关注视野,对其中的议题、方法及应用等内容进行评析,同时介绍了手册尚未关注到的三个前沿研究课题。

---

* 本文是 2019 年国家社会科学基金青年项目"基于多模态语料库的阿尔茨海默症老年人语用能力蚀失研究"(编号:19CYY018)的部分成果。

** 作者简介:黄立鹤,同济大学外国语学院副教授,研究方向为多模态语用学、老年语言学。邮箱:cranehlh@tongji.edu.cn;祝琳,同济大学外国语学院硕士研究生,研究方向为语用学。

1 手册综述的语用学研究领域与方法

手册共分为总论加上四个正文部分。

总论有两篇文章构成。第一篇是本书三位编者合写的引言,标题为"广义视角下的语用学"。此篇开宗明义,将语用学视为研究各类社会情境中语言使用的学问,这也决定了本手册在内容、方法和视角上的开阔视野。在简略回顾英美学派和欧洲大陆学派的发展历史后,编者指出:本手册试图融合各种不同的语用学研究传统,邀请各领域的专家,站在广义语用学的高度,向读者展现相关研究的最新成果。可见,该书的特点是秉承"大语用观",认为语用学可为语言使用涉及的各个方面提供解释。这一点在题为"语用学及语言学研究中的跨学科问题"的第二篇文章中得到了很好地体现。该文由国际著名语用学家 Jacob L. Mey 从语言学研究历史发展的高度审视语用学演变的问题。作者明确指出,理想化、抽象化的语言研究并不符合在各种语境下鲜活语言使用的实际,各种理想化的模型与研究人类语言使用的人文学科性质格格不入。奥斯汀开启的言语行为研究及舍尔、格赖斯、莱文森等学者的相关研究呈现出了实质性的学科交叉倾向;萨克斯等学者采用的会话分析方法注重语境因素,真正赋予了语用学人文学科性质。语言学旨在描述和分析人们的语言行为,是语用学的一部分,而语用学包含着人们使用语言及进行其他社会行为时的所有情境。在该思路下,广义语用学自然具备学科交叉的属性,而语言学范畴下的语用学(linguistic pragmatics)旨在研究"各种社会情境下人类交际中的语言使用情况"。读者阅读本手册后面部分时,就会对三位编者及 Mey 关于语用学广义性的立场有更为清晰的认识。

其后的 38 个章节属于专题部分,包括了研究方法、涉及领域、跨学科范式、研究应用四个部分。

1.1 方法与模态:语用学研究的数据类型与多样来源

第一部分题为"方法与模态",分为两个子部分。之所以使用模态(modalities)一词,笔者认为是为了突显当前语用学研究数据类型与来源的多样性。

第一个子部分是对自然发生话语、诱导采集话语以及语料库语料这三种数据类型的探讨。田野笔记与音视频采录是采集自然发生数据的两种常用方法。田野记录具有便捷、直接、易于操作的特点,但也存在着过分依赖记录者记忆、无法回溯验证数据以及经过记录者主观"过滤"等缺点;音视频采录客观性较强,但对某些机构性话语(如法庭、医院等)而言,因涉及法律法规或个人隐私,有时较难进行采录。与自然发生数据相对的是诱导数据,采集该类数据的方法有结构化访谈、使用诱导工具等。这些诱导工具包括:书面话语填充、角色扮演、(不)礼貌事件回顾、等级量表评估以及内省口头汇报、书面多项选择与话语填充、强制判断法及生理测量等。基于语料库的语用学研究日益受到重视,但该类研究很大一个问题是并非所有语用现象都有规约化、相对固定的形式标记,这给语料标注、建库、检索等都带来很大困难。即便如此,仍有学者尝试开发了一些语用标注体系及相应的语料库。

第二个子部分主要介绍非言语交际与语用学研究的关系。第一篇介绍英国手语,对手语语用现象进行研究的课题包括:(不)礼貌、指称、话轮、修补、韵律等。第二篇关注身势①与语用学研究。包括 Kendon, McNeil 及 Goodwin 等在内的诸多学者认为,身势是人们语言使用的一部分,应该把身势视为与言语共现资源(coverbal),而不是非言语行为(nonverbal)。身势与语用学研究结合的经典案例是身势对语力的作用研究,自20 世纪 90 年代起,一些学者对意大利语、德语、加泰罗尼亚语、英语等言语行为与身势之间的关系进行了研究。在我国,顾曰国(Gu,2013)、黄立鹤(2018)从多模态视角对汉语言语行为进行了研究。另外,国际语用学界已经开始关注特殊人群语用交际中的动作研究,如自闭症及失语症儿童、中风或脑功能区受损患者等;我国学者(如曾小荣、马博森,2015;顾曰国,2019;黄立鹤,2019;马博森、曾小荣、龚然,2020)也已开始运用多模态方法开展包括儿童及老年人等人群的语用交际特征研究及康复干预。第三篇是对副语言的探讨。关于副语言(paralanguage)的范畴,Poyatas 将其定义为语言使用中的发音特征,即集中于对韵律的探讨,并不包含面部表情、手势动作等;Abercrombie 则将言语交际中语言本身之外的、说话人能够用来表意的其他资源均归入副语言范畴中。此文从本手册内容安排的实际角度出发,采用的是前者立场,通过实例分析了语音、韵律等因素在表意上的重要作用。

1.2 方向与领域:语用学研究的经典命题与新兴议题

第二部分重点阐述了语用学研究所涉及的方向与领域,其中既有经典命题,也有新兴议题,共分为五个子部分。

第一子部分题为"语用学与变异",话题涉及"历史语用学"、"变异语用学"、"后殖民主义语用学"、"性别与社会语用学"及"双语与多语"五个方面。"历史语用学"一文指出,语用演变涉及社会阶层、性别、年龄等多个层面,这些因素需与话语行为、话语风格等结合起来考虑才能真正揭示共时特征与历时变化之间的关系;"变异语用学"注重语言之间的语用变异(variation),旨在描述地区、性别以及社会经济地位等因素影响下人与人之间交际模式的变异现象;后殖民主义社会的重要特征是多语与多种族,"后殖民

---

① 原题为 Gesture and Pragmatics。按照 Kendon(2004)的观点,gesture 是任何可见的身体动作,而不仅限于手势,此处译为"身势"。

主义语用学"部分从该特征入手,分析后殖民主义社会中人们交际的重要语言特征;"性别与社会语用学"介绍了语言与性别的关系,并着重探讨了礼貌与权力两个主题;"双语与多语"则主要阐述了双语以及多语作为个人语言能力以及社会语用现象的发展、特点与影响。

第二子部分为"语用学与文化",主要在不同语言文化背景下审视语用研究,下分"中介语语用学""跨文化语用学""身份与群体关系""民俗语用学"。"中介语语用学"重点分析学习者在社会文化背景下学习语言学知识、社会文化传统习俗及相关知识的过程,学习者之间的差异及影响学习过程的因素等;"跨文化语用学"探讨不同文化背景下语言使用的特点特征;"身份与群体关系"从社会结构、言语交际及语篇等多角度分析语言使用者的"身份"及其特征。此文指出,身份研究日益复杂化,其中从多模态角度进行研究逐渐成为热点;"民俗语用学"是指非语言学者对语言使用的研究,介绍了相关经典课题、研究方法、数据来源等问题。

第三子部分为"语言语用学"(linguistic pragmatics)。前文已述,本手册秉持广义语用学观,语言学范畴下的语用学研究是其中的一部分。此文主要探讨传统语用学的经典课题,包括意图、言语行为、时间指称、形式与自然语言、语用预设与顺应(accommodation)、语法化等方面。

第四子部分题为"认知与语用学",涉及"元表征""关联""语用学中的隐喻"与"语用充实"等话题。"元表征"一文主要介绍言语交际中的隐含意义、意图推导等问题,并涉及关联论、格赖斯意义理论等;"关联"一文从心理属性、认知机制及言语交际等方面入手,探讨了关联这一语用学经典话题;"语用学中的隐喻"针对隐喻这一交际及认知现象,涉及隐含意义、指称过程、归约性及语义—语用交互等问题;"语用充实"(enrichment)是指在语用交际中某些结构在特定语境中发生意义扩充、延伸或意义缩小、收窄的语用加工过程,从字面含义到隐含意义的语用推理需要"充实"这一过程的参与。

第五子部分题为"互动语用学",下分"会话""话语""礼貌"与"引语"四篇文章。"会话"一文指出,从历史上看,研究者不满足于仅运用言语行为理论等语用学核心工具分析真实会话,从而引入会话分析等新工具。作者认为,研究者应当思考如何将已有结论推广至教育教学中,实现理论走向实践;"话语"一文介绍了研究者在话语分析时需要考虑的三个方面,即"文本结构""社会实践"与"行为";"礼貌"一文综述了(不)礼貌语言特征与"面子"之间的关系以及与"面子"相关的礼貌原则;"引语"部分则主要阐述直接引语和间接引语的结构特征及语用功能等方面。

1.3 语用学的跨学科研究格局

第三部分是跨学科视阈下的语用学研究,显示了当今语用学走向跨学科、秉持宽广视野的研究格局。该部分共有"临床语用学""语用学与神经语言学""民族志研究""社会符号视角下的语言使用"和"演化视角下的语言语用学"五篇文章。"临床语用学"阐述了语用障碍的特征描述、诊断评估与治疗等;"语用学与神经语言学"探讨将语用学引入神经语言学之后的相关理论问题、操作方法等;"民族志研究"讨论了符号互动论的语用学基础并介绍了相关实证研究及成果;"社会符号视角下的语言使用"从社会符号学视角入手,阐述了以不同感官模态为基础的各种符号系统之间的差异与联系;"演化视角下的语言语用学"从交际有效性及模式复杂性入手,讨论了与语用学相关的一系列进化语言学领域的问题,引入了从进化论角度看语言学问题的新视角。

1.4 语用学研究的应用领域

第四部分介绍语用学研究的应用领域,包括"语用学与本体论""语用学与翻译""法律翻译语用学""社会媒体"与"语用学与教学"五篇文章。"语用学与本体论"从本体论视角对言语交际进行了分析并讨论了语用本体论等相关话题,阐释了本体论与语用学的相互关系及发展方向;"语用学与翻译"阐释了以语用为导向的翻译理论、翻译中语用学概念及理论的适用性问题;"法律翻译语用学"就法律语言中语用意义的理解进行了分析;"社会媒体"讨论了新媒体附加于传统语用学研究的限制因素,指出社会媒体正成为语用学的热点研究领域;"语用学与教学"部分则介绍了中介语语用学及二语教学中的语用维度问题。

2 手册内容评析与语用学研究的三个新兴领域

总体而言,本手册视野开阔、内容前沿、可读性强,对语用学的学科发展脉络进行了清晰的梳理,对日益丰富的语用学学科内涵做了全景式介绍,对诸多前沿性的语用学研究领域进行了愿景展望。值得一提的是,本手册每一篇文章之后均有作者的推荐书目,为感兴趣的读者深入研讨该话题提供了阅读指引。

2.1 手册的突出特点

本手册最为突出的特点就是涵盖话题丰富、阐述理论全面、介绍方法新颖,这一点在同类手册中出类拔萃。三位主编所秉持的广义语用学的学科视野,可谓在题材选取、内容阐述及方法介绍上体现得淋漓尽致。读者阅读后会发现,本手册既包括从微观角度对语言结构、语用意义的探究,也包括从广义的社会文化路径探讨宏观语境;既覆盖了传统语用学研究的经典课题,也反映了近年来语用学研究领域的新课题、新方法与新成果。

同样值得称道的是本手册在语用学前沿应用领域的详细介绍。应用是理论研究的必要过程，对应用领域、具体方法及相关问题的阐述有助于进一步明晰语用学研究的发展方向。本手册在第四部分论及本体论、翻译、社会媒体、教学等领域，展现了常见的语用研究应用范畴。同时，在第三部分学科交叉中涉及的临床语用学、神经语用学、民族志研究等，也勾画了不少应用图景。

另外，本手册介绍的一些研究内容和方法是国内语用学研究刚刚起步或尚未涉及的，特别是在学科交叉视野下的语用研究及诸多应用领域，需要引起国内学者的特别注意。

2.2　三个新兴领域与手册编写缺憾

当然，本手册也存在一些小缺憾，如未能关注到若干个在国际语用学新兴发展的领域。

第一，语料库语用学发展方兴未艾，但该手册只在第一部分介绍数据与方法时对其有所涉及，而语料库语用学的基本思路、操作方法、研究问题及经典案例等未能单独成章进行详细论述，这似乎与语料库语用学目前的地位不甚相符；"手册"之所以为"手册"，应旨在为研究者随时提供研究参考，并且在介绍一些研究方法时提供详细的可操作性介绍，如相关研究工具的介绍等，但此方面似乎也未能在该手册中得到充分体现。语料库语用学对语用学整体学科的发展具有重要意义，包括提供新的研究范式，验证、修正和提出新的理论等。因此，目前很有必要进一步确立语料库语用学的学科地位，推进语料库语用学的深化发展。另外，与国际语用学界相比，我国的语料库语用学研究显著偏少，应当引起重视（李民、陈新仁，2019）。

第二，虽然手册中的多篇文献提及多模态视角对语用学研究的重要意义，但尚未上升到"多模态语用学"的高度。事实上，近十年来，多模态语料库语言学正逐步兴起，运用多模态语料库语言学方法对语用课题进行研究，既可以为语用研究增加定量分析的客观性，从较大程度上弥补传统语用研究的不足，也能借助多模态语料库语言学强劲发展的推力，弥补传统文本语料库无法体现诸多重要言语交际信息的缺陷，在研究方法上对语用学研究进行升级，从而对相关语用学理论进行拓展、修正。当然，多模态语料库方法只是多模态研究范式中的一种路径，研究语用课题也可以采用其他的多模态研究路径，包括多模态话语分析、多模态互动研究等。使用多模态研究范式的各种路径，对语用课题进行新的考察、促进新的发现、产生新的理论，这正是构建"多模态语用学"的逻辑（黄立鹤，2018）。多模态语料不仅可以体现诸多原先未能记录的信息，而且可以呈现语言与语境或其他因素之间的关系，对研究者从人们普通行为的高度更为全面、准确地解读语言使用意义十分关键。目前，这一新的研究领域在国际上已经受到学者们的关注。多年来，每届国际语用学大会上都有不少学者在多模态视角下研讨语用课题。

第三,该手册没有对特殊群体语用问题给予足够的关注。随着语用学知识体系日臻完善,对特殊群体(包括但不限于正常儿童、健康老年人以及罹患自闭症、痴呆症、精神疾病等人群)语用交际及其背后机制的研究日益丰富,相关研究已成为语用话语领域重要的议题。需要注意的是,对该群体语用交际的研究,并不完全属于临床语用学范畴。以老年人语用交际研究为例,基于临床语用视角的研究是对语言障碍患者语用产出的描述、评估和干预,焦点是病理语言现象。但是,对正常、超康健老人、成功老龄老人的语用交际现象及语用能力变化等方面研究,却不在临床语用学范畴之内。世界老龄化趋势促成了老年语言学的兴起,相关研究旨在探索老年人因正常认知老化、生理器官衰退、罹患精神或神经退行性疾病而引发的各类语言现象。其中,对老年人语用交际特征的研究兼具理论与应用价值,已成为老年语言学核心范畴之一(黄立鹤、朱琦,2019)。研究议题至少包括但不限于:正常及特殊群体老年人的语用交际特点有哪些?老年群体的语用能力如何衡量?如何利用语用交际特征加强对认知能力减退或相关临床疾病的预判?在研究视野与方法上,在多模态语用学框架下考察老年人的正常语用交际特征及语言能力受损情况下的语用代偿现象,都是目前新兴的研究课题(黄立鹤,2019)。

总的来说,《劳特利奇语用学手册》反映了目前国际语用学研究的经典课题与新兴领域,既能为刚入门语用学的初级研究者提供教科书式的信息及鸟瞰式的综述,也可为资深研究者提供特定领域的研究思路和灵感,是一本值得细读并且需要经常翻阅的语用学研究文献。

参考文献

[1] Gu, Y. 2013. A conceptual model of Chinese illocution, emotion and prosody [A]. In Chiu-yu Tseng (ed.). *Human Language Resources and Linguistic Typology* [C]. Taipei: Academia Sinica, 309-362.

[2] Kendon, A. 2004. *Gesture: Visible Action as Utterance* [M]. Cambridge: Cambridge University Press.

[3] 顾曰国,2019.老年语言学发端[J].语言战略研究,(5):12-33.

[4] 黄立鹤,2018.基于多模态语料库的语力研究:多模态语用学新探索[M].上海:上海外语教育出版社.

[5] 黄立鹤,2019.多模态语用学视域下的言语行为与情感因素:兼论在老年语言学中的应用[J].当代修辞学,(6):42-52.

[6] 黄立鹤、朱琦,2019.老年语言学研究的语用维度:视角、方法与议题[J].华东师范大学学报(哲学社会科学版),(6):129-137.

[7] 李民、陈新仁,2019.语料库语用学研究的国际热点解析[J].现代外语,(1):122-133.

[8] 马博森、曾小荣、龚然,2020.国外自闭症人群多模态话语及智能辅助诊断与干预研究[J].语言战略研究,(2):51-60.

[9] 曾小荣、马博森,2015.物体指称行为中的涉手模式分析[J].当代语言学,(3):331-347.

《语用翻译学:寓意言谈翻译研究》简评*

泉州师范学院　王才英**

A Review of *PRAGMATRANSLATOLOGY*: *A Study of Translation of Metaphorical Talk*

侯国金,2020.《语用翻译学:寓意言谈翻译研究》,北京:北京大学出版社。

美国哲学家莫里斯(1901—1979)和卡纳普(1891—1970)在20世纪30年代前后首先提出语用学概念。语用学涉及语言学、哲学、心理学和符号学等学科。经过近百年的发展,语用学与其他学科联姻,逐渐形成了新的学科。语用翻译学(pragmatranslatology)便是其中之一。最早把语用学和翻译结合起来的是国外的哈蒂姆、梅森、格特、希基和韦伯等和我国的张亚非、何自然、曾宪才、钱冠连、赵彦春、侯国金、曾文雄、李占喜、莫爱屏等。近几年,语用翻译学在翻译学中的作用越来越大,正如侯国金教授在《语用翻译学:寓意言谈翻译研究》的第99页中写道,"语用翻译学不仅要深化语用学研究以及翻译学研究,更要从语用学的经典理论和新视角考察诸多翻译问题,从而更好地解决其他一般翻译问题,并能解决翻译的疑难杂症"。这本专著是他的语用翻译学研究的系列成果之一,是语用翻译学的集成之作。

全书共分为五个部分:第一部分是"语用学说略",作者列举了语用学的定义、语言哲学基础、学科定位、意义、含意等。第二部分是"翻译学说略",作者列举了翻译的定

---

* 本文是2020年度中青年教师教育科研项目(社科类)一般项目"新媒体修辞语境下的国家形象建构"(编号:JAS20262)、福建省教育科学"十三五"规划常规课题"信息技术与中学英语视听说教学的融合研究"(项目号:FJJKXB19-545)及2019泉州师范学院线上线下精品课程的部分成果。特别感谢华侨大学语用修辞研究创新团队(50X17191)。

** 作者简介:王才英,泉州师范学院外国语学院副教授,研究方向:翻译学和生态语言学。邮箱:804028787@qq.com。

义、可译性与不可译性、归化与异化的互补、翻译与创作的关系。第三部分首先讨论了语用翻译学的作用,即语用翻译学可助力我国"一带一路建设""中国文化走出去""讲好中国故事""中国形象建设"以及"翻译强国";其次是语用翻译学的确立、发展及研究对象以及基本语用译观。作者论述了三大语用翻译观,也即"关联顺应译观""构建主义译观"以及"语用标记等效译观",认为语用翻译学在理论上可调和翻译研究的语言派和文化派之争,在实践上能解决随意言谈(含寓意言谈)的翻译等效问题。第四部分是语用翻译学的个案研究,主要阐述了颜色词、隐喻、转喻、花径等翻译问题。第五部分则是语用翻译学的翻译评论。

可见该书不是纯粹的大而上的语用翻译理论研究,也不是形而下的单纯译技讲解。它是语用翻译理论与具体翻译策略和方法的融合。该专著有以下特点:

(一) 拓宽了语用翻译研究的广度

我们可以发现该书已经超越语用翻译的经典译观:关联顺应译观、构建主义译观和语用标记等效译观,还拓展到了语用修辞理论及其翻译实践,话语的"原意言谈""随意言谈"到"寓意言谈"在语用翻译理论关照下的翻译处理。可以说,该著是翻译语用学的继承和发展,书中大篇幅研究标记程度较高的"寓意言谈"翻译的语用策略和途径便是最有力的证据。如第 139 页的例 13:

(女儿对爸爸说:"到我的房间辅导我作业吧。"他说:"我不想进狗窝!")
译 1:I don't want to go to your room.
译 2:I don't want to go to your dirty room.
译 3:I don't want to go to your room as dirty as a doghouse.
译 4:I don't want to go to your doghouse.

该例"爸爸"使用"狗窝"一词是随意言谈的寓意言谈或隐喻式,比较起来,译 4("your doghouse")最契合或等效于原文;译 1("your room")属于无标记,译 2("your dirty room")属于弱标记,译 3("your room as dirty as a doghouse")属于中标记。

(二) 挖掘了语用翻译研究的深度

如第四章观照了六种常见颜色词的原意用法、随意用法(隐喻和转喻用法等),作者分别讨论了容易翻译类、较难翻译类、极难翻译类颜色词,并提供了相应译法,犹如颜色词译法小百科。以"红"为例,原意用法如"red ink",直译为"红墨水","red blood cell"直译为"红血球"。随意用法如"red card",直译为"红牌子、红卡片",用于足球等运动,是一级随意用法,可意译为"因犯规而被罚下场",而用于非体育领域(如学校生活)则是二级随意用法,可意译为"劝退、除名、开除、退学";若进一步寓意化,当属三级随意用法,可意译为"心理上的疏远、撤销、拉入黑名单、断绝关系"等;而形如"I'll give John a red card, a redder one at that."中的"redder"则可以说是四级随意用法(比较"我会给约翰一张红牌,一张更红的红牌",第148页)。

(三) 丰富了语用翻译研究的语料

书中语料多源于经典名著。如在讨论关联顺应时(第123页),作者选用了世界名著《大卫·科波菲尔》中的例子:

How many winter days have I seen him, standing blue-nosed in the snow and east wind?
译1:在许多冬日里我都看见他,鼻子冻得发紫,站在飞雪和东风中。
译2:在多少个冬日里,我看见他站在飞雪和寒风中,鼻子冻得发紫。

译2中的"寒风"对应原文的"east wind",此乃语用翻译的上策,因为中国的东风与英国的东风不同,前暖后冷。因此,翻译时要动态关联顺应原文和译文的相关语境和结构,在翻译重构中找到平衡。又如杜甫《春夜喜雨》中:

"野径云俱黑,/江船火独明"(第295页)
译文:Out there, the fields, the paths, by dark clouds blanketed; / Here in my river boat, the only light, burning bright.

原文中的"火"属范畴—属性转喻,意为"灯";如果直译为"fire",英美读者有可能误解为火盆类。

书中也有日常生活语例,如:

"Unfortunately our new physics teacher is a fossil."(第240页)。
译1:不幸的是,我们的新物理老师很老。

译2：不幸的是，我们的新物理老师<u>很老很古板</u>。

译3：不幸的是，我们的新物理老师<u>(简直)是一块化石</u>。

译3是译者通过语言策划使能喻和所喻完全匹配，是对人物性格的画龙点睛妙译，再现了原文的意思和语效。又如：

"她每天都为<u>柴米油盐酱醋茶</u>操心。"(第297-298页)

译1：She has to worry about <u>firewood, rice, cooking oil, salt, soybean sauce, vinegar, and tea</u> every day.

译2：She has to worry about <u>daily necessities</u> every day.

译3：She is concerned about <u>bread and milk of the household</u> every day.

译4：She is concerned about <u>bread and butter of the household</u> every day.

中国人喜欢把日常必需品转喻为"柴米油盐酱醋茶"，译1的直译显然不符合英语习惯。译2中的"daily necessities"回译为"生活必需品"，是用上位范畴词代替了原文的下位范畴词，但译文在语效方面欠生动。译3和译4因为译语文化碰巧有一个转喻表达式和原文的转喻表达式相同，也就是在英文语境"bread and milk of the household"和"bread and butter of the household"恰巧等效于原文的"柴米油盐酱醋茶"。因此，译3和译4的转喻译法关联顺应了中英文的语义、语力和语效。

还有来自电影电视剧的语例，如：

"雨来刚到堂屋，见<u>十几把雪亮的刺刀</u>从前门进来"(第280页)

译1：No sooner had Yulai entered the central room than over <u>ten enemy soldiers</u> came in from the front door with shiny bayonets fixed to the end of their guns.

译2：No sooner had Yulai entered the central room than over <u>ten bright bayonets</u> came in …

原文中的"十几把雪亮的刺刀"转喻了"敌兵"，译2保留了喻体"十几把雪亮的刺刀"("over ten bright bayonets")，这样既保留了原意，又取得了等值于原文的语效。

还有多语语料，如韩语的"帽子、母子"(mutsa)(第15页)。为了说明"语用变通"，作者还列举了多国语言拍照时等效于中国人照相的"茄子"语例，如韩语的"泡菜"(kimqi)，日语的"地图"(qizi)，英语的"奶酪"(cheese)，法语的"狨猴"(ouistiti)(第65页)。

总之，书中古今中外的语料作者信手拈来，用以说明语用翻译学的译理和译观显得自然圆润，具有释理性、互通性、趣味性。

（四）使用了通俗隽永的语言

全书虽有大量来自翻译学、语言学、修辞学等的术语，但作者通过深入浅出的语言解构和重构了那些受制于语法、语义、修辞、认知和语用的各种随意言谈和寓意言谈，阐释和论述了各种疑难寓意言谈（个案）的翻译策略。如"在外语教学中，常常碰到一些生僻或似是而非、似非而是的英语语句或表达式。不考虑哪些望文生义而贻笑大方的情况，假如某学生看到下面的语句，可能先经历望文生义，然后自我否决，达到正确的解读，这是外语学习中的特殊花径。"（第325页）在这段文字中"花径"是一种构式（手法），也是一种语用手段，还是一种有趣的修辞方式。"花径"这个词初读可能不一定好理解，但作者先铺垫了其意思，以便于理解。再如：

It's a good father that knows his son.
译1：理解自己儿子的父亲才是好父亲。
译2：就算是最好的父亲也未必了解自己的孩子。

上文通俗的语言解释再加上相关译例能够帮助读者更好地理解"花径"的含义。该例初读英文可能会翻译/误解成译1，但其实指/应译成译2。

（五）对比评析了书中的译例

书中对译例的解析并不是单纯的批评，也不是纯粹地抛出正确得体的译文，而是有破有立，既指出译文中的不足，又指出如何按照书中的某条译观使得译文准确得体。如《孟子·梁惠王上》的

"老吾老，以及人之老；幼吾幼，以及人之幼。"（第307页）
译1：We should respect other old people the same way as we do our own, and love other children the same way as we do our own.
译2：We should treat other people's fathers and sons like our own father and son.

译 3：We should <u>father</u> other people's fathers, and <u>son</u> other people's sons.

原文中的"老、幼"是形容词活用为动词的语法转喻，是行为转喻和符号指称转喻。译 1 没有转喻，欠生动，语效低(参见转喻译观之 5，也即"用释义白话来翻译，以求转喻所喻指之意")；译 2 更经济，但语效低(参见转喻译观之 5)；译 3 有转喻，同原文语效，因为"father other people's fathers"受到拈连(syllepsis)和轭配(zeugma)机制驱动，是转喻性翻译策略(参照转喻译观之 1b，即"没有现成转喻，但进行转喻移植，即直译原文转喻的字词")。书中此类译例不胜枚举，可以帮助读者知其然并知其所以然。

(六) 内容及其编排适合阅读

作者在例子后面直接注明该例句的关注点，再用一小段文字解释所参照的译观及几个译文之间的对比，这样就一目了然。另外，书中的语用翻译学术语都旁注了英文对应表达式，方便读者对照学习和研究。

当然，随着翻译技术的不断推进，书中提到的译观有待进一步推进和阐释，如语用标记等效译观能否通过翻译技术进行比较科学的量化？遇到翻译问题时，我们应如何孰先孰后、孰重孰轻地考量书中提到的三种语用翻译观呢？

正如书中前言所说，"Translate or die"(不译则亡)，全球化时代越来越需要各种领域和各种形式的翻译。愿借侯国金教授通俗隽永的语言、生动活泼的举例铺就的语用翻译路径，引领我们走向物质、服务、信息和思想交流的翻译之旅，更好地解决翻译中的疑难杂症，更好地服务"中国文化走出去"，更好地实现"翻译强国"。

《面向"一带一路"建设的外语规划研究》介评*

四川外国语大学英语学院 杨金龙**

1 引 言

随着"一带一路"倡议的深入开展,我国与沿线国家在金融、交通、教育和文化等各个领域的合作与交流日益繁荣。在"一带一路"倡议的政策沟通、设施联通、贸易畅通、资金融通和民心相通中,语言是实现"五通"的重要基础之一,是促进人文交流、服务互联互通建设的重要支撑。在此背景下,语言规划界就相应的语言服务需求(赵世举,2015)、跨境语言文字概况(黄行,2015)、国家外语能力建设(沈骑,2015)、语言生活层级建设(卢俊霖、祝晓宏,2017)、关键土著语言规划(王雪梅、邓世平,2020)等话题进行了深入探讨。相较之下,外语规划方面的中、微观研究,尤其是对接企业、教育和文化等领域的调研与规划研究相对薄弱。

2020 年 9 月,由东南大学外国语学院院长陈美华教授著、外语教学与研究出版社出版的《面向"一带一路"建设的外语规划研究》一书问世。该作由北京语言大学李宇明教授作序,从地位规划、语种规划、功能规划和习得规划的,对我国"一带一路"沿线省份和重点行业领域的外语需求与服务现状进行了广泛调查,为相关政府、企业和教育等领域面向"一带一路"建设的外语规划提供了数据支撑与实践启示。

---

* 基金项目:本文为国家语委"十三五"2019 年度重点项目(ZDI 135—100)"新时代城市语言文明建设研究",以及四川外国语大学教学改革项目(JY1965230)"'人类命运共同体'视域下复合型国际事务人才的'全人'培养模式探究"的阶段成果。
** 作者简介:杨金龙,博士,在站博士后,副教授,硕士研究生导师。主要研究方向为语言政策与规划、教育语言学、语用学。邮箱:yangjinlong1011@126.com。

2　内容介绍

除序言与前言外,全书共十三章。其中,第一章为全书的绪论部分,第二章为相关研究综述,第三章和第四章为研究方法与分析框架,第五章至第十章为领域外语规划下的实证调查研究,第十一、十二和十三章为研究启示与结语部分。下文对该作的内容进行简要介绍。

2.1　绪论

该作的第一章为研究绪论部分。作者对"一带一路"、外语规划等核心概念进行介绍与梳理,并交代研究背景、研究目的与全书的框架结构。该章指出,在"一带一路"深入发展的背景下,调研和分析重点行业领域的语言应用、外语服务和外语人才培养,考察政府、企业、学校和家庭各个层面的外语规划实践,最终提出面向"一带一路"建设的外语规划初步构想与对策建议是本研究的主要目标。

2.2　相关文献综述

该作的第二章对"一带一路"倡议下的外语规划研究进行梳理。作者从外语规划与非传统国家安全、"一带一路"与外语规划、"一带一路"新格局与领域外语规划三个维度出发,分别对外语地位规划、外语语种规划、外语功能规划、外语习得规划,以及领域外语规划的相关研究成果进行归纳总结。作者指出,服务于"一带一路"倡议的领域外语规划研究仍然阙如,难以对一些重点行业领域的外语规划提供支持,相关调研与思考亟待开展,因而引入本研究的主要设计思路。

2.3　研究方法与分析框架

该作的第三、四章主要阐述研究方法与分析框架。在第三章中,作者基于"一带一路"倡议下外语规划研究重理论、轻实践的现状,对不同领域的实证调研方法予以设计。其中,面对企业外语需求、外语服务、学校外语规划、国家和省域外语规划以及家庭语言规划五个不同领域的研究目标,研究者分别采用半结构化访谈、语料库、网络调研和民族志研究等方法进行实证调查与分析。

第四章对"一带一路"建设的重点领域进行逐一阐述。作者认为,领域外语规划是本研究的主要构建思路,因此,对涉及"一带一路"建设的相关领域及其外语规划实践应分别予以分析。在本章中,作者首先梳理了中资企业参与"一带一路"建设的现状,随后就金融企业、文化企业、地方政府、教育部门和学术研究机构这五大领域在"一带一路"

建设中的重要作用和参与现状分别予以分析，并据此引入本研究的实证调研部分。

2.4 领域外语规划下的实证调查研究

　　第五章至第十章为该作的实证研究部分。研究者通过前章提及的各类研究方法，分别对"一带一路"倡议下各领域的外语规划现状进行实证调查、分析与讨论。其中，第五章重点关注"一带一路"倡议下的企业外语需求现状。作者将技术传播的概念引入到外语人才培养的思考当中，认为技术传播作为企业命运和国家经济发展的重要因子，其中涉及的技术写作、软件技术开发和跨文化沟通等能力并未引起中国外语教育工作者的关注，相关研究与人才培养相对薄弱。由此，作者以"一带一路"建设关键领域的企业员工、大学英语教师和英语专业学生为研究对象，分别进行半结构化访谈。研究发现，技术传播作为一个跨学科领域，对企业员工的技术协作、沟通技巧、视觉设计、信息开发和逻辑思维能力等品质有综合考量。因此，高校外语人才培养应关注人文学科与科学技术的结合，切实服务于现阶段的国家战略需求。

　　第六章聚焦"一带一路"倡议下公共行政领域的外语规划调查。作者选择江苏、陕西、云南、黑龙江、山西、湖北的省政府官网、外办官网以及商业厅官网平台中关于"一带一路"的新闻报道作为研究语料，采用定量与定性相结合的方法对相关语料进行横向对比分析。研究发现，目前各省份对接"一带一路"倡议的语言服务结构不均衡，外语经济服务的新闻数据量最高，外语人才服务、应用服务和学术服务则相对滞后。

　　第七章旨在调查"一带一路"倡议下文化企业的外语服务现状。文化企业是弘扬民族优秀文化、实施文化"走出去"战略的重要媒介，而涉及其中的语言服务业发挥着关键作用。作者认为，由于文化企业的概念较为宽泛，故本章聚焦于文化企业中的语言服务企业。作者从国家的宏观层面，江苏、甘肃与广西省域的中观层面，以及三例语言服务企业的微观层面出发，分别进行数据收集与分析。研究发现，目前我国的语言服务行业缺乏政府扶持与顶层设计，造成行业发展方向不明确、优质翻译人才匮乏和行业标准不完善等问题。

　　第八章聚焦"一带一路"倡议下的学校外语规划现状。作者认为，学校是语言管理和实践发展的关键领域之一，科学的学校外语规划与实践是共建"一带一路"、培养高层次语言人才的关键。本章通过网络和电话调查、访谈等方法，对我国东北、西北、西南、华中、华东和华北6个地区的24所大学、12所高中进行了调查，并分别对外语语种规划、外语地位规划和外语习得规划三个方面进行了分析讨论。基于调查结果，作者提出应开设更多针对"一带一路"沿线国家的外语选修课程；将地理、市场等因素纳入到外语教育规划的考虑范畴；将经贸、法律和文化等方面的课程纳入到外语人才培养体系当中。

　　第九章调查了"一带一路"倡议下国家和省域的外语规划现状。本章运用文献分析、调查以及个案研究方法,从教育、外贸和文化三个领域出发,对"一带一路"倡议下的国家外语规划现状,以及江苏省、福建省和陕西省的省域外语规划现状进行调查。基于调查数据的横向对比与分析,作者对"一带一路"沿线相关语种的人才储备、人力资源管理与培训和外语相关产业结构优化三个方面提出了调适建议。

第十章主要涉及"一带一路"倡议下的家庭外语规划研究。作者基于 Splosky(2004)语言规划三元构成理论,构建家庭语言规划模型,并从其中的语言信念与语言管理两个方面进行实证调研。研究通过半结构化访谈、实地观察,对我国长江中下游某城市 40 个中小学家庭的父母进行调研。研究结果表明,大部分父母重视家庭英语规划,也有个别家庭关注到了法语、德语和日语规划,但从"一带一路"建设的需求来看,家庭语言规划仍未给予针对性的多语种习得支持。

2.5 研究启示与讨论

该作的第十一、十二、十三章为研究启示、讨论与结语部分。作者基于不同领域的外语规划调查,从"一带一路"倡议下的领域外语能力和外语规划两方面分别予以思考。其中,在第十一章中,作者从"一带一路"倡议下的国家外语能力需求出发,对我国目前各领域的外语人才培养进行讨论,认为我国的外语能力框架构建可以《欧洲语言共同参考框架》为模板,从非通用语建设和领域外语能力建设两方面进行相应的人才体系构建;在第十二章中,作者结合调查数据与相关文献、政策文本梳理,从外语地位、语种、功能和习得四个方面对"一带一路"倡议下的外语规划分别予以讨论,并在第十三章中对全文做出总结。

3 简评

综览全书,我们认为,陈美华教授的新作《面向"一带一路"建设的外语规划研究》在以下两个方面为我国外语规划研究注入了新的活力:

(一)该作以领域语言规划为抓手,观照到了"一带一路"相关行业、领域的方方面面。自上世纪六十年代以来,语言规划研究逐渐受到社会语言学和语言社会学者的关注,成为语言学研究的重要领域之一。然而,不论语言规划研究的视域、对象和方法如何拓充与发展,就语言规划的类型或分析框架而言,仍多借鉴 Kloss(1969)、Cooper(1989)、Baldauf(2005)、Ager(2005)等提出的语言本体规划、地位规划、习得规划、以及声望规划。本世纪初,语言规划研究在中国"语言生活派"的给养下,内涵与外延进一步丰富。基于语言生活层级观的思考,李宇明(2013)引入"领域语言规划"的概念并进行展望。

目前,以领域语言规划为指导的相关研究仍处起步阶段,仅有部分学者在国际学术交流(沈骑、夏天,2013)、法律(董晓波,2015)和汉语传播(余江英,2019)等领域做了相应的调研或探讨。陈美华教授《面向"一带一路"建设的外语规划研究》一书结合"一带一路"倡议下外语服务的行业现实所需,对中资企业、政府、学校、文化和家庭等不同领域的外语规划实践予以调研,较全面地将领域语言规划框架付诸外语服务调查的各个方面。正如李宇明教授在该作的序言中所提:随着语言学的发展方向由结构研究转向话语研究,必然涉及各领域、各行业和各社会话题中的语言运用问题。可见,不同行业、领域下的外语规划研究正当时,而陈美华教授的新作为以"领域"为抓手的外语规划研究提供了新的路径思考。

(二) 该作对技术传播为导向的复合型外语人才培养作出了重要思考。随着"一带一路"倡议与"人类命运共同体"思想在全球范围内的不断深化认同,我国比以往任何时候都更迫切需要提高国际影响力、加强国际对话与多边合作。为迎合国际局面与国家战略,学界围绕"新文科"建设(如王军哲,2020;王俊菊,2021 等)、外语人才的跨学科或超学科培养(如申丹,2007;张德禄、吴连春,2021 等)和区域国别人才培养(如宁琦,2020;郑春荣,2020 等)等路径作出大量讨论。但就如何对接企业技术需求,将外语人才的语言优势转换至国际贸易领域的生产实践当中,相关研究仍较薄弱。

针对外语人才在国际合作相关行业中实践能力不足的问题,《面向"一带一路"建设的外语规划研究》一书的第五章以企业外语需求调研为基础,将技术传播的概念引入到我国的外语人才培养议题当中。该作认为,在推进"一带一路"倡议过程中,企业之间的国际贸易合作是重要驱动力,而与之相关的知识分享、科学研究和信息传播等均涉及技术传播人才的话语实践能力。由此,该作第五章立足学校人才培养与企业人才需求之间的对接问题,对"一带一路"信息技术与通信行业的企业员工进行半结构化访谈,并据此提出了以技术传播为导向的复合型外语人才的培养路径,为我国的语言政策与语言教育研究开拓了新思路。

4 结语

"一带一路",需要语言铺路(李宇明,2015)。2020 年 9 月陈美华教授的新作《面向"一带一路"建设的外语规划研究》以"一带一路"倡议下的领域语言规划为抓手,对中资企业、政府、学校、文化和家庭等不同领域的外语规划实践予以实证调研,较全面地将领域语言规划框架付诸外语服务调查的各个方面。此外,该作还将技术传播的概念引入到我国的外语人才培养议题当中,为我国的语言政策与语言教育研究注入了新的活力。美中不足的是,该作第三、四章的研究方法与研究框架部分,与第五章至第十章的实证调研对象似乎并未呈现一一对应关系,为读者梳理、理解作者研究思路造成些许困扰。但瑕不掩瑜,该书的出版对领域语言规划下的研究与实践工作仍具有重要的启发和指导作用。

参考文献

[1] Ager, D. 2005. Image and prestige planning[J]. *Current Issues in Language Planning*, 6(1): 1-43.

[2] Baldauf Jr., R. B. 2005. Language planning and policy research: An overview[C]. In Hinkel, E. Handbook of Research in Second Language Teaching and Learning[A]. Mahwah, NJ: Erlbaum, 957-970.

[3] Cooper, R. 1989. Language Planning and Social Change[M]. Cambridge: Cambridge University Press.

[4] Kloss, H. 1969. Research Possibilities on Group Bilingualism: A Report[M]. Quebec: International Cerner for Research on Bilingualism.

[5] Splosky, B. 2004. Language Policy[M]. Cambridge: Cambridge University Press.

[6] 陈美华. 2020. 面向"一带一路"建设的外语规划研究[M]. 北京:外语教学与研究出版社.

[7] 董晓波. 2015. 法律领域的语言规划研究:问题与方法[J]. 外语教学理论与实践,(4):37-43.

[8] 黄行. 2015. 我国与"一带一路"核心区国家跨境语言文字状况[J]. 云南师范大学学报(哲学社会科学版),(5):1-8.

[9] 李宇明. 2013. 领域语言规划试论[J]. 华中师范大学学报(人文社会科学版),(3):86-92.

[10] 李宇明. 2015. "一带一路"需要语言铺路[N]. 人民日报(理论版),2015年9月22日.

[11] 卢俊霖、祝晓宏. 2017. "一带一路"建设背景下"语言互通"的层级、定位与规划[J]. 语言文字应用,(2):67-73.

[12] 宁琦. 2020. 区域与国别研究人才培养的理论与实践——以北京大学为例[J]. 外语界,(3):36-42.

[13] 申丹. 2007. 外语跨学科研究与自主创新[J]. 中国外语,(1):13-18.

[14] 沈骑. 2015. "一带一路"倡议下国家外语能力建设的战略转型[J]. 云南师范大学学报(哲学社会科学版),(5):9-13.

[15] 沈骑、夏天. 2013. 国际学术交流领域的语言规划研究:问题与方法[J]. 外语教学与研究,(6):876-885.

[16] 王军哲. 2020. 新文科背景下外语类院校一流本科建设探索与实践[J]. 外语教学,(1):3-6.

[17] 王俊菊. 2021. 新文科建设对外语专业意味着什么?[J]. 中国外语,(1):1+24.

[18] 王雪梅、邓世平. 2020. "一带一路"沿线关键土著语言规划:内涵、原则与框架[J]. 外语界,(6):63-69.

[19] 余江英. 2019. 领域汉语传播规划研究:目标与任务[J]. 语言文字应用,(2):10-19.

[20] 张德禄、吴连春.2021.超学科知识的融合模式及教学模式探索[J].中国外语,(1):45-52.
[21] 赵世举.2015."一带一路"建设的语言需求及服务对策[J].云南师范大学学报(哲学社会科学版),(4):36-42.
[22] 郑春荣.2020.全球治理视域下国别区域人才培养探析[J].中国外语,(6):20-25.

图书在版编目(CIP)数据

外国语文研究：语言与传播 / 陈新仁主编. —南京：南京大学出版社，2021.9
ISBN 978-7-305-24818-4

Ⅰ. ①外… Ⅱ. ①陈… Ⅲ. ①外语教学－教学研究－文集 Ⅳ. ①H09-53

中国版本图书馆 CIP 数据核字(2021)第 146056 号

出版发行	南京大学出版社
社　　址	南京市汉口路 22 号　　邮　编　210093
出 版 人	金鑫荣

书　　名	**外国语文研究——语言与传播**
主　　编	陈新仁
责任编辑	董　颖　　　　　编辑热线　025-83596997

照　　排	南京南琳图文制作有限公司
印　　刷	江苏凤凰数码印务有限公司
开　　本	787×1092　1/16　印张 12.75　字数 256 千
版　　次	2021 年 9 月第 1 版　2021 年 9 月第 1 次印刷
ISBN	978-7-305-24818-4
定　　价	45.00 元

网址：http://www.njupco.com
官方微博：http://weibo.com/njupco
官方微信号：njupress
销售咨询热线：(025) 83594756

＊版权所有，侵权必究
＊凡购买南大版图书，如有印装质量问题，请与所购
　图书销售部门联系调换